Alternative Krishnas

Alternative Krishnas

Regional and Vernacular Variations on a Hindu Deity

Edited by
Guy L. Beck

State University of New York Press

Cover art: Kajal Beck

Published by
State University of New York Press, Albany

Printed in the United States of America

For information, address State University of New York Press, Albany, NY
www.sunypress.edu

Production by Judith Block
Marketing by Susan M. Petrie

Library of Congress Cataloging-in-Publication Data

Alternative Krishnas : regional and vernacular variations on a Hindu deity / Guy L. Beck, editor.
p. cm.
Includes bibliographical references and index.
ISBN 0-7914-6415-6 (Hardcover : alk. paper)—0-7914-6416-4 (pbk).
1. Krishna (Hindu deity)—Cult. 2. Hinduism—Customs and practices. I. Beck, Guy L., 1948–

BL1220.2.A57 2005
294.5'512—dc22

2004015115

10 9 8 7 6 5 4 3 2 1

Contents

Acknowledgments

This book represents a joint effort that began with the 1999 Annual Meeting of the American Academy of Religion in Boston. First I would like to thank Tracy Pintchman, the organizer, for so kindly inviting me to preside over a panel session held there on "Alternative Krishnas." After the session, the members of the panel gathered for lunch at a nearby Indian restaurant. To my surprise, I was unanimously nominated to pursue publication of the panel papers as a book. I then gave my solemn promise to execute the order. There was a kind of consensus that State University of New York Press would be the ideal place for publication. Yet the five papers presented on the panel—Glen Alexander Hayes, June McDaniel, Tracy Pintchman, Anne E. Monius, and Valerie Ritter—needed to be augmented to reach book size. After considerable looking about, three additional papers were submitted by A. Whitney Sanford, Christian Lee Novetzke, and Jerome H. Bauer. Including my own, this brought the total number to nine, an auspicious Indian number. I would thus like to personally thank all of the contributors for producing what I consider a first-rate group of essays.

I would also like to sincerely thank Ms. Nancy Ellegate and the staff at State University of New York Press for their interest and pursuit of this project.

Lastly, I wish to thank Kajal Beck, my artist wife, for contributing the cover art, and Śrī Harishankar Mathur for the translations at the end of chapter five.

And as they say in India, Jai Sri Krishna!

Chapter 1

Introduction

Guy L. Beck

Krishna is the name of one of the most popular and beloved deities in the Hindu pantheon. The many intriguing and delightful features of this divine character match with one of the literal meanings of his name, "all-attractive." Whether known as an incarnation of the god Vishnu or worshiped himself as the Supreme Deity, Lord Krishna has found the widest representation in Indian culture. Indian scholar Bimanbehari Majumdar has underscored Krishna's magnitude in *Krishna in History and Legend*: "As Vishnu pervades all the worlds and through them causes himself to be permeated, so does Krishna permeate Indian art, literature, ethics, philosophy and religion." Yet we are also advised that, "no figure in the history of Indian culture has given rise to so much controversy as Krishna."[1]

The actual tradition of "Krishna" fits more specifically within the broad umbrella category of "Vaishnava" in Hindu India, understood to encompass also the veneration of Vishnu, Nārāyaṇa, Lakshmī, Rādhā, Rāma, Sītā, the remainder of the *avatāras* (incarnations) with their female consorts, saints, and sectarian leaders and followers. The other principal Hindu divisions are Śaivism, including Śiva and the worship of his many manifestations as supreme deity, Śaktism, encompassing the Goddess Devī as supreme feminine power such as Durgā or Kālī, Smārta traditions that venerate a sequence of five major deities, the Advaita nondualist traditions including neo-Vedānta, lesser-known sects, modern synthetic movements, and local cultic forms. While the personality and worship of the deity Krishna forms a very significant division within Vaishnavism, his complete profile has, as suggested above, remained problematic and elusive.

Through the centuries the enigmatic and shifting identity of Krishna has ranged from pure fantasy to mere history, from cowherd friend to dynastic king, from butter thief to philanthropist, from flute musician to charioteer, from wrestler to peacemaker, from flirtatious paramour to polygamist, from philanderer to Ideal Man, from *ksatriya* warrior to yoga philosopher, from non-Aryan tribal deity to Aryan superman, from cunning military strategist to avatāra of Vishnu, from Jesus clone to "Supreme Personality of Godhead," and from epic hero to the creator of the universe as well as the source of all religious incarnations in the world. Many Hindus embrace one of these forms of Krishna and distance others, and so it is clear that Krishna represents many different things to many different kinds of people, each in a unique way part and parcel of a whole which has never been fully grasped in entirety.

As may be surmised, the "Krishnaite" traditions are by no means uniform, and so for our purposes are tentatively divided into normative and alternative. The so-called normative Krishna is based primarily on a canon of early Sanskrit texts, while an alternative Krishna may or may not include these along with specific regional or vernacular texts and traditions. The word "alternative" means, in the strictest sense, that besides a standard norm there are other choices or options available. In our case, besides an alleged normative Krishna, there are several other types of Krishnas that have flourished in different parts of India among various ethnic groups and sectarian divisions.

As a collection of essays describing "alternative Krishnas," this book is an attempt to supply some of the more elusive yet compelling missing pieces to the complete jigsaw puzzle of "Krishna." Yet to fully appreciate the range of choices presented within this volume, one needs to clarify the standard or normative Krishna, if indeed there is one. As a term, "standard" refers to "regular, orthodox, conventional." Is there such a Krishna to be found, or is this option merely an artificial construction drawn from other diverse types? If we look carefully at the "orthodox" literature in Sanskrit pertaining to the life of Krishna we indeed already find an assortment of "types" or even "archetypes" of the person of Krishna that have become overlaid upon each other throughout the passage of many centuries. In this case the category "alternative" could be problematic in that it may refer simply to additional varieties of the ever expanding multiple expressions of this rather amazing personality known as Krishna. Nonetheless, as it stands there is a kind of normative Krishna that has become accepted at least by the more orthodox schools and among sectors of the pan-Indian public. The Sanskrit/vernacular divide is not meant to be contrastive, but serves to widen the lens on the broader meaning of Krishna in India. While a few of the alternatives may appear to dispute the primacy of the standard or orthodox Krishna, the intention of the book is to give voice to some other religious traditions of Krishna worship, regional and vernacular, that have run parallel to the mainline.

The earliest classical sources for a "standard" life of Krishna include the *Mahābhārata* epic as well as the *Hari Vaṃśa, Vishnu Purāṇa*, the *Brahma Purāṇa*, and the *Bhāgavata Purāṇa* (also known as the *Śrīmad Bhāgavatam*). Taken together, these will be referred to as the Sanskrit "canon." The *Hari Vaṃśa*, attached as an appendage to the much earlier *Mahābhārata*, is dated roughly within the first three centuries CE, and the *Vishnu Purāṇa* before 500 CE. While the *Brahma Purāṇa* is perhaps only a few centuries later, the *Bhāgavata Purāṇa*, as the principal literary source for the childhood pastimes of Krishna, most probably reached its final form in the ninth century CE. Many other Purāṇas and supplementary texts were written to corroborate material contained in the above canon. While the dating of Krishna's life is accepted by pious tradition to be around 3000 BCE, there is also believed to have been a strong oral tradition of his life handed down until the written format was commenced sometime before the Christian era.

One may affirm with considerably more assurance that there is such a thing as an historical "orthodox Jesus," in that various councils of Christian theologians through the centuries have determined a standard Jesus, binding on the believers, that has been drawn from the very limited body of material in the New Testament. Despite this, the so-called search for the historical Jesus has occupied some of the most brilliant minds in modern Christendom, from its initial frenzy in the nineteenth century to the current revival from the 1950s, and especially with the Jesus Seminar in Berkeley beginning in 1985. One may also acknowledge an "orthodox Muhammad" in the Islamic tradition, strictly based on the Quranic writings, the Sunna, and the Hadith. Historical studies, with their recurrent problems, have followed in search of the historical Buddha, Lao Tzu, and Confucius. As founders of major world religions, Jesus, Muhammad, and the Buddha have also been treated in a spate of biographies in recent years, with focused attention on minute details as shifted through historical and literary evidence.

In the Western examples, a rigid demarcation between orthodox and heterodox was often established and implemented by central ecclesiastical authorities, such that alterations in the depictions of these religious founders were declared heresies and abolished in one manner or another. The case is quite different with the personality of Krishna, for there has never been a central tribunal of orthodoxy in Hinduism that would have enforced or mandated a particular version of the Krishna personality for all Hindus, that is, limiting its sources to the Purāṇas only, the epics only, the Sanskrit literature only. Thus what might have been deemed heretical in terms of the Krishna image and personality has survived in both urban and rural locations, everywhere largely untempered by orthodox enforcement. Later Vaishnava Sampradāyas, religious schools claiming orthodoxy, shaped their formations of Krishna by selection of specific texts, both in Sanskrit and in vernacular languages, along with additional materials conforming to the teachings of the founder saints. And while they often debated with each other to affirm and develop their own doctrinal theologies, the regional or alternative Krishna traditions were not persecuted as in Inquisitional Christianity or radical Islamist regimes.

The empirical evidence of inscriptions, dated monuments, and original manuscripts is not perhaps as strong for Krishna as in some of the other examples of religious figures. However, most scholars of Hinduism and Indian history accept the historicity of Krishna—that he was a real male person, whether human or divine, who lived on Indian soil by at least 1000 BCE and interacted with many other historical persons within the cycles of the epic and puranic literatures. And while not the founder of Hinduism as such, Krishna is probably the most important "historically divine" figure in Hindu India today, with Lord Rāma of the *Rāmāyaṇa* story the only possible rival for popularity. By "historically divine" is meant a god or divine being that is both worshiped as a transcendent God and believed to have appeared in human form in historical time.

Despite the obvious importance of Krishna for the history of India and Hinduism, there is as yet no serious "biography" much less a "standard" one. Modern apologists representing the various faith-based communities of Hinduism or Krishna worship, while accepting the historical divinity of Krishna, have generally limited their sources of historical authority to the Sanskrit canon (S. Radhakrishnan, Swami Prabhupada, Devi Vanamali, Swami Cinmayananda, Maharishi Mahesh Yogi, etc.). Many secular or lay authors who have attempted to portray a life of Krishna have also drawn exclusively from the epic and Purāṇic sources (Menon, Sheth, Frith), yet have usually consigned Krishna purely within the realm of myth, legend, and even fairytale. Moreover, the widely popular Indian TV serial of *Shri Krishna* (Bombay: Sagar Enterprises, 1989) of 106 episodes by famed *Ramayan* director Ramanand Sagar was "mainly based on Shrimad Bhagvat Maha Puran by Bhagwan Veda Vyās, with material from other Purāṇas," reinforcing standard images of Krishna throughout India and the world. With the exception of Hiltebeital (1976), Kinsley (1979) and Hawley (1983), who have each focused on a specific dimension of Krishna's life using canonical as well as noncanonical sources, most academic scholars of Hinduism have also remained within the domain of the Sanskrit canon for any kind of biographical reconstruction. Thus Krishna, whose actual historical presence is no longer in dispute, has all but evaded the eyes and ears of serious scholarship to such an extent that his "real life" has become virtually shrouded in mystery. The Krishna of Indian piety and imagination has eclipsed the objective historical Krishna by leaps and bounds.

According to even the most circumspect approach, however, the purported life of Krishna had more of the "stuff" of real history than most religiously historical figures, though much of this information appears exaggerated at first glance. According to the accounts in the Sanskrit canon, as well as depictions in sculpture and other visual art, Krishna ruled his own kingdom and was the descendent of an illustrious dynasty that has been carefully chronicled and preserved by scribes and Purāṇic authors. In fact, Krishna is the only deity in the Hindu pantheon whose entire earthly life, from birth to death, has been presented in Sanskrit literature. His life spanned over one hundred years according to the *Vishnu Purāṇa*. This would place Krishna's life considerably longer than the lives of either Jesus (thirty-three years), Muhammad (sixty-two years), Confucius (seventy years), the Buddha (eighty years), or Mahavira (seventy-two years). Krishna had more wives (16,108), children (180,000 sons, according to *Vishnu Purāṇa* 5.32), and grandchildren than any other known religious figure, except perhaps some of the mythical Chinese emperors of yore. Krishna's earthly career covered more geographical territory than any of the others, including the entire region of northern India. There are far more material pilgrimage sites and shrines commemorating specific events in Krishna's life than for any other sacred figure in world religions. Furthermore, there are more references to Krishna's life in literature, both classical and vernacular, than any other historical or semihistorical religious personality.

Then why is there hesitation to conduct comprehensive biographical documentation? Perhaps the reason can be summed up in the expression that is used as the title for the first chapter of Professor Majumdar's book: "Chronological Puzzles," referring to the enormous number of contradictions and discrepancies surrounding the chronology of Krishna's life as depicted in the Sanskrit canon. In order for Krishna to have conducted all of the activities described therein at the specific ages mentioned, he either needed to duplicate himself or else perform certain acts way out of their normal human range of possibilities (i.e., become a grandfather at age thirteen, or join the Mahābhārata war at age ninety-four!). If Noah of the Bible can live 475 years, or Abraham can father a child at 100 years of age, then perhaps those who study Western traditions can empathize. These kinds of problems, and others, have posed as nearly insurmountable hurdles for even the most ambitiously devout scholar of any religious tradition. Yet the much talked about "problem" of constructing the historical life of Jesus from the Synoptic Gospels, of Muhammad from the Qur'an and Hadith, compared to the task of the Krishna historian, is quite rudimentary, indeed even a picnic.

The gradual stages of historical development by which Vishnu ascended to prominence after the Vedic period are important precursors to the ascendancy of Krishna as the Supreme God. The earliest Vaishnavas, early followers of Vishnu and Nārāyaṇa, were the Bhāgavatas and Pāñcarātras, both of whom rejected the Vedic sacrificial cult and embraced the path of devotion, or *bhakti*. But while the former group accepted the *varṇa* system and brahmanical status, the latter rejected it and originally flourished among ascetics and those influenced by the Tantric tradition. Vishnu and Nārāyaṇa were previously worshiped separately by the Bhāgavatas and Pāñcarātras, yet the new amalgam, with the further addition of Vāsudeva-Krishna, developed rapidly to become the most important theistic division of Sanskritic Hinduism.

The relationship of Krishna with these Vaishnava traditions is complex and develops over a long period, but is at least initially established by the time of the Bhagavad Gītā or the *Mahābhārata*, around 200 BCE in its final form. Thus, before the Christian era, the "historical" figure and evolving deity of a cowherd clan by the name of Krishna was annexed into the Bhāgavata religion as Vāsudeva-Krishna, first as an incarnation of Vishnu-Nārāyaṇa, then gradually as identical with him as in the Bhagavad Gītā, and finally, as his superior by the time of the *Bhāgavata Purāṇa* in its final form in the ninth century.

By the medieval period, orthodox sectarian Vaishnavism had developed into four major Vaishnava Sampradāyas, disciplic lineages or schools that were each founded by a renowned scholar who wrote learned Sanskrit commentaries on the Upanishads, the *Vedānta Sūtra*, and the Bhagavad Gītā. The four founders, ranging in time from the eleventh century to the fourteenth, were Rāmānuja, Madhva, Nimbārka, and Vishnuswami. Each conferred authentic—that is, Sankritic—sanction to the emerging bhakti movements devoted to the expression of bhakti as the superior means of achieving *moksha*, or liberation. In these schools, the status of Krishna ranges from avatāra (incarnation) of Vishnu, to identity with Vishnu on the highest level. In each case he is connected directly with the Supreme Being and co-eternal with the Upanishadic Brahman. In modern times the Gauḍīya Sampradāya, linked to Madhva Sampradāya but established by Caitanya and his followers in sixteenth-century Bengal, includes the recent worldwide movement know as ISKCON (International Society for Krishna Consciousness) in which Krishna is most clearly declared the "Supreme Personality of Godhead," surpassing Vishnu.

Many scholastic works in Sanskrit by the above founders established the orthodox sampradāyas and the legitimacy of bhakti toward Krishna or Vishnu as superior to other paths employing knowledge (*jñāna-mārga*) and works (*karma-mārga*). The complete raison d'etre for these lineages, however, either at their inauguration or within their development, was not simply to perpetuate a Sanskrit canonical Krishna, but to uplift the status of bhakti vernacular writings within the canonical sphere. For example, in the Rāmānuja or Śrī Sampradāya there were the Tamil poems of the Āḷvār saints like Āṇṭāḷ and Nāmmāḷvār, for Madhva the devotional songs and poems in Kannada language of the Haridāsa Kuṭa saints like Vyāsatīrtha and Purandara Dāsa, for Vishnuswami and the Vallabha Sampradāya the Hindi or Braj Bhāshā poems of the Aṣṭachāp poets like Sūr Dās, and for Nimbārka Sampradāya the Braj Bhāshā poems of Śrī Bhaṭṭa and Śrī Harivyāsadeva. The later Gauḍīya tradition, while containing many Sanskrit treatises by the Six Goswamis of Vrindaban, included on an equal level the Bengali poems of Chaṇḍīdās, Vidyāpati, and Narottama Dās, among many others. Within all four of the major "orthodox" traditions of Vaishnavism, there were significant elements of vernacular and regional input. Thus there is no surviving official "Sanskrit-only" tradition of Krishna theology and worship that has been mandated by any central or sectarian Hindu authority. As such, no living "orthodox tradition" of Krishna worship rejects vernacular expressions. In terms of orthodoxy there are only specific religious lineages that have propounded a specific form of Krishna as most effective in a salvational scheme of sectarian devotion. The rest is alternative! The so-called normative, classical tradition of Krishna mythology and worship as allegedly disseminated throughout India by brahminical culture and the Sanskrit canonical literature is in reality more of an academic construct useful for theorists and historians to analyze and evaluate the historical developments of ideas in India.

Nonetheless, drawing upon the classical Sanskrit sources, including especially the *Bhāgavata Purāṇa* but also the epics and other Purāṇas, a brief biographical portrait of the normative Krishna is presented below for purposes of providing a frame of reference for comparison with the papers presented in this volume.

Krishna is most generally accepted within the Hindu tradition as the eighth of ten incarnations of Vishnu, descending on earth at the beginning of the present age of Kali Yuga, and at the end of the previous age of Dvāpara Yuga, in about 3000 BCE. Whenever there is a general rise in unrighteousness, Lord Vishnu is believed to descend as an avātara (incarnation) in order to punish the miscreants and deliver the righteous devotees from the cycle of rebirth. At this particular juncture there was a preponderance of demons from former times that had taken birth as evil kings and were threatening the stability of Hindu Dharma. Planning his strategy of descent, Vishnu is said to have pulled two hairs from his head, one black (Krishna) and the other white (Balarāma).

Many centuries ago descendants of the Yādava family had settled around the town of Mathurā in North India. Overthrowing his pious father Ugrasena, the evil King Kaṁsa was the principal villain and reason for the descent of Vishnu. With the support of his father-in-law King Jarāsandha of Magadha, he precipitated a reign of terror in the region. Krishna, while understood to have taken a divine birth, was born to Devakī, the sister of Kaṁsa, and her husband Vasudeva of the same illustrious Yādava family, a lunar dynasty descended from the Moon. In a situation of similar intrigue to the Jesus narrative, Krishna's parents had to face a horrible ordeal. Kaṁsa had heard in a vision that the eighth son of Devakī would ultimately kill him, and so he had Devakī and Vasudeva imprisoned in a Mathurā jail, where he murdered six of her sons out of fear. Kaṁsa was told that the seventh child had aborted. However, this child, known as Balarāma who was another avātara of Vishnu sent to help Krishna, had actually been miraculously transferred to the womb of Vasudeva's second wife Rohinī. When Krishna finally took birth, divine intervention allowed for the blackish-colored child to be carried out of jail and switched with a female child in the nearby village of Gokula, where his new "foster parents" Yaśodā and her husband Nanda lived as wealthy dairy farmers. Thus when Kaṁsa tried to kill the eighth child of Devakī, lo!, it was a girl and had to be spared.

Krishna's early life was spent growing up with his elder brother Balarāma, who was white colored, in an idyllic rural setting. Yet Krishna and his family were besieged by demons sent by Kaṁsa, who had gotten wind of a miraculous child in the Braj area. Krishna, as a beautifully divine child, was naturally adorable to everyone in the village, but could also wield frightening consequences on the evil beings that entered his turf. This series of demons included a witch, whirlwind, cow, serpent, bird, sea dragon, ox, horse, and goat, all of which were destroyed by the child prodigy and his brother. Further exploits included lifting Govardhan Hill to protect the villagers from the rainfall of a jealous Lord Indra, and stealing the clothes of the cowherd girls of the village of Vrindāvana where his family had subsequently settled. As Krishna approached his teenage years, he gained a reputation for dallying with the local cowherd maidens and wives by enchanting them with his flute, leading ultimately to a midnight Rāsa Dance in which he multiplied himself in order to satisfy their amorous desires. All of these childhood pastimes created an unprecedented outpouring of affection and deep attachment for Krishna by the villagers that became a paradigm for religious devotion in Vaishnava traditions.

At one point, Kaṁsa invited Krishna and Balarāma to Mathurā to witness a fourteen-day sacrifice, using this as a ruse to destroy them. Akrūra, a devotee of Krishna, was sent by Kaṁsa to collect the brothers in Vrindāvana and warned them of Kaṁsa's evil designs. The residents of Vrindāvana experienced deep emotional trauma upon the departure of the two brothers, yet were assured of their return after helping the Yādava clan. In Mathurā, Krishna and Balarāma performed a few healing miracles, killed an evil elephant, defeated two wrestlers, and ultimately killed Kaṁsa along with his eight evil bothers. After this, Vasudeva and Devakī, released from prison, proceeded to arrange for their sons' education in the sixty-four arts and archery at the hermitage of the sage Sāndīpani Muni. After their return, it became difficult for the brothers to remain in Mathurā. The evil Jarāsandha, king of Magadha and father of two of Kaṁsa's wives, led a large coalition of kings with their armies into revenge on the Yādavas, who were temporarily impoverished and thus retreated. Krishna quickly built a new capital city of Dvārakā on an island off the Northwest coast of India, where his parents Vasudeva and Devakī were kept safely. Through a series of events, Krishna and fellow Yādavas accumulated wealth and built up a large kingdom and army. Krishna then married Rukmiṇī as his chief queen, but went on to also marry many other women (i.e., Jambavatī, Satyabhāmā, Kālindī, Satyā, Kaikeyī, etc.), who either fell in love with him or else were given by grateful kings or princes in return for his valor and good deeds. In one unprecedented event in all world religious history, Krishna married the sixteen thousand daughters of Nārakāsura who were released by him from captivity, and built each of them a palace in Dvārakā where he multiplied himself in order to satisfy all simultaneously! In terms of progeny, it is mentioned that Krishna had ten sons from each of eight wives.

The remainder of Krishna's story is bound up with the fate of the five Pāṇḍava brothers and their common wife Draupadī. The Pāṇḍavas, including Yudhiṣṭhira, Bhīma, Arjuna, Nakula, and Sahadeva, were also Yādavas, being the sons, by divine intervention, of Pāṇḍu and his wives Kuntī and Mādrī. Krishna took pity on their miserable plight of being cheated by the Kauravas out of their wealth and kingdom in a loaded dice game. Despite the efforts of Krishna to negotiate peace between the rival family groups—the Pāṇḍavas and their allies versus the Kauravas including the one hundred sons of Dhritarāṣṭra and Gandhārī—steps were taken toward an all-out war on the battlefield of Kurukshetra in northern India. Krishna lent his skill as a charioteer to Arjuna, and the stage was set for the epic eighteen-day war chronicled in the *Mahābhārata.* After speaking the famous Bhagavad Gītā discourse to Arjuna who had suddenly been overcome with grief and panic about performing his duty in battle, Krishna and the Pāṇḍavas fought relentlessly and scored a victory in that war. The Yādava clan returned to Dvārakā to celebrate, yet evil omens lay ahead. Gandhārī, angered at her loss of sons and kin, cursed Krishna to die in the forest, and the entire Yādava Dynasty to be destroyed within thirty-six years. Such was the case, as the Yādavas killed each other in drunken quarrels, and Krishna was struck with an arrow in the foot (Achille's Heel!) by the hunter Jara who mistook him for a deer. Arjuna then cremated Krishna's body and our hero rose up as Vishnu to return to the heavenly Vaikuṇṭha and receive worship there as Nārāyaṇa. Krishna's brother Balarāma who had stayed with him throughout most of his life except for the war, died just before him at the same location and rejoined Vishnu.[2]

The lengthy and variegated life of the normative Krishna, spanning nearly 120 years, was thus drawn to a close. The evil King Kaṁsa and many of his cohorts were certainly vanquished, yet it is believed that with the withdrawal of Krishna and Balarāma from the world, the evil and decadent fourth age of Kali Yuga commenced in which we are presently embroiled.

While there are nonetheless multiple images and roles of Krishna already contained in the normative depiction, this volume seeks to describe alternative versions of Krishna that lie outside the parameters of the above canonical paradigm and especially of the four orthodox Vaishnava Sampradāyas. As we shall observe, there are numerous variations on the Krishna theme throughout India, manifested almost solely in vernacular languages and in so-called folk cultural traditions that occupy smaller regions or localities, but which are no less significant or compelling. The nine chapters of the present volume present such assorted regional and vernacular variants of the Krishna story, ranging from Bengal to Mahārāṣṭra and Benares, from Jainism to Tamilian South India, and from Braj traditions to a modern depiction. Each in its own way contributes toward a complete and perhaps more robust understanding of the full identity of this complex deity and personality.

The first two chapters focus on Krishna in West Bengal. Chapter 2, "Contemporary Metaphor Theory and Alternative Views of Krishna and Rādhā in Vaishnava Sahajiyā Tantric Traditions," by Glen Alexander Hayes, illustrates how the Vaishnava Sahajiyās, a medieval Bengali Tantric tradition, developed "alternative" Krishna traditions using the vernacular language of Bengali and distinctly regional metaphors of body, world, and being. Vaishnava Sahajiyās transformed Krishna and Rādhā from a divine being and consort into the inner masculine and feminine essences of every man and woman.

By examining selected Sahajiyā texts of the seventeenth century, it will show how such alternative views of Krishna and Rādhā reflect Bengali religious, social, linguistic, cultural, and geographical contexts. Using insights from recent studies of conceptual metaphor and folklore, this chapter explains how "alternative" worldviews and practices are connected to underlying linguistic and metaphoric worlds. This sheds light not only on important roles of language and culture in the history of religions, but also on the powerful influences of vernacular imagery and deeper conceptual structures.

As chapter 3, "Folk Vaishnavism and the Ṭhākur Pañcāyat: Life and Status among Village Krishna Statues" by June McDaniel discusses further the Krishna of West Bengal by showing how Krishna is understood by folk Vaishnava devotees in a certain district to be a living presence in his various statues. In some villages, the New Year is celebrated by having a "Ṭhākur Pañcāyat," or a meeting of deities in the form of statues. The statues are carried in procession, feasted, and left to discuss the village budget and future celebrations. Based on field work primarily in Moyda village north of Calcutta, this chapter describes these events and examines assumptions inherent in this meeting of deities, and the various moods and forms of living statues. It also contrasts the alternative folk understanding of the embodiment of deities with the orthodox tradition of Gauḍīya Vaishnavism in Bengal—that is, a kind of Vaishnava "animism" versus the normative brahmanical system of deity installation.

Chapter 4, "Domesticating Krishna: Friendship, Marriage, and Women's Experience in a Hindu Women's Ritual Tradition," by Tracy Pintchman, uncovers an alternative Krishna tradition in one of the very centers of Hindu orthodoxy, Benares. According to Brahmanical Hindu traditions, the god Vishnu weds the plant goddess Tulsi every year on the eleventh day of the bright fortnight of the month of Kārtik in the fall season. In Benares, the main celebration of this wedding takes place in Śrī Maṭh, where Rāmānandī monks perform the wedding with great pageantry. In homes throughout the city and on the ghats of the Ganges River where women perform this marriage, however, there is an alternative understanding of this event. According to these women's traditions, this is not Vishnu's wedding but Krishna's, and the marriage of Krishna and Tulsi is the culmination of a full month of *pūjā* in which female devotees "raise" Krishna from infancy to adulthood, marrying him and his bride and sending them off to their home in Vaikuṇṭha, the Vaishnava heaven. Based upon extensive fieldwork in Benares as well as on a number of literary sources including both Sanskrit Mahātmyas and vernacular texts, this chapter focuses on this alternative understanding of the marriage of Tulsi, furthering our understanding, through anthropological modes of gender analysis, of Hindu women's "folk" ritual practices and mythological traditions.

The next two chapters cover alternative images of Krishna in Braj, his place of birth and childhood. Chapter 5, "Krishna as Loving Husband of God: The Alternative Krishnology of the Rādhāvallabha Sampradāya," by Guy L. Beck, introduces the alternative Krishna theology of the Rādhāvallabha Sampradāya headquartered in the Braj region. As part of the larger bhakti movement of medieval North India, this group shared many externals with other mainstream Hindu groups (temple worship, male lineages, seasonal festivals, etc.), yet bore some striking differences from the normative Krishna traditions found in the epics and Purāṇas and in the orthodox *sampradāyas*. Essentially rejecting most of the normative Sanskrit literature and ritual practice of Vaishnavism, Rādhāvallabha theology stood more in debt to local folk expressions found in the region of its origin, which it combined with its own unique religious perspective. This alternative Krishna is depicted in the literature of the founder Śrī Hita Harivaṁśa (sixteenth century CE) and his followers as the servant and husband of God, in this case the Goddess Rādhā. Opposing mainstream Vaishnava Sampradāyas that recognized Krishna as either avatāra of Vishnu or Supreme Being, the Rādhāvallabha tradition claimed that Rādhā is the Supreme Being, with Krishna as her most loving companion and eternal spouse. The devotees relish the bliss of the divine conjugal union as the highest spiritual attainment. The literature of the sect is almost entirely in Braj Bhāshā, a medieval dialect of Hindi said to be the actual language spoken in the heavenly abode of Krishna, and is ranked higher than the Sanskrit canon, which is relegated to mundane concerns compared to the elevated and erotic subject matter of their own poetry. Based on fieldwork in Vrindaban and literary study, this chapter discusses theological issues surrounding the placement of Rādhā above Krishna, and presents three poetic songs (*Vyāhulau Utsav ke Pad*, "Wedding Festival Songs") of the sect in translation in which the wedding of Rādhā and Krishna is described and praised.

In chapter 6, "Holī through Daūjī's Eyes: Alternate Views of Krishna and Balarāma in Daūjī," A. Whitney Sanford describes how the Holī celebration in Daūjī, the center of Balarāma devotion in India, located in the region of Braj, displays an alternative vision of the traditional relationship between Krishna and his elder brother Balarāma or Daūjī. These raucous and unique Holī festivities establish Balarāma in his seemingly paradoxical role as profligate—though at the same time protective and generative—elder brother in contrast to his more innocently playful younger brother Krishna. The traditional images of Balarāma and Krishna are routinely portrayed as pastoral. Yet Braj pastoralization, which is ironically an urban phenomenon, encompasses a different set of conflicts, chief among which is the disjunction created by Balarāma's (anomalous) rusticity in relation to Krishna's rural persona, which masks an urbane sophistication. Balarāma's earthly image conveniently frees Krishna to exist in that pastoral ideal in which nature never presents danger and erotic dalliances have no unwanted consequences. Balarāma is important in a symbiotic but necessarily hierarchical relationship with Krishna. This family relationship appears in multiple dimensions (e.g., theological, iconographic, and communal) and provides a flexible structure through which divergent groups and practices can be related to the center, inevitably a form of Krishna. These Holī festivities in Daūjī specific to Daūjī provide a variant understanding of Krishna and his relationship to his Braj environs and family.

In chapter 7, "A Family Affair: Krishna Comes to Paṇḍharpūr and Makes Himself at Home," Christian Lee Novetzke discusses an alternative form of Krishna in Western India. Pilgrims, on their triumphant entrance into Paṇḍharpūr in Mahārāṣṭra, sing praises to their God of many names: Viṭṭhal̤, Pāṇḍuraṅga, Śiva, Vishnu, or simply Mother. They venerate an image of Śiva at a simple temple, half submerged in Chandrabhāga's water, before they enter Viṭṭhal̤'s opulent home. Several scholars have suggested that the conical headdress that crowns the image of Viṭṭhal̤ in his temple is really Śiva's *liṅga,* while others have argued that sometimes a hat is just a hat. Charlotte Vaudeville described this religion known as Vārkarī as a Śaiva-Vaishnava synthesis, suggesting that a predominantly Śaiva tradition had been flavored by nominal Vaishnavism. However, the nature of Viṭṭhal̤ and his worship, with his bride Rukmiṇī and his pastoral mythology, make him decidedly Krishnaite. And while the foundational poets of the Vārkarī religion, namely Jñāndev and Nāmdev, worshiped both Śiva and Vishnu and were initiated into Śaiva Tantric lineages, Jñāndev translated and commented on the Bhagavad Gītā in Marāṭhī while Nāmdev, according to some, inaugurated Vaishnava Bhakti in northern India. This chapter posits that their devotion actually superceded sectarian differences or was altogether unaffected by them. Through an examination of how Nāmdev and others conceived of Viṭṭhal̤ in their early songs, this chapter attempts to demonstrate that more important than sectarian affiliation was the construction of a religious tradition that reflected the plurality of beliefs of the tenth to twelfth centuries. Nonetheless, by the middle of the seventeenth century, some three hundred years after Nāmdev and Jñāndev, the Vārkarī religion was transformed into the sectarian Krishna Bhakti tradition flourishing today.

Chapter 8, "Dance before Doom: Krishna in the Non-Hindu Literature of Early Medieval South India," by Anne E. Monius, reflects the growing interest in South India as a fertile source for alternative Hindu and non-Hindu traditions. Based on literary analysis and research into Tamil folk Vaishnava traditions, this chapter explores the scenes of Krishna's dance in two early medieval texts (fifth to sixth century CE), Buddhist and Jain, that share a non-Hindu Krishna tradition. In the Buddhist *Maṇimēkalai*, the king of Pukār frolics with his queen in the royal garden; seeing three birds dancing about a tank, he cries: "This is the kuruvai dance danced by Māmaṇivaṇṇaṉ, his elder brother, and Piññai!" Later, the king's son is brutally slaughtered in a case of mistaken identity. In the primarily Jain *Cilappatikāram*, the herdswoman Mātari calls for the local girls to perform "one of the boyhood dances of Māyavaṉ and Balarāma with Piññai" to ward off impending evil. Immediately following the end of the dance, the heroine learns of her husband's untimely demise and predicts that she will burn the city of Maturai to the ground. Both texts serve to downplay the effectiveness of the dances of the gods for bringing positive results, and yield instead to larger impersonal forces like *karma* and destiny.

In chapter 9, "Hero of Wonders, Hero in Deeds: Vāsudeva Krishna in Jaina Cosmohistory," Jerome H. Bauer draws us into the realm of Jainism, where Jaina teachers have masterfully adapted the "Hindu" Krishna stories popular among their laity by retelling them to conform to Jaina orthodoxy and to promote orthopraxies. Accordingly, Jaina Krishna mythology presents an alternative Krishna, which stands alongside the well-known Hindu stories simultaneously popular among the Jaina laity. Krishna in the Jaina tradition is no more a god than any other human being capable of liberation from karma and rebirth, but neither is he an ordinary human being. Krishna Vāsudeva is, on the one hand, a model Jaina layman and king and, on the other hand, a Śalākāpuruṣa, an Illustrious Person, with an illustrious destiny. As such, he has the role of *karmavīr* or "action hero," rather than *dharmavīr*, the role played by the Tīrthaṁkaras (exemplary saviors) and other renunciants. As karmavīr, he is also *āścaryavīr*, "wonder hero," an apparent worker in miracles. For example, the Śvetāmbara canon tells a unique story of a singular wonder worked by Krishna whereby he journeys across spatiotemporal boundaries to rescue the heroine Draupadī. While Hindu theologians are divided on the issue of whether Krishna, as an avatāra of Vishnu, controls, or is controlled by, the law of karma, the Jainas have no doubt. Krishna must go to Hell, for his (necessary) deeds of violence, committed to uphold the order of society and divine custom, and for his well-known sexual misconduct, as troubling for Jaina teachers as it is for their Christian and Muslim counterparts. Sin is real, and must be worked off, even by such an exalted personage as Krishna, whose penultimate destiny is to become an exalted Jaina teacher, the twelfth Tīrthaṅkara of the coming age, and whose ultimate destiny is liberation. This chapter examines Krishna's role in Jaina cosmohistory, drawing upon both Śvetāmbara and Digambara texts as well as the testimony of current lay practitioners.

Chapter 10, "Epiphany in Rādhā's Arbor: Nature and the Reform of Bhakti in Hariaudh's *Priyapravās*," by Valerie Ritter, explores the development of a modern Hindi variant of the Krishna theme. *Priyapravās* ("The Sojourn of the Beloved") is an epic work in Khari Boli or Modern Hindi by Ayodhyāsiṁh Upādhyāy ("Hariaudh") that is well known for its revision of the character of Rādhā, presented through a virtuosic use of Sanskritic literary forms. In this poetic work, Hariaudh recasts the carnal relationship between Rādhā and Krishna in an intellectual context of reformism and cultural defensiveness. His revision entailed changes in the bodily-ness of Vaishnava devotion and the interpolation of an explicit message of social service. This chapter addresses the reformist antecedents of this text, and its relation to revisionist religious thinking of the period. Additionally, Hariaudh's method of positioning the text between "tradition" and "modernity" by means of literary tropes will be examined. This analysis of *Priyapravās* may yield insight into the problems of conceiving both a "modern" Hinduism and "modern" Hindi literature in this period of incipient nationalism.

One of the tasks of the phenomenology of religion is to cultivate an openness to a variety of perspectives on the same subject of inquiry, with the underlying axiom in place that an object of study is by no means exhausted with one or more "orthodox" views, and that the views of the most authoritarian believers or controllers of the mythic image of a deity are just one among many. What ultimately counts is the total picture as gleaned from multiple source readings, including those from diverse social classes, language groups, religious sects, and other branches of the social order. Thus an examination of regional variants of a living Hindu tradition facilitates a deeper and truer understanding of the phenomenon we call Krishna in India. It is hoped that these nine perspectives will help to round out a more complete portrait of Krishna within India and beyond.

Notes

1. Bimanbehari Majumdar (1969), 1.
2. This brief summary of the life of Krishna was constructed from entries found in Vettam Mani (1975), 420–29.

References

Anand, D. *Krishna: The Living God of Braj*. New Delhi: South Asia, 1992.

Archer, W. G. *The Loves of Krishna in Indian Painting and Poetry*. New York: Grove, 1957.

Bryant, Edwin F. *Krishna: The Beautiful Legend of God* (Śrīmad Bhāgavata Purāṇa Book X). London: Penguin, 2003.

Case, Margaret. *Seeing Krishna: The Religious World of a Brahmin Family in Vrindaban*. New York: Oxford University Press, 2000.

Das, Bhagavan. *Krishna: A Study in the Theory of Avatāras*. Bombay: Bharatiya Vidya Bhavan, 1962.

Dutt, Manmatha Nath, trans. *Harivaṁśa*. Calcutta: Elysium, 1897.

Frith, Nigel. *The Legend of Krishna*. New York: Schocken, 1976.

Ganguly, Kisari Mohan, ed. and trans. *The Mahābhārata of Krishna-Dvaipāyana Vyāsa*. 4 vols. New Delhi: Munshiram Manoharlal, 2002.

Haberman, David L. *Journey through the Twelve Forests: An Encounter with Krishna*. New York: Oxford University Press, 1994.

Hawley, John Stratton. *At Play with Krishna: Pilgimage Dramas from Brindavan*. Princeton, NJ: Princeton University Press, 1981.

———. *Krishna, the Butter Thief*. Princeton, NJ: Princeton University Press, 1983.

Hiltebeitel, Alf. *The Ritual of Battle: Krishna in the Mahābhārata*. Albany: State University of New York Press, 1990.

Kinsley, David R. *Divine Player: A Study of Krishna's Life*. Orient, 1979.

———. *The Sword and the Flute: Kālī and Kṛṣṇa, Dark Visions of the Terrible and the Sublime in Hindu Mythology*. Berkeley: University of California Press, 1975.

Majumdar, Bimanbehari. *Kṛṣṇa in History and Legend*. Calcutta: University of Calcutta, 1969.

Mani, Vettam. *Puranic Encyclopedia: A Comprehensive Dictionary with Specific Reference to the Epic and Puranic Literature*. New Delhi: Motilal Banarsidass, 1975.

Menon, Ramesh. *Blue God: A Life of Krishna*. Writers Club, 2000.

Mukerjee, Radhakamal. *The Lord of the Autumn Moons*. Bombay: Asia, 1957.

Prabhupada, A. C. Bhaktivedanta Swami. *Krishna the Supreme Personality of Godhead: A Summary Study of Śrīmad Bhāgavatam's Tenth Canto*. Los Angeles: Bhaktivedanta Book Trust, 2003.

Preciado-Solis, Benjamin. *The Kṛṣṇa Cycle in the Purāṇas: Themes and Motifs in a Heroic Saga*. Delhi: Motilal Banarsidass, 1984.

Raghunathan, N., trans. *Śrīmad Bhāgavatam*. 2 vols. Madras: Vighnesvara, 1976.

Sanyal, J. M. *The Śrīmad Bhāgavatam of Krishna-Dwaipāyana Vyāsa*. 5 vols. Calcutta: Oriental, 1952.

Sheth, Noel, S.J. *The Divinity of Krishna*. New Delhi: Munshiram Manoharlal, 1984.

Singer, Milton, ed. *Krishna: Myths, Rites, and Attitudes*. Chicago and London: University of Chicago Press, 1966.

Tripurari, B. V. *Form of Beauty: The Krishna Art of B. G. Sharma*. Novato, CA: Mandala, 1998.

Vanamali, Devi. *The Play of God: Visions of the Life of Krishna*. San Diego, CA: Blue Dove, 1995.

Wilson, H. H., trans. *The Vishnu Purāṇa*. Calcutta: Punthi Pustak, 1961.

Chapter 2

Contemporary Metaphor Theory and Alternative Views of Krishna and Rādhā in Vaishnava Sahajiyā Tantric Traditions

GLEN ALEXANDER HAYES

In this chapter I would like to consider how recent advances in the study of metaphor can help us to appreciate alternative views of Krishna among the Vaishnava Sahajiyās of medieval Bengal, a Tantric Yogic movement that flourished from the sixteenth through nineteenth centuries CE.[1] Information gleaned from their wonderful if challenging esoteric texts can illustrate not only "alternative" views of Krishna in a major vernacular literature, but also show how the use of modern conceptual metaphor theories can help us to better understand the imaginative worlds expressed by vernacular texts and traditions. Of course, one may speculate just why Vaishnava Sahajiyās developed "alternative Krishna traditions." What must they have found in the classical stories of the Dark Lord and his consort Rādhā to have moved them to create such alternative visions and ritual systems? Why did they appropriate so much of the Caitanya movement and Gauḍīya Vaishnava *rāgānuga bhakti sādhana*—causing so much controversy with orthodox Vaishnavas?[2] We'll never know for sure, since most of the hundreds of surviving Sahajiyā manuscripts are concerned more directly with matters of ritual, gurus and students, visualization, and subtle yogic physiology. But some, such as the *Amṛtaratnāvalī* of Mukunda-dāsa (ca. 1600 CE) and the *Vivarta-vilāsa* of Ākiñcana-dāsa (ca. 1650 CE) provide us with glimpses into this complex process of appropriation and development of "alternative" traditions.

Since the late Edward C. Dimock Jr., in his now-classic *The Place of the Hidden Moon*,[3] has presented many of the basic beliefs and practices of Vaishnava Sahajiyā traditions and has discussed the problematics of determining their origins, these won't be covered in this chapter. However, there are some basic points for us to consider. The Sahajiyās may be considered—in the very broad sense—an alternative Krishna tradition for two major reasons. First, they adapt classical devotional interpretations of Krishna, transforming him from a supreme being (as Bhagavān, quite distinct from ordinary human beings) into the inner cosmic form (*svarūpa*) of every human male. Rādhā is transformed from the consort, or *hlādinī-śakti*, of Krishna into the svarūpa of every woman. For Sahajiyās, in other words, the goal is not to worship Krishna or imitate Rādhā and the *gopīs* in a dualistic *bhakti* sense, but rather *to become* Krishna or Rādhā themselves, in a monistic Tantric manner. Second, by expressing these alternative and antinomian notions of Krishna and Rādhā in vernacular Bengali verse, and embedding these narratives in specific Sahajiyā teaching lineages, they move Krishna and Rādhā even further from the Sanskrit-based and classical formulations into the local realities of Bengali men and women.

As Dimock has shown, Krishna and his erotic encounters with Rādhā would seem to be natural choices for adaptations by late medieval Sahajiyā tantrics as they sought to express the need to reverse the phenomenal flow of creation—engendered as the cosmic "play" (*līlā*) of male and female powers—"upwards against the current" (*sroter ujāna*) back to the unitive state of Sahaja, the "Innate" or "Primordial" condition. Of course, the popular notion of Caitanya as the dual incarnation of both Rādhā and Krishna, developed by Krishnadāsa Kavirāja in his *Caitanya-caritāmṛta*, was also taken up by Sahajiyā gurus like Ākiñcana-dāsa and Mukunda-dāsa as a clear reflection of their own belief that all Sahajiyās must themselves realize the indwelling of both male and female powers within their own physical bodies.

If we can set aside the controversy of possible Sahajiyā influence on orthodox Vaishnavism,[4] we can turn our attention to how alternative traditions of Krishna are expressed in some Sahajiyā texts, and to do this we need to explore the metaphors that lie at the heart of the texts. This is because religious metaphors provide us with windows into the core beliefs and imageries of the sacred. To begin with, the basic Vaishnava notion of *avatāra* is itself a wonderful metaphoric process, for it enables an abstract, cosmic, divine being to be expressed in more earthly, concrete terms—one of the basic functions of religious metaphor. Whether it is Vishnu taking form as a fish or a boar or a man-lion or Krishna taking form as a baby, a friend, or a lover, it is this shape-shifting nature of Vishnu and Krishna that lends itself to Tantric reinterpretation and metaphorical elaboration.

Until recently, metaphor has been studied by Western scholars primarily as a linguistic and poetic device. However, metaphor was given extensive treatment in classical Indian aesthetics and dramaturgy in terms of *rūpaka*, *alaṃkāra*, and *dhvani* (ideas which continue in Gauḍīya Vaishnava and Sahajiyā aesthetics).[5] But over the past several decades a decidedly modern theory of "conceptual metaphor" has emerged, based on the efforts of a wide range of scholars, including linguists, philosophers, literary critics, folklorists, cognitive scientists, and anthropologists.[6] In my own efforts to better understand the content of medieval Sahajiyā texts, I have found the recent studies of Mark Johnson, George Lakoff, Mark Turner, Barre Toelken, and Samuel Levin to be quite useful in evaluating the potency of conceptual metaphor in religious texts. Alternative religious traditions are alternative not only because they are developed in (and respond to) different social, cultural, and historical contexts, but also because they make distinctive uses of metaphors in their attempt to construe and express sacred realities and beings. These are not metaphors just in the sense of literary and poetic devices; the modern understanding of conceptual metaphors connects metaphors to fundamental cognitive, physiological, and neurological processes.

As linguist George Lakoff and philosopher Mark Johnson observe in their wonderful groundbreaking collaboration *Metaphors We Live By*, "metaphor is pervasive in everyday life, not just in language but in thought and action. Our ordinary conceptual system, in terms of which we both think and act, is fundamentally metaphorical in nature."[7] According to Johnson, metaphor is

> conceived as a pervasive mode of understanding by which we project patterns from one domain of experience in order to structure another domain of a different kind. So conceived, metaphor is not merely a linguistic mode of expression; rather, it is one of the chief cognitive structures by which we are able to have coherent, ordered experiences that we can reason about and make sense of. Through metaphor, we make use of patterns that obtain in our physical experience to organize our more abstract understanding.[8]

I would argue that this methodology can help us to better understand the richness of metaphors in alternative religious traditions.[9] In order to appreciate the basic theory, a bit of linguistic terminology must be used, that involving so-called target and source domains. Regarding the LOVE IS A JOURNEY metaphor (which exists in variants worldwide, and is found in Sahajiyā texts as well), Lakoff observes:

> The metaphor involves understanding one domain of experience, love, in terms of another domain of experience, journeys. More technically, the metaphor can be understood as a mapping (in the mathematical sense) from a source domain (in this case, journeys) to a target domain (in this case, love). The mapping is tightly structured. There are ontological correspondences, according to which entities in the domain of love (e.g., the lovers, their common goals, their difficulties, the love relationship) correspond systematically to entities in the domain of a journey (the travelers, the vehicle, destinations, etc.).[10]

Thus, for most metaphors, the basic taxonomy is: TARGET-domain IS SOURCE-domain, and much of the theory explores these "ontological correspondences," as well as their various meanings. This same basic relationship can be applied to virtually any metaphor, for example: ARGUMENT IS WAR or IDEAS ARE FOOD. The multiple meanings found in the source domain (war, food) may have complex relationships with those in the target domain (argument, ideas), and a wide range of semantic and lexical implications or entailments are the result. Thus, we can have, respectively, expressions like "He attacked my position" and "Your thesis is hard to digest."

When we examine important Sahajiyā religious metaphors (and there are many), such as THE BODY IS A RIVER SYSTEM or REALITY IS FLUID or SAHAJA IS A CONTAINER or SADHANA IS A JOURNEY we find that important aspects of the source domain (the relatively "concrete" notions of a river system, fluid, container, journey) tend to be applied to the target domains (the more abstract notions of body, reality, Sahaja, and *sādhana*) in ways that attempt to maintain metaphorical consistency. In other words, the details of a river system (e.g., banks, landing stairs, waters, villages, ponds, current, boats) are connected to the body in a way that the Sahajiyās thus envision these details as part of the subtle inner body. In other words, the "cognitive topology," the "nooks and crannies" as it were, of the source domains (the "concrete" image) tend to constrain and structure how the target domain (the "abstraction") is perceived and experienced. This is one reason why we must pay attention to the specifically local images that are used to express cosmic abstractions like Krishna, Sahaja, or the subtle body; it also suggests why the Sahajiyā subtle physiology is typically envisioned not as fiery energy centers (*cakras*) and the ascending cosmic power of *kuṇḍalinī-śakti*, but rather as the movement of fluids along a river, past villages, and into a series of inner ponds. There is a metaphorical consistency that leads to what might be called "coherent metaphoric worlds."[11]

Metaphors are thus useful because they enable what Mark Johnson calls "the imaginative structuring of experience" in human life, which consists of "forms of imagination that grow out of bodily experience, as it contributes to our understanding and guides our reasoning."[12] And it is here then where we can gain an appreciation for the use of alternative local, folk, and vernacular expressions, for it is this very function of metaphor that allows mystics such as the Sahajiyās to "imaginatively structure" their yogic, emotional, and sexual experiences. This is based upon what modern theorists call "image schemata," essentially "a recurring, dynamic pattern of our perceptual interactions and motor programs that gives coherence and structure to our experience".[13] Some such schemata, such as the "verticality schema" (and the meaning or value of "up" versus "down") or the "container schema" (which can "mark off" a mental space and turn an idea or experience into a "vessel") are perhaps universally found with humans, but it is likely that there are important local and individual expressions—issues that scholars are still working out.

Metaphors thus work together with bodily experience and image schemata to create "coherent metaphoric worlds," allowing us to interact with, and even to "enter" those worlds. It is precisely this process of what Lakoff and Johnson call "mapping" that we can find in alternative Sahajiyā notions of subtle physiology and ritual process, of identifying men with Krishna and women with Rādhā. This mapping (itself a spatial metaphor) allows for not just analysis and manipulation of the embodied condition and the material world, but for gradual transformation of the bodies of the male and female practitioners and the attainment of Sahaja.

Although the preceding discussion of contemporary metaphor theory is necessarily brief, and the issues are often quite subtle and nuanced, I trust that it has shown how metaphors may be related to language, thought, imagination, and basic experience. In addition to being useful literary devices, metaphors are embedded in our ways of thinking about ourselves, others, and the world. Like the operating system of a computer that runs quietly "in the background" of what we see on the screen, metaphors and image schemata exist underneath our words and thoughts and actions. As it turns out, they are very "real." Lakoff observes that "metaphors impose a structure on real life, *through the creation of new correspondences in experience. And once created in one generation, they serve as an experiential basis for that metaphor in the next generation.*"[14] This is precisely what seems to have happened in medieval Sahajiyā communities, as influential gurus developed distinctive alternative metaphoric worlds based on their own yogic experiences, expressed them orally and in written texts, and then passed them down to their own students. Through their development of such worlds they were able to express and disseminate their alternative Krishna traditions to others in greater Bengal.

When we consider the often lovely inner worlds depicted in Sahajiyā texts (e.g., beautiful groves and villages, radiant lotus clusters, "The Place of the Hidden Moon," "The Pond of Divine Love") we need to bear in mind that these visionary worlds are connected to underlying metaphorical structures and experienced by Sahajiyās as very real—more "real" than the outer realm of zamindars, geckoes, and monsoons. Sahajiyās did not just attempt to construe their esoteric language so that it made sense in the ordinary world; rather, to paraphrase literary critic Samuel Levin,[15] they construed the world to make sense of the esoteric language. It is thus this profound "process of construal" that we must be sensitive to, by noting regional phrasings, local references, and above all metaphorical consistencies (or, in some cases, inconsistencies).

For esoteric mystical traditions like the Sahajiyās, ritual practices—ranging from the beginner's practices of singing and dancing adapted from Gauḍīya Vaishnava *vaidhi-bhakti* to the Tantric sexual rituals practiced at the advanced stage of *siddha*—thus allow for a visualized inner cosmos and body that is construed in terms of the metaphors, be they "rivers," "ponds," "flowers," or "villages." There is, of course, a physical component, as parts of the human body and material world are homologized with the metaphors, such as the vagina with a lotus, the penis with a honeybee, the urethra with a river, and so forth. This esoteric "process of construal," then, allows for not just metaphoric language based on concepts, but also for religious realities and concepts "created" by the metaphoric language. The religious adept is thus "projected into," engages, and responds to, such metaphoric worlds as coherent reality, not at all fictive illusion.[16]

Folklorist Barre Toelken, in his wonderful study of European and American folksongs and ballads, *Morning Dew and Roses*, argues that "We will not want to read meaning into a song, but rather attempt to read meaning out by carefully noting . . . the relationship of the metaphor to the assumptions in its culture and by charting its coherent relationships to the song in which it appears."[17] When reading such material (or listening to it), the scholar should be sensitive to the "range of metaphorical possibilities" within the text and the culture, and will discover that this range can span "almost explicit metonymy to complex suggestive metaphor."[18]

In the case of Sahajiyā texts, which are often riddlelike in their use of uninflected language and esoteric vocabulary, there is an interesting range of imagery and metaphor, much of which is "hydraulic" in nature, based on sexuality, fluids, rivers, ponds, and flowers. We also find such imageries in other Bengali vernacular Tantric traditions, such as Bāul, Śākta, and Kartābhajā songs.[19] This consistency suggests that such choices are neither coincidental nor random. In explaining the polysemy of Euro-American "riddle songs," Toelken observes:

> The more fully we can perceive the vernacular system from which the song grows and in which such references make sense, the more we will realize that there is not a strict code of any sort, but rather a field of metaphorical possibility, a pool of culturally recognizable resources in the language and in everyday jokes and formulations.[20]

Thus, in a way, we return to Lakoff and Johnson's basic point about metaphor, that the relationship between the target and source domains (between the denotative and connotative, "love" and "journey," or "woman" and "lotus flower") is not simple and predictable, and certainly not a simple or even predictable "code."

The *Amṛtaratnāvalī* or "Necklace of Immortality" of Mukunda-dāsa was composed approximately in 1650 CE, and in its more than three hundred couplets we find a rich trove of metaphors and Bengali cultural references—as well as the tantric visualizations and ritual procedures that are its main focus. As with other Bengali vernacular tantras, it expresses a worldview emphasizing embodiment, the transformative and salvific powers of ritual sexual intercourse, and the importance of "substance" in the religious quest. The very title, "Necklace (*ratnāvali*) of Immortality (*amṛta*)," is itself a polysemic metaphor, for it suggests not only the uses of jewels and bodily ornamentation in tantric ritual, but the more fundamental notion that the practitioner must "fashion" and then figuratively "wear" an encircling *maṇḍala* made out of the "jewels" or *ratna* which, in the esoteric language of the text, are yogically reversed sexual fluids. Called *vastu* or "stuff" by Mukunda-dāsa, these fluids are created and joined when the male practitioner, as Krishna, joins with his female partner who is visualized as Rādhā. The process is one in which the male is believed to draw the female sexual fluid (*rati*) from the woman's vagina into his penis, where it joins with his semen (*rasa*) and is then caused to move upward along the "crooked river" (*bāṅkānadī*), through four inner ponds (*sarovara*), and finally up to Sahaja itself. (Some have playfully termed this the "reverse-fountain-pen technique," but it is a variant of the tantric practice of "reverse suction," such as the *vajrolī-mudrā* of Siddha traditions).[21] As abstract and mystical as these inner places may be, they are all accessible through the fluids of the human body, connected to the very "stuff" (vastu) of this world.

That Mukunda-dāsa and other medieval Vaishnava Sahajiyās would use a substantive term like vastu in their description of subtle physiology is significant, for it illustrates the use of several different kinds of *ontological* metaphors identified by Lakoff and Johnson: entity, substance, and container metaphors. Abstractions like the Sahajiyā experience of a "divine body" (*deva-deha*) and associated states of consciousness are expressed and made more accessible through the use of such images. As Lakoff and Johnson note:

> Our experience of physical objects and substances provides a further basis for understanding—one that goes beyond mere orientation. Understanding our experiences in terms of objects and substances allows us to pick out parts of our experience and treat them as discrete entities or substances of a uniform kind. Once we can identify our experiences as entities or substances, we can refer to them, categorize them, group them, and quantify them—and, by this means, reason about them.[22]

Because of the use of such "substantive" metaphors to express mystical experiences, the metaphoric world of the *Necklace* has a particular character or quality that distinguishes it from the metaphoric worlds of some Sanskrit-based Tantric or Krishna traditions, which often use different kinds of metaphors. Whereas the metaphoric world of the *Necklace* is expressed primarily through metaphors of substances and fluids, other types of Tantric worlds, for example, those expressed using the better-known systems of cakras and kuṇḍalinī-śakti, use metaphors of energy, sound, power, and light.[23] Although this is not the place to explore the many fascinating issues arising from such differences (and similarities), it should be clear that, once a basic metaphorical world is established, certain entailments and outcomes are possible—while others are not. In other words, a cosmophysiology based primarily (though not exclusively) upon fluids and substances will probably have some dynamics or "feel" (to use a modern sensory metaphor) that vary from one based primarily upon energy, sound, and light.

Mukunda-dāsa is quite clear about the importance of substance and fluid, for early in the text (NI:7–12), immediately after offering homage to notable Gauḍīya Vaishnava authorities like Caitanya, Nityānanda, and the Gosvāmins, he discusses the importance of *rasa*, understood on several levels—as a religio-aesthetic experience, as a sexual substance, and even as an alchemical term (as mercury).[24] However, since the basic meaning of rasa is "juice" or "essence" (as from a sugar cane), this allows Mukunda-dāsa to develop entailments based upon the core image of a "sweet fluid" that causes delightful sensations when "tasted." Thus, rasa can be the rapturous aesthetic or devotional experience of "sweet" emotions, and it can also be the essence that derives, not just from a cane, but from the penis. Furthermore, those who experience rasa are called *rasikas* ("aesthetes," "connoisseurs," or "tasters"), and Mukunda-dāsa compares their experiences to floating upon a river (NI:8–9):

> Those devotees who are *rasikas* seek the subtle inner Body (*śrī-rūpa*).
> Their minds are constantly bobbing (*ḍubāya*) about in the *rasa*.
>
> With minds submerged (*magna*) in *rasa*, they float along.
> *Rasa* can only be produced by keeping the company of *rasikas*.

Both meanings of rasa—as aesthetic experience and sexual substance—share similar entailments, for both "experience" and "semen" can "flow" like a river. This riverine entailment or extended meaning of the basic substance/fluid metaphor also helps to suggest why the subtle physiology of the *Necklace* consists of a system of a river and ponds, and not the more familiar *suṣumṇā-nāḍī* and cakras of other traditions: fluids naturally run through rivers and streams and into ponds. Recalling the earlier metaphors of love and sādhana as a journey, which defines a path and surfaces, if mystical experience is being expressed in terms of fluidic metaphors, then the later stages of the process of liberation may be expressed as passage along a river, being contained by the two banks of the river, flowing into a pond, and leaving the waters through landing-stairs (*ghāṭ*) to enter neighboring celestial villages (*grāma*). Of course, much of this also reflects the natural topology and climate of deltaic Bengal, with its innumerable streams, rivers, and bodies of water. In other words, the experiences of substances, fluids, rivers, and bodies of water may have been adopted as metaphors and then projected in order to refer to, categorize, group, and quantify profound mystical and sexual experiences.

I hope that these brief comments regarding contemporary metaphor theory have been of some use as we consider the nature of alternative Krishna traditions. Bengali vernacular Tantric traditions are wonderful examples of the dynamic nature of the history of religions, but there is still much interesting work to do. As depicted in the Bengali verses of Mukunda-dāsa, the transformation of men and women into Krishna and Rādhā is a complex esoteric process. Thanks to their gurus, fellow adepts, and ritual processes, the Sahajiyās envision and experience a very special body that they can use for realizing the "original" cosmic state of Sahaja. And just as sensible people in the ordinary world like to dress appropriately for any given occasion, Mukunda-dāsa has thoughtfully provided that subtle body with its own *Necklace of Immortality*.

Notes

Some portions of this chapter have appeared in my essay "Metaphoric Worlds and Yoga in the Vaiṣṇava Sahajiyā Tantric Traditions of Medieval Bengal," in *Yoga: The Indian Tradition*, edited by Ian Whicher and David Carpenter (2003), 162–84; other portions will appear in a forthcoming work, "The Guru's Tongue: Metaphor, Ambivalence, and Appropriation in Vaiṣṇava Sahajiyā Traditions," in *In the Flesh: Eros, Secrecy, and Power in the Tantric Traditions of South Asia*, edited by Hugh B. Urban, Glen Alexander Hayes, and Paul Muller-Ortega (forthcoming).

1. Standard scholarly works on the Vaishnava Sahajiyās in English are Shashibhusan Dasgupta (1969), especially 113–56; Manindramohan Bose (1930, reprint 1986); and Edward C. Dimock Jr. (1966, reprint 1989). Scholarly works in Bengali include: Manindra Mohan Basu (Bose) (1932); Paritos Dāsa (1972 and 1978) and Gopinath Kaviraj (1969–75), which covers the Vaishnava Sahajiyās in various places. An excellent introduction to Tantra in general is provided by David Gordon White, "Introduction," in *Tantra in Practice* (2000), 3–38. White has also provided an intriguing study of Tantric sexuality in *The Kiss of the Yoginī: "Tantric Sex" in Its South Asian Contexts* (2003). Also valuable are recent works by Hugh B. Urban, including *Tantra: Sex, Secrecy, Politics and Power in the Study of Religion* (2003); *The Economics of Ecstasy: Tantra, Secrecy, and Power in Colonial Bengal* (2001a), and the companion volume of translated texts, *Songs of Ecstasy: Tantric and Devotional Songs from Bengal* (2001b). Superb studies of Hindu Tantrism may be found in Douglas Renfrew Brooks, *The Secret of the Three Cities: An Introduction to Hindu Śākta Tantrism* (1990) and Paul Eduardo Muller-Ortega, *The Triadic Heart of Śiva: Kaula Tantricism of Abhinavagupta in the Non-Dual Shaivism of Kashmir*, State University of New York Series in the Shaiva Traditions of Kashmir, edited by Harvey P. Alper (1989). For my own works, see references.

2. See Glen Alexander Hayes (fall 1999), 77–90.

3. See references for full citation.

4. For an overview, see Glen Alexander Hayes (fall 1999).

5. For a brief survey of Western views through the mid-twentieth century, see Terence Hawkes (1972). On the basic traditions of Sanskrit aesthetics, see A. K. Ramanujan and Edwin Gerow (1974), 115–43.

6. Perhaps the most comprehensive collection of essays, examining metaphor from a range of disciplines, may be found in Andrew Ortony, ed. (1993). Another valuable collection is Sheldon Sacks, ed. (1979). The URL for the Center for the Cognitive Science of Metaphor Online is http://philosophy.uoregon.edu/metaphor/metaphor.htm. This has many links to other related sites.

7. George Lakoff and Mark Johnson (1980), 3. Other relevant studies in contemporary metaphor theory include Mark Johnson (1987); George Lakoff and Mark Turner (1989); George Lakoff (1987); and George Lakoff and Mark

Johnson (1999). Finally, an intriguing recent work in cognitive science and linguistics is also worth noting: Gilles Fauconnier and Mark Turner (2002). I am indebted to these works for helping me to appreciate the pivotal role of metaphor in the medieval Vaishnava Sahajiyā traditions.

8. Mark Johnson (1987), xiv–xv.

9. George Lakoff (1993), 203–4. See Michael J. Reddy, "The Conduit Metaphor: A Case of Frame Conflict in Our Language about Language," in Andrew Ortony, ed. (1993), 164–201.

10. George Lakoff (1993), 207.

11. This phrase was introduced by Tony K. Stewart of North Carolina State University at a conference held at the University of Pennsylvania on September 12–14, 1997, entitled *Constrained by Choice? The Places of Bengali Vernacular Tantra.* I am indebted to Dr. Stewart for his insights into the uses of contemporary metaphor theory.

12. Mark Johnson (1987), 215.

13. Mark Johnson (1987), xiv.

14. George Lakoff (1993), 241.

15. See Samuel Levin, "Language, Concepts, and Worlds: Three Domains of Metaphor," in Andrew Ortony, ed. (1993), 121.

16. This is very much what goes on in the Gauḍīya Vaishnava practice of *rāgānuga-bhakti-sādhana*, adapted by Sahajiyās for beginners. In this, one envisions, and gradually identifies with, a character in the mythical love play of Rādhā and Krishna. See David L. Haberman (1988).

17. Barre Toelken (1995), 34.

18. Barre Toelken (1995), 35–36.

19. For an excellent recent study of the Kartābhajās and a collection of translated songs, see Hugh B. Urban (2001b).

20. Barre Toelken (1995), 39.

21. David Gordon White (1996).

22. George Lakoff and Mark Johnson (1980), 25.

23. This is not to say that Mukunda-dāsa does not make some use of these other metaphors, especially sound and color/light, or that other traditions eschew metaphors of fluid and substance. However, Mukunda-dāsa clearly emphasizes the primacy of the substance/fluid metaphors over these others. I will explore these issues further in a forthcoming work.

24. See Monier Monier-Williams (1976), 869, cols. 2–3. On the Gauḍīya Vaishnava and Vaishnava Sahajiyā interpretations, see Edward C. Dimock (1966, reprint 1989), 20–24. An extensive treatment of alchemy may be found in David Gordon White (1996).

References

Basu (Bose), Manindra Mohan. *Sahajiyā Sāhitya*. Calcutta: University of Calcutta, 1932.

Bose, Manindramohan. *The Post-Caitanya Sahajia [sic] Cult of Bengal.* Calcutta: University of Calcutta, 1930, Reprint ed. Delhi: Gian, 1986.

Brooks, Douglas Renfrew. *The Secret of the Three Cities: An Introduction to Hindu Śākta Tantrism.* Chicago: University of Chicago Press, 1990.

Dasa, Paritos. *Caitanyottara prathamā cariti sahajiyā puṅthi.* Calcutta: Bharati Book Stall, 1972.

Dasgupta, Shashibhusan. *Obscure Religious Cults*, 3d ed. Calcutta: Firma K. L. Mukhopadhyay, 1969.

Dimock Jr, Edward C. *The Place of the Hidden Moon: Erotic Mysticism in the Vaiṣṇava-sahajiyā Cult of Bengal.* Chicago: University of Chicago Press, 1966; reprint ed. Phoenix, 1989.

Fauconnier, Gilles, and Mark Turner. *The Way We Think: Conceptual Blending and the Mind's Hidden Complexities.* New York: Basic, 2002.

Haberman, David L. *Acting as a Way of Salvation: A Study of Rāgānuga Bhakti Sādhana.* New York: Oxford University Press, 1988.

Hawkes, Terence. *Metaphor.* London: Methuen, 1972.

Hayes, Glen Alexander. "Boating upon the Crooked River: Cosmophysiological Soteriologies in the Vaiṣṇava Sahajiyā Tradition of Medieval Bengal." In *Shaping Bengali Worlds, Public and Private.* Tony K. Stewart, ed. South Asia Series Occasional Paper No. 37. East Lansing: Asian Studies Center/Michigan State University, 1989), 29–35.

———. "The Churning of Controversy: Vaiṣṇava Sahajiyā Appropriations of Gauḍīya Vaiṣṇavism." *Journal of Vaiṣṇava Studies* 8:1 (fall 1999), 77–90.

———. "Cosmic Substance in the Vaiṣṇava Sahajiyā Traditions of Medieval Bengal." *Journal of Vaiṣṇava Studies* 5:1 (winter 1996–97), 183–96.

———. "The Guru's Tongue: Metaphor, Ambivalence, and Appropriation in Vaiṣṇava Sahajiyā Traditions." In *In the Flesh: Eros, Secrecy, and Power in the Tantric Traditions of South Asia.* Hugh B. Urban, Glen Alexander Hayes, and Paul Muller-Ortega, eds. Oxford: Oxford University Press, 2004.

———. "Metaphoric Worlds and Yoga in the Vaiṣṇava Sahajiyā Tantric Traditions of Medieval Bengal." In *Yoga: The Indian Tradition.* Ian Whicher and David Carpenter, eds. London and New York: Routledge Curzon, 2003, 162–84.

———. "The Necklace of Immortality: A Seventeenth-Century Vaiṣṇava Sahajiyā Text." In *Tantra in Practice,* David Gordon White, ed. Princeton, NJ: Princeton University Press, 2000, 308–25.

———. "On the Concept of Vastu in the Vaiṣṇava-sahajiyā Tradition of Medieval Bengal." In *Religions and Comparative Thought: Essays in Honour of the Late Dr. Ian Kesarcodi-Watson.* Purusottama Bilimoria and Peter Fenner, eds. Sri Garib Dass Oriental Series No. 62. Delhi: Sri Satguru Publications/Indian Books Centre, 1988, 141–49.

———. "Shapes for the Soul: A Study of Body Symbolism in the Vaiṣṇava-sahajiyā Tradition of Medieval Bengal," Ph.D. Dissertation, University of Chicago, 1985.

———. "The Vaiṣṇava Sahajiyā Traditions of Medieval Bengal." In *Religions of India in Practice.* Donald S. Lopez, Jr., ed. Princeton Readings in Religion. Princeton, NJ: Princeton University Press, 1995, 333–51.

Johnson, Mark. *The Body in the Mind: The Bodily Basis of Meaning, Imagination, and Reason.* Chicago: University of Chicago Press, 1987.

Kaviraj, Gopinath. *Tantrik sādhana o siddhānta,* 2 vols. Burdhwan: Bardhaman Visvavidyalaya, 1969–75.

Lakoff, George. "The Contemporary Theory of Metaphor." In *Methaphor and Thought,* 2d ed. Andrew Ortony, ed. Cambridge: Cambridge University Press, 1993, 202–51.

———. *Women, Fire, and Dangerous Things: What Categories Reveal about the Mind.* Chicago: University of Chicago Press, 1987.

Lakoff, George, and Mark Johnson. *Metaphors We Live By.* Chicago: University of Chicago Press, 1980.

———. *Philosophy in the Flesh: The Embodies Mind and Its Challenge to Western Thought.* New York: Basic, 1999.

Lakoff, George, and Mark Turner. *More than Cool Reason: A Field Guide to Poetic Metaphor.* Chicago: University of Chicago Press, 1989.

Monier-Williams, Monier. *A Sanskrit-English Dictionary.* Reprint ed. Oxford: Clarendon, 1976.

Muller-Ortega, Paul Eduardo. *The Triadic Heart of Śiva: Kaula Tantricism of Abhinavagupta in the Non-Dual Shaivism of Kashmir,* State University of New York Series in the Shaiva Traditions of Kashmir. Harvey P. Alper, ed. Albany: State University of New York Press, 1989.

Ortony, Andrew, ed. *Metaphor and Thought.* 2d ed. Cambridge: Cambridge University Press, 1993.

Ramanujan, A. K., and Edwin Gerow. "Indian Poetics." In *The Literatures of India: An Introduction,* Edward C. Dimock Jr. et al., eds. Chicago: University of Chicago Press, 1974, 115–43.

Sacks, Sheldon, ed. *On Metaphor.* Chicago: University of Chicago Press, 1979.

Toelken, Barre. *Morning Dew and Roses: Nuance, Metaphor, and Meaning in Folksongs.* Urbana and Chicago: University of Illinois Press, 1995.

Urban, Hugh B. *The Economics of Ecstasy: Tantra, Secrecy, and Power in Colonial Bengal.* New York: Oxford University Press, 2001a.

———. *Songs of Ecstasy: Tantric and Devotional Songs from Bengal*. New York: Oxford University Press, 2001b.

———. *Tantra: Sex, Secrecy, Politics and Power in the Study of Religion*. Berkeley: University of California Press, 2003.

White, David Gordon. *The Alchemical Body: Siddha Traditions in Medieval India*. Chicago: University of Chicago Press, 1996.

———. "Introduction." In *Tantra in Practice.* David Gordon White, ed. Princeton, NJ: Princeton University Press, 2000, 3–38.

———. *The Kiss of the Yoginī: "Tantric Sex" in Its South Asian Contexts*. Chicago: University of Chicago Press, 2003.

Chapter 3

Folk Vaishnavism and the Ṭhākur Pañcāyat
Life and Status among Village Krishna Statues

June McDaniel

In West Bengal, Krishna is understood by Vaishnava devotees to be a living presence in his various statue forms. In some villages, the New Year is celebrated by having a Ṭhākur Pañcāyat, or council meeting of deities in the form of statues. The statues are carried in procession, feasted, and left to discuss the village budget and future celebrations. This chapter will examine assumptions inherent in this meeting of deities and the various types and moods of living statues. It will also contrast the orthodox Gauḍīya Vaishnava tradition with alternative "folk" understandings of the nature and manifestation of the god Krishna.

The April New Year in the rural district of 24 Parganas is celebrated as the Vaishnava Goṣṭho holiday. In Moyda village, people who have done service to the town's Krishna temple carry their personal statues of Krishna in a procession. These include the deity's various forms: Śyāmasundara, Gopīnātha, Madanmohana, Rādhā-Krishna, and others. Statues from all over the village come to the central temple of Krishna as Rādhāvallabha.

There is much concern as to whether the various statues of Śyāmasundara, Gopīnātha, Murāri, Madanmohana, Rādhā-Krishna, and others will come first or last. The statues are first left alone to discuss business, and then seated at a feast in their honor, with the highest-status deities at the head of the table. Those who serve each statue show their devotion to their house deity. The order at the procession and the seats at the *pañcāyat* meeting and feast are dependent on the temple service and donations of food and money of their owners, who are most anxious to show their dedication to their house deities by placing them above other house deities. Though all of the deities are forms of Krishna, some are claimed to be superior to others on the basis of mood (*rasa*), craftsmanship, and elaborate worship by their devotees.[1]

The statues are believed to discuss the village budget and plans for next year's celebration when they get together. Though there is a pecking order, it is believed that the gods are sociable. According to one village informant, "God-statues (ṭhākurs) are like cows; they all like to meet together and they like to go to the assembly of gods. When they pass the homes of Śiva and Kālī, they bow and salute them; gods are respectful of other gods." There is no rivalry on this day between Vaishnava and Śākta followers.

Vaishnava "animism," the embodiment of a living Krishna in statues and other objects, is widespread in rural West Bengal. While classical Gauḍīya Vaishnavism emphasizes theological Sanskrit texts, literary knowledge, and complex categories of drama and emotion, folk Vaishnavism focuses on miracles, possession, and the use of Harinām (chanting the name of Krishna) to dispel evil spirits, disease, and bad luck. It also includes living statues who act in the world. While some statues are particularly alive and can give special insight into Krishna's experience or can grant boons, others do nothing, get ignored, and eventually are given to temples—the "old-age homes" for unwanted living statues.

Bengal Vaishnavism is often equated with the Gauḍīya Vaishnava tradition, yet there are several other Vaishnava traditions in West Bengal. Historically, there are the Parama-Bhāgavatas, for whom Krishna was an incarnation,[2] and the erotic Vaishnavism of the *Gītagovinda* (twelfth century) and the songs of Caṇḍīdāsa and Vidyāpati, which later influenced the tradition of Sahajiyā Vaishnavism.

Gauḍīya Vaishnavism is considered the classical or orthodox form of Vaishnavism in West Bengal, a monotheistic tradition with Krishna as both transcendent creator god and male person fascinated by the emotional depths of his consort, Rādhā. Sahajiyā Vaishnavism, the alternative Krishna tradition discussed in the previous chapter, is considered heretical by the Gauḍīya school. It is a dualistic and often Tantric tradition which has many doctrines and forms of textual interpretation. Some of their prominent beliefs are that worlds and deities dwell within the human body, the importance of the feminine principle (*śakti*), and the use of sexual and other bodily rituals for grasping the immanent divine couple.

Still another form of Vaishnavism is that which is practiced in Bengali villages by people who have not been trained in the ritual and doctrinal knowledge of the former schools. This may be called *deśī* or folk Vaishnavism, and its doctrines would be closest to the much disputed "little tradition" of Hinduism. Rather than the monotheistic Gauḍīyas or dualistic Sahajiyās, folk Vaishnavism is polytheistic, or more properly henotheistic: Krishna is the most important god in a large pantheon of gods, ancestors, village guardians, and irritable ghosts. Unlike the relatively static Krishna of normative theology, this alternative Krishna often changes roles—he may be a fertility god of the fields, or a protector of villagers (like the Krishna of the *Bhāgavata Purāṇa* who protected villagers from the great snake Kāliya). He is a god of blessings and miracles, animals and thieves, a hero and a trickster. He spends a lot of time in statues and rocks.

While both Gauḍīyas and folk Vaishnavas have a range of beliefs about the manifestation and embodiment of Krishna in the world, they differ on some crucial points. In Gauḍīya theology, Krishna may be present in both human and statue form. In humans, such presence denotes an *avatāra*, a person in whom the god is fully or partially present. A person may be a *pūrṇa avatāra*, a perfect avatār in whom all of the god's powers are fully present, or an *aṃśa avatāra*, one who is like a limb or a part of the god, where only a portion of the god's power is manifest. Such avatāra forms may be limited in time: in the *prabhava* form, the full form and power of the deity are present temporarily (as in the story of Mohinī), while in the *āveśa* form, a portion of the deity's power comes down during possession or trance, and some aspect of the deity is present for the space of the trance.[3]

The god may also be present in statues, called *mūrti* or *vigraha*, the concrete and artistic form of the deity. The god may enter as a result of ritual, yet this is understood as his *prasāda* or grace, and his choice rather than his obedience to human ritual action. The god may also exist in a rock or statue or other locale spontaneously, without the use of ritual.

When Krishna has been called down into a mūrti, that particular figure of stone, wood, metal, or other substance becomes inwardly pure, full of truth, consciousness, and bliss.[4] The mūrti is both physical and supernatural, the body and soul of the deity. The god indwells in spiritual form, not visible to the mortal eye.[5] He can only be seen by divine vision (*divya-dṛṣṭi*). As the form that is worshiped (*arcā-mūrti*), it is the god in physical form, and the temple or shrine becomes his divine world.

In Gauḍīya Vaishnavism, the condition of being in the presence of the statue, having its *darśana*, is important, because each statue is understood to express a specific rasa or mood of Krishna. The concept of dramatic rasas derive from Bhārata Muni's *Nāṭya-Śāstra*, where eight basic sentiments are described: erotic, comic, pathetic, furious, heroic, terrible, disgusting, and marvelous. However, Vaishnava writers have reorganized these basic emotions in various ways. According to Rūpa Goswāmin, *bhakti*, or devotional love, is the root or primordial rasa, and the other moods are subsumed under this root of bhakti-rasa.[6] Rūpa wrote of five basic rasas of devotion: pure love, affection, friendship, parental love, and erotic love. Other Vaishnava writers have placed a greater emphasis on Bharāta's model. The rasas act as triggers of *bhāvas*, or human states of intense emotion, such that the act of visiting various enlivened statues can generate the desired emotions in devotees who are able to perceive the divine nature of the statues.

The substance of the statue is understood to give special blessings. Wood brings long life, clay brings pleasures in every world, gems bring prosperity, gold brings strength, silver brings fame, copper brings many children, and stone brings wealth and property.

Folk Vaishnavism, on the other hand, is rarely concerned with rasas and bhāvas. It is much more concerned with pleasing the god so that he will do special favors for the devotee. The miracle worker and saint are more important than the scholar (*śāstrī*) and *gosvāmin*, and Krishna will bless his devotees in worldly life, in bringing rain, good crops, or love and happiness.

In folk Vaishnavism, we see the statues imbued with a different kind of life. Village Krishna statues are believed by devotees to get upset if treated poorly, and experience the statue equivalent of "anxiety attacks" unless they are a militant form of deity. This is one reason why they are often placed in cages behind bars in larger towns—they are too sensitive to defend themselves against thieves or Muslims seeking to knock their noses off. Such behavior is a form of deity torture, as the gods are stuck in their statue bodies and cannot leave when they choose. Home deities are often treated like disabled family members—they are fed, bathed, dressed, entertained, and tucked in at night. Vaishnava devotees have explained that they must feed the deity, for Krishna cannot feed himself, and he would starve otherwise.

During the Bangladesh war, when Hindus in East Pakistan fled with only what they could carry, many families chose to carry their statues rather than food, clothing, or money. As one informant in Calcutta said of his statue: "He is a family member—leaving without him would be like leaving a child behind, or an elderly grandfather. You wouldn't leave a member of your family to enemies in a war."[7]

The god may also be present in rocks, plants, or parts of the natural landscape. The *śālagrāma* stone is a dark stone found along the banks of the Gaṇḍakī River. They are *svayambhū*, spontaneous dwelling places of Krishna or Vishnu in his various forms—Nārāyaṇa, Vāsudeva, Keśava, Saṁkarṣaṇa, and so on. Krishna's form may be determined according to the stone's characteristics. He lives within the stone of his own choice, without the need for ritual invocation, and the stones possess sanctity and merit. They can be touched by women and impure *śūdras* without reducing their powers. Smaller stones are considered to be more auspicious, and while their worship is *nitya*, or compulsory, śālagrāmas may not be bought or sold.

According to some classical Purāṇic sources, certain śālagrāmas give special benefits. For instance, the Rājarājeśvara śālagrāma with seven cakra marks and an umbrella gives its owner the wealth of kings, while the Narasiṁha gives renunciation, the Vāsudeva fulfills desires, the Aniruddha comforts householders, and the Śrīdhara gives wealth.[8]

In folk Vaishnavism, however, śālagrāmas have a variety of other powers. They bless people with wealth and fertility, and can create through spontaneous generation. One traditional way to test a śālagrāma is by the test of multiplication: put the stone on a pile of rice and measure the rice, seeing if it multiplies due to its proximity to the stone.[9] Or the stone may act as a field guardian or *kshetrapāla*, and that field should remain fertile and healthy. Sometimes in Northwestern India the stones may be placed in groups of five and called *pāṇḍavas*, though this is rare in West Bengal. Śālagrāmas are also said to protect against witches, who get hypnotized by the stones, confused by their holes and veins.

The śālagrāma may also bless people by being dipped in water, and the water sipped three times. For the stone to be happiest and to work best, it should be married to the Tulsi plant. Ideally, there should be a garden wedding, with brahmin priests present. The stone may then bring visions and luck.

Stones and statues of gods and goddesses are loosely called "ṭhākurs," or lords, by many village people. Āmār Ṭhākur, "My Lord," does not generally refer to a deity in heaven, but rather to a deity on earth: the stone or statue in the house worship room (*ṭhākur ghar*). Ṭhākurs have both upward and downward mobility. A rock or other object may be determined to be the dwelling place of a deity, placed in a house to be worshiped, and gain the respect of the family. If that family is blessed with luck, especially cures of disease, then the family deity may be worshiped by the village.

As a village deity, the stone may get its own temple and a full-time priest. People from other villages may come over with offerings. It can get a reputation as a deity that is alive and awake, and its temple can become a place of pilgrimage. Sometimes it may be taken in procession to other villages, which keep an empty seat (*āsana*) for its visit.

There is also a downward mobility among ṭhākurs, however. When a stone or statue has not been doing its job, and the town or family has been unlucky, the statue may be understood as weak (however, if there are real disasters, the statue may also be viewed as strong but angry, and needing propitiation). If the statue is determined to be weak, or its worshipers leave and nobody else wishes to take on the responsibility of caring for it, it loses status. It may be consigned to the Ganges River or some other body of water, or it may be put into a temple of some other deity as an additional god or goddess, also cared for by the priest. Some temples become a sort of "old-age home" for ṭhākurs, with unwanted gods donated along with money for their upkeep. There are sections in some temples for old goddess stones, *liṅgas*, Nārāyaṇa stones, small statues, and even photographs. However, I have found the topic of getting rid of unwanted ṭhākurs to be an embarrassing one for informants, perhaps comparable to getting rid of unwanted relatives. People are uncomfortable at leaving their grandfather's goddess in the spare room or sending her off to live on a temple's charity.

In some cases, a deserted temple with a living deity may have the equivalent of "home health care"—a group or society may decide to hire a brahmin to visit the temple each day to feed and care for the deity. This is because the ground on which the temple sits is sacred ground, and it has been revealed that the deity wishes to stay in its own temple, on its own ground. Within native Ādivāsī communities, a major situation exists in which old deities are lost through forced migration (especially during the building of roads and dams), when the traditional home lands must be left, and the rocks and ground sacred to the deities must also be left behind.

If localized Ādivāsī deities are viewed as more powerful than the pan-Indian Hindu deities, there may be competition; sometimes they may even chase them out of town. According to a folk ballad of the Santal rebellion, when the Santals rose up and invaded Hindu Bengal,

> the pillaging of the insurgents on the people of Banskuli was so severe that even the village tutelary deity, Kambasini, fled away from her shrine . . . the god Gopal [Krishna] of Bhanderban became panic-stricken.[10]

However, some Krishna statues are known for their bravery. In 1669 CE, the image of Krishna known as Śrīnāthjī was removed from Govardhan in the Braj area to be hidden in Mewar in Rajasthan. The priests of this deity wanted to protect the statue from the menace of Aurangzeb and his Muslim armies, but "when they reached the village of Sinhad (or Siarh), . . . Śrīnāthjī's cart got stuck beneath a pipal tree and could not be moved any further. This was taken as a sign that the deity wished to settle at that spot. It was installed in a hastily constructed shrine, which was later replaced by a temple."[11] The township that grew up around this shrine became known as Nāthadvāra ("Gateway to God") and has always been protected by the presence of Krishna. Other statues are known for their more sensual nature: one Krishna statue shared the bed of a Delhi princess, and she later became absorbed into it;[12] an image of Jagannāth followed a gardener's daughter as she sang a verse from the *Gītagovinda*.[13]

In closing, some further distinctions between orthodox Gauḍīya Vaishnava thought and folk Vaishnavism regarding the nature of the god Krishna and his manifestation in the physical world may be mentioned. In orthodox Gauḍīya or Bengal Vaishnavism, Krishna is the only true god, creator of the universe. According to Rūpa Goswāmin, one of the principle theologians of Gauḍīya Vaishnavism, Krishna's *svarūpa* or true form manifests in three ways. His *svayam-rūpa* or transcendent form is self-existent, not dependent on anything. His *tadekātma-rūpa* is identical in essence to his true form, though it differs in appearance (and would include such forms of Krishna as Nārāyaṇa and Vāsudeva). His āveśa form has Krishna appearing though in varying degrees of possession, and through such qualities as śakti, *jñāna*, and bhakti.[14]

Krishna's avatāras may be in any of the latter categories, in varying degrees of descent, in order to perform action in the world. An avatāra can be a *puruṣa avatāra*, one of Krishna's emanations for the sake of creation; a *guṇāvatāra* or deity of qualities, such as Brahma, Vishnu and Śiva; or it may be a *līlāvatāra*, manifesting Krishna's joy in creativity (these include avatārs of *kalpas* and *yugas*). Each avatāra has his own locale in the heaven of Mahāvaikuṇṭha.[15] Such *līlās* are both real and eternal, and exist in both the manifest and unmanifest worlds; Krishna can live in both eternal Vrindāvana and earthly Mathurā. According to Jīva Goswāmin, another orthodox theologian, the avatāras descend for the welfare of the world, and Krishna takes on a specific form for the purpose of the descent. While he is actually unembodied, he temporarily possesses a physical form or mūrti. Such mūrtis possess varying degrees of power and beauty or rasa.

However, in the folk understanding, Krishna is an immanent god, found in matter and in the human heart. He blesses sacred places and sacred objects, and can be found in special temples, streams, and mountains. He is not far away, but close at hand, within the matter of which the devotee is made. While the orthodox understanding of the Krishna mūrti holds that an all-powerful transcendent god dwells within the statue, who can come or go at any time according to his will, the folk understanding is that the Krishna mūrti contains an aspect of Krishna who has lost much of his divine power by entering the statue, and is now trapped within his material form. This Krishna is not all-powerful, but weakened and dependent upon his caretaker. That is why mūrtis must be turned over to temples, to be fed and cared for by priests, and why they are fearful of invaders.

In early Christian theology, Christ was said to have undergone *kenosis*, the "self-emptying" of his divinity, by his descent into the physical world.[16] This was why he was able to become fully human. The folk Krishna, too, has lost his vast spiritual strength by his entrance into the material world, and thus he becomes dependent upon the Krishna *bhaktas* or devotees who serve him. Unlike the powerful Gauḍīya Krishna who rules the universe, this alternative or folk Krishna has humbled himself as a prisoner within matter.

Notes

1. This *Ṭhākur Pañcāyat* was described to me by the anthropologist Tushar Niyogī, who had attended this festival, as well as other local informants.
2. According to S. K. De (1961), this is documented by inscriptions.
3. See the discussion in S. K. De (1961), 243–45.
4. S. K. De (1961), 284.
5. S. K. De (1961), 287.
6. S. N. Ghosal (1974), 38.
7. Interview, Administrator, Calcutta, 1984.
8. Gautam Chatterjee (1996), 67–69.
9. J. Abbott (1974), 249.
10. R. M. Sarkar (1986), 39.
11. A. W. Entwistle (1987), 184.
12. J. Tod (1884), 143.
13. J. Tod (1884), 143.
14. S. K. De (1961), 240.
15. S. K. De (1961), 242.
16. *Kenosis* is a term in Christian theology that refers to the self-emptying of Christ. The concept is described in one of Paul's letters: "For the divine nature was his from the first; yet he did not think to snatch at equality with God, but made himself nothing, assuming the nature of a slave. Bearing the human likeness, revealed in human shape, he humbled himself, and in obedience accepted even death" (Philippians 2:5–11). It was used primarily by writers of the Patristic period, though later writers have also made reference to it.

References

Abbot, J. *The Keys of Power: A Study of Indian Ritual and Belief.* Secaucus, NJ: University Books, 1974.

Chatterjee, Gautam. *Sacred Hindu Symbols.* New Delhi: Abhinav, 1996.

De, S. K. *Early History of the Vaiṣṇava Faith and Movement in Bengal.* Calcutta: Firma KLM, 1961.

Entwistle, A. W. *Braj: Centre of Krishna Pilgrimage.* Groningen: Egbert Forsten, 1987.

Ghosal, S. N. *Studies in Divine Aesthetics.* Visvabharati: Shantiniketan, 1974.

Sarkar, R. M. *Regional Cults and Rural Traditions: An Interacting Pattern of Divinity and Humanity in Rural Bengal.* New Delhi: Inter-India, 1986.

Tod, J. *Annals of Rajasthan.* Calcutta, 1884. Cited in James Hastings, *Encyclopedia of Religion and Ethics* "Images and Idols, Indian." 143. Vol. 7. New York: Scribner's, 1915.

Chapter 4

Domesticating Krishna:
Friendship, Marriage, and Women's Experience in a Hindu Women's Ritual Tradition

TRACY PINTCHMAN

In his well-known book on Krishna, *The Divine Player: A Study of Kṛṣṇa Līlā*, David Kinsley emphasizes the nature of Krishna as a playful deity who remains eternally unbound by the social and moral norms that condition the human realm. As a mischievous child, Krishna lies, steals, and bucks authority, all in the name of play. His childish world *is* play, reflecting the nature of the divine world as completely pleasurable, a realm where "fullness and bounty make work superfluous" (Kinsley 1979, 67). The erotic love play in which Krishna later engages with his alluring mate Rādhā and a number of cowherdesses (*gopīs*), is similarly an expression of divine sport, "far removed from the harsh world of work and worrisome duty" (86). Predominant traditions in North India portray both Rādhā and the cowherdesses as married to men other than Krishna, so their love play is clearly illicit. Krishna embodies the otherworldly joy of the transcendent realm, and such joy is not, nor can it ever be, subject to the social and moral constraints that restrict the human realm.

There is certainly a great deal of truth to these insights. Like much of the Western academic work devoted to the study of Krishna devotional traditions, however, Kinsley's scholarship focuses on materials that we know or may presume to be male authored.[1] Those interested in a woman's point of view often turn to works attributed to female saints, like Āṇṭāl and Mīrabāī, who have led extraordinary lives. One might well wonder, however, how "ordinary" female Hindu householders might appropriate imagery of Krishna's *līlā*. Caroline Walker Bynum notes that women's images and symbols tend to be continuous with women's ordinary experience rather than break with that experience (1996, 74). The devotional realm of Krishna's transgressive erotic sport, by contrast, seems far removed from the types of relationships and experiences that are of central social importance to most Hindu women.

In this chapter, I will explore Hindu women's ritual devotions to Krishna in the city of Benares, North India, during the month of Kārtik (October–November).[2] In so doing, I will focus on how women shape imagery of Krishna's līlā in this context in ways that tend to reflect their own devotional and social values and preoccupations. During the month of Kārtik, Benarsi Hindu women meet daily to perform a *pūjā* in which they raise Krishna from childhood to adulthood, marrying him off to the plant goddess Tulsi toward the end of the month. The world of Kārtik pūjā embraces predominant imagery of Krishna's playful behavior as transgressive. Simultaneously, however, it supplements such imagery with alternative imagery, reconfiguring Krishna traditions in ways that Sanskritic theologies may not emphasize but that resonate with women's ideals and concerns.[3]

The Month of Kārtik and Women s Kārtik Pūjā

In Benares, Kārtik is celebrated as a deeply sacred month, and many Benarsis with whom I spoke counted Kārtik among the three or four most religiously important months of the year.[4] It is associated primarily with the worship of Vishnu and therefore is most meaningful to Vaishnavas, although many non-Vaishnavas also participate in religious practices associated with the month. A rich variety of ritual observances bring the month to life in Benares in people's homes, in temples, and along the *ghāṭs*, the banks of stone steps and landings that run along the banks of the Ganges River at the edge of the city.

The merits of Kārtik are especially lauded in scriptures called Kārtik Māhātmya, "Glorification of Kārtik." Beginning in late September, if one happens to be browsing through one of the many bookstalls that line the alleys in downtown Benares, one will inevitably come across devotional pamphlets that contain a Hindi rendition of this text. The *Kārtik Māhātmya* consists of materials excerpted from the Sanskrit Purāṇas, which comprise the most recent scriptural layer of the Brahmanical Hindu canon. There are two versions of this text. One is derived from the *Skanda Purāṇa* and consists of *Skanda Purāṇa* 2.4.1–36. The other includes the twenty-nine chapters from *Padma Purāṇa* 6.88–6.117, along with another Kārtik-related Purāṇic chapter or section included as a thirtieth chapter or an addendum. The *Padma*

Purāṇa's version of the text is the one that seems to be most widely sold in Benares. The two versions are not identical, but they do share a good deal of content. Both versions of the text include passages that glorify Kārtik, explain its religious importance, describe ritual practices that should be undertaken during Kārtik, and narrate stories related to the month. Throughout the month these texts are recited aloud in homes and temples all over Benares.

The key religious injunction pertaining to the month has to do with the maintenance of a religious practice known as the Kārtik *vrat* (Sanskrit *vrata*). The term "vrat" can be translated as "vow" or "votive observance," but in fact vrats encompass a variety of elements, and different vrats may emphasize different ones.[5] They are most popularly associated with fasting, and the Kārtik vrat, like other vrats, entails abstention from certain foods.[6] Even more central to this vrat, however, is Kārtik *snān*, daily ritual bathing throughout the month. In Benares, most Kārtik votaries bathe in the Ganges River. Such ritual bathing is considered especially meritorious when performed before sunrise.

Kārtik is sandwiched between the hot and humid rainy season and the chilling cold that often comes in late December and January, when temperatures can fall near freezing at night. Although it is usually still rather hot in Benares when Kārtik begins, by the end of the month mornings have become chilly, requiring one to wear a shawl. The streets are dark and peaceful in the early morning hours. If you were to make your way from the dense neighborhoods of the city to the Ganges's edge at this time, almost every being you would pass would be sleeping: people, water buffalo, dogs, all slumbering quietly by the side of the road. The first active souls you would be likely to encounter would be Kārtik votaries on their way to the river to perform their morning ablutions. Indeed, while silence reigns in the city streets, it is a very different story at the ghāṭs. From about 3:00 AM on, Kārtik votaries come to the river's edge to fulfill their vow of daily, early-morning bathing throughout the month. The ghāṭs get more and more crowded with bathers as the month progresses. One sees both men and women splashing in the waters and dressing discreetly by the river's edge, but one sees mostly women. Men on the ghāṭs tend to perform their morning rituals and then leave, headed to home and work, with only a few men remaining to meditate by the side of the river, drink tea, or watch the goings on. After bathing, however, many women and girls gather in groups along the ghāṭs to perform a special pūjā as part of their observance of the vrat. Although both men and women may engage in ritual bathing and other practices associated with the Kārtik vrat, this pūjā is exclusively for women. While the *Kārtik Māhātmyas* advocate worship of Krishna during the month of Kārtik, they do not seem to describe anything like this pūjā. Indeed, I have not located any explicit scriptural reference to this form of worship.

Not all female Kārtik votaries participate in Kārtik pūjā, but as far as I could observe, all Kārtik pūjā participants are female Kārtik votaries. Participants construct several icons (*mūrtis*) out of Ganges mud, including those of Vishnu and Lakshmī, Śiva, Ganesha, Rādhā-Krishna, Tulsi, the Moon-god Candrama, the Sun-god Surya, and the Ganges herself. Forming a circle around the clay icons, they perform pūjā while singing songs particular to this occasion. Many deities are honored, but several of the songs focus specifically on Krishna, and informants told me that the pūjā itself is largely dedicated to Krishna with the other deities called to be present chiefly so that they, too, can participate as devotees.

Why Krishna? Participants offered a wide array of different and sometimes contradictory interpretations regarding various dimensions of the pūjā, and it would be misleading to suggest that all participants view the pūjā in the same way. However, more than half of the thirty-six women whom I formally interviewed indicated that they consider Kārtik pūjā to be in some way related to Krishna's *rāsa-līlā*. On one level, of course, the term *rāsa-līlā* refers to the famous circle dance of Krishna mythology, in which Krishna danced in the middle of a circle of cowherdesses, or gopīs, making love with each of them. This erotic dance is considered by many Kārtik pūjā participants to be the model for the pūjā. Some participants maintained that the rāsa-līlā took place during the month of Kārtik, describing Kārtik pūjā as a form of worship enacted in commemoration of the earthly rāsa-līlā performed in Braj in ancient times. Just as the gopīs gathered around Krishna in a circle in the original circle dance, so Kartik pūjā participants gather in a circle around icons of Krishna and other deities; and just as the gopīs adored Krishna with song and dance, pūjā participants worship him with song and devotional offerings. Popular understandings of the rāsa-līlā often place Krishna together with his alluring mate Rādhā at the center of the circle, and participants in the pūjā generally understand Rādhā to be at Krishna's side while the pūjā is taking place.[7]

In interviews, a number of informants compared their role in the pūjā to that of the gopīs who took part in rāsa-līlā and described themselves as imitating the gopīs' devotions to Krishna. Various elements of the pūjā also suggest this association. Songs sung during the pūjā, for example, often invoke the term *sakhī*, "female friend," a term used to refer to Rādhā's faithful female servants who accompany and serve the divine couple, and in Kārtik pūjā circles women refer to themselves and each other with the same term. Popular Krishna traditions equate Rādhā's sakhīs with the gopīs, and pūjā participants generally do the same. While the link between Kartik and the rāsa-līlā episode of Krishna's life is especially strong, however, several informants associated Kārtik with Krishna's entire līlā, his "play," in Braj—that is, Krishna's entire life as a cowherd from his birth until his departure as an adult for Dvārakā. In this regard, informants tended to use the same term, "rāsa-līlā," to refer not only to the specific episode of the rāsa-līlā, but to Krishna's entire līlā, that is, his entire youthful life in Vrindāvana.[8] Participants understand their role in the pūjā as related to this more expansive sense of the term as well, comparable to that of the gopīs who cared for Krishna during all his years as a youth in Vrindāvana. Within Kārtik pūjā, this role takes on a progressive character, marking Krishna's development from infancy to adulthood and culminating in the arrangement and celebration of Krishna's marriage to Tulsi.

In the pūjā, Krishna is considered to be present in child form as well as adult form during most of Kārtik, since the month is dedicated to raising him from infancy to a marriageable age. During this period, when the daily pūjā comes to an end, participants gather together all the clay icons in the cloth on which the pūjā is performed. They then swing the baby Krishna, along with all the other deities involved in the pūjā, offering Krishna milk and singing a lullaby to pacify him. After this, the clay icons, cloth, and all items offered during the pūjā are immersed in the Ganges, marking the end of the pūjā, and participants disperse. This basic rhythm defines the course of the pūjā for approximately the first twenty days of the month.

About two-thirds of the way through the month, pūjā participants celebrate Krishna's *janeū* or *upanāyana*, his religious initiation ceremony, which designates Krishna's transformation from child to young man. For this occasion, a brass image is used in place of the usual clay one. Pūjā participants prepare Krishna for his janeū with appropriate songs; they bathe him with turmeric and water, dress him, and offer him janeū threads and betel nut. A male priest is then called to the circle to recite mantras appropriate to the occasion. For several days following the initiation ceremony, women sing marriage songs in the pūjā circle before beginning the pūjā itself, signaling an impending wedding. During these days, participants assume the roles of family members on both bride's and groom's sides, discussing wedding arrangements, arguing about dowry, and so forth. Designated participants also gather money from the entire circle of participants to purchase gifts and other items needed for the wedding. Several pūjā participants told me that the janeū and marriage ceremonies, both Hindu rites of passage *(saṁskāras)*, are inextricably linked; traditionally, after the performance of a boy's janeū, it is time for the parents to begin seeking a bride for him. Often in contemporary India if a Hindu groom has never undergone a formal janeū ceremony, such a ceremony will be performed just before his wedding takes place. Indeed, janeū and marriage are so linked, at least in the minds of many pūjā participants I spoke with, that the janeū is also referred to as the "half marriage."

The wedding itself is celebrated in grand fashion. After concluding the daily pūjā, participants clear and purify a space for the marriage pavilion. The groom Krishna, represented on this occasion as in the janeū by a brass icon instead of a clay one, is brought to the pūjā circle and prepared for the wedding. The bride, a potted Tulsi plant, is also brought to the circle, draped in appropriate red and gold wedding garb, and adorned with tinsel, small mirrors, and other decorations. Gifts are placed before the bride and groom and displayed as dowry offerings, and, as in the janeū a male priest is called in briefly to recite appropriate wedding mantras and to collect the dowry items as a donation *(dān)*.

Krishna's wedding to Tulsi takes place on the eleventh of Kārtik's light fortnight, so the full-moon night that marks the end of the month is still several days away. During these final days of Kārtik women's daily pūjā continues, but wedding songs are no longer sung, and no clay images are made. Instead, the pūjā is done with a plastic or metal box, said to contain the merit that participants have accumulated during the month by their participation in worship activities.

Many Kārtik pūjā participants maintain that although Tulsi is wed to Krishna on the eleventh of the month's light fortnight, she does not depart with her new husband for her *sasurāl*—the home of the groom and his extended family, which becomes the bride's new home—until the night of the full moon, Kārtik Pūrṇimā. Tulsi's sasurāl is understood to be Vaikuṇṭha, the Vaishnava heaven. Several participants with whom I spoke insisted that the five days between Tulsi's marriage and Kārtik Pūrṇimā days mark the period that Krishna and Tulsi spend in the Kohabar, a room in the house that is decorated for the wedding and set up for wedding-related pūjā. In some Benaras households, newlyweds exchange *dahi-guṛ*, yogurt mixed with molasses, in the Kohabar of the bride's natal home after the wedding, before departing for the bride's sasurāl, where the newlyweds then take up residence. I was also told that in parts of Bihar, a neighboring state that is the natal home of many Kārtik pūjā participants, the groom remains at the bride's house for nine days, and the *suhāgrāt*, the consummation of the marriage, is celebrated in the Kohabar. Others insisted that this period had nothing at all to do with the Kohabar, claiming instead that Tulsi is too young to leave for her sasurāl at the time of her wedding. Hence she remains at her natal home until Kārtik Pūrṇimā, the night of her *gauna*. A gauna occurs when a bride is too young to move to her husband's house at the time of her marriage; when she matures, there is a gauna ceremony, in which she is ceremoniously brought from her natal home to live at her conjugal home. In any case, many informants maintained that Krishna and Tulsi consummate their marriage on the night of Kārtik Pūrṇimā before departing for Vaikuṇṭha.

Domesticating Krishna

In her work on elderly Jewish women living in Jerusalem, Susan Starr Sered notes that in male-dominated religious traditions, women's religion is not independent of the normative tradition, and women's beliefs tend not to differ radically from those shared by their male kin. But, she observes, in such contexts women have a tendency to "subtly alter, elaborate, reinterpret, reshape, and domesticate" normative traditions into forms that are "meaningful to and consistent with their perceptions, roles, identities, needs, and experience" as women (Sered 1992, 49–50). I would submit that Kartik pūjā traditions tend to embrace normative, Sanskritic Krishna traditions and women's alterations of these traditions simultaneously, even where the former might seem to contradict the latter. In other words, Kārtik pūjā does not supplant normative imagery of Krishna's behavior as transgressive, but it supplements such imagery with alternative appropriations of Krishna materials that are allied more closely with householder women's worldly preoccupations. In so doing, it provides space for women to engage Krishna traditions in ways that resonate with their own lives. Here I want to consider two aspects of Kārtik pūjā and how these intersect with women's values and concerns: the way that pūjā participants appropriate the figure of the sakhī or gopī as a role model, and imagery of Krishna's līlā as culminating in his marriage to Tulsi.

Being a Sakhī: Friendship and Worship in Kārtik Pūjā

As noted above, in Kārtik pūjā women consider themselves to be human embodiments of the gopīs or sakhīs who frolicked with Rādhā and Krishna in ancient times. Bengal Vaishnavism details five basic devotional attitudes (*bhāvas*) foundational to Krishna worship—peaceful, amorous, parental, friendlike, and servantlike—with various legendary characters prominent in Krishna mythology said to exemplify each of these bhāvas. Vaishnava theology has upheld the gopīs as ideal exemplars of spiritual intimacy with Krishna especially through the amorous or erotic (*mādhurya* or *śṛṅgāra*) devotional sentiment.[9] While a few of the women I interviewed denied that Krishna's relationship with the gopīs was sexual, most accepted that it was. But they did not emphasize the erotic stance as particularly relevant for *human* devotional posturing. Instead, they spoke overwhelmingly of their own devotional role in terms of simple service (*sevā*), and they tended to stress the *devotional*, not erotic, nature of the gopīs' attachment to Krishna as exemplifying religious ideals.

In North India, traditional Hindu morality concerning women's behavior favors chastity, sexual modesty, and service (sevā) to others. Romantic love either before or outside of marriage is discouraged. It may be that an emphasis on such cultural values makes illicit sexuality unattractive to women as a devotional paradigm. Hindu reform movements of the nineteenth and early twentieth centuries, which formed in response to colonial British criticisms of Indian cultural and religious formations, could also be an influence here. Reformers tended to be highly critical of elements of Hinduism that they perceived to be crude or unsophisticated, including the sexual aspects of Krishna traditions.[10] It could be that such criticisms have affected the way that contemporary Hindu women consciously perceive the devotional implications of the gopīs' erotic stance toward Krishna.

In Kārtik pūjā, to imitate the gopīs also means to assume a parental (*vātsalya*) posture, entailing as it does symbolism of raising a child from infancy to adulthood, undertaking the responsibility of performing daily care, arranging one's child's janeū and marriage, and so forth. In his research on Krishna līlā performances in Braj, John Stratton Hawley notes that many of the people he spoke with tended not to maintain distinctions between parenting (vātsalya) and amorous (mādhurya) sentiments when it comes to Krishna devotion; he quotes one informant who describes these two devotional sentiments as being like two light bulbs that can be lit up with a common switch of love (1983, 263–64).[11] Indeed, popular religiosity tends to remain largely unconcerned with sorting out the devotional sentiments or differentiating one bhāva from the other, and that is certainly the case here. While Krishna's foster mother Yaśodā is the ideal exemplar of the parental sentiment, the many gopīs who cared for Krishna as a child, fed him, played with him, and adored him as if he were their own child, also exemplify this devotional posture.

Devotion to Krishna in his child form thrives throughout North India, so it is not extraordinary in the context of Hindu devotional practice. However, the emphasis placed on nurturing the child Krishna in *this* tradition clearly reflects the enormous social and emotional significance that Hindu women in North India tend to ascribe to motherhood and the raising of children, especially sons. Paralleling human experience, within the pūjā the parental dimension of devotion entails not just nurturing Krishna from childhood to adulthood, but also fulfilling parental responsibility through the arrangement and execution of Krishna's marriage.

To be a sakhī in the worship circle also entails working with other women. This is an inherently collective ritual, and several women told me you cannot do this worship alone. You need your sakhīs, for both historical reasons (Krishna's sakhīs worshiped him collectively) and practical ones (you might forget some of the songs; there is a lot to do, so it is best to divide up the work; and so forth). And to worship with other women brings participants pleasure. On several occasions, in fact, women highlighted to me the enjoyment they derived from collective female participation in the pūjā. One worshiper, for example, noted, "Where there are four or five people in a group, then you like doing worship (*pūjā-pāṭh*), singing, dancing. You get so much pleasure. If I sing by myself—say, if you are singing by yourself, then there is no one to listen. If there is no audience, then why sing? . . . And where there aren't four, five, or six sakhīs, there is no fun in singing and dancing."

North Indian Vaishnavism stresses the bonds that the gopīs share not only with Krishna, but also with Rādhā, whom they accompany and serve during Rādhā's love play with Krishna. Kārtik pūjā participants, however, also tended to stress to me the bonds that participating women share with one another and the pleasure that women derive from gathering together as women. The act of worshiping Krishna in a ritual context that includes other women engages human ideals pertaining not only to devotion, but also to friendship and feelings of emotional relatedness between and among women. When in the course of interviews I asked participants about the meaning of the term "sakhī" as it is used in the pūjā, in fact, many participants defined it first in terms of human friendship, bringing up the term's connection to Krishna mythology only at my prompting.

One of the most basic aspects that women articulated to me about being a sakhī in the worship circle involves the sentiment of love (*prema*) that such a role requires. As one participant put it, the term "sakhī" means "Love (prema). Just love." As previously noted, the gopīs typically are held to be exemplars of devotional love for Krishna. However, when participants spoke about the feelings of love associated with being a sakhī in this context, they emphasized the term's association not with love for Krishna (although that is certainly important in the pūjā), but with love *for one's coworshipers*. While the term "sakhī" has specific associations with Krishna's gopī-girlfriends, it is also a commonly used term for "female friend," and in Kārtik pūjā, women interpret their role as sakhīs in social, as well as devotional, terms. For at least some participants, love for fellow worshipers is one of the defining features of what it means to be a sakhī in the pūjā. When I asked one informant why women refer to each other in the pūjā circle by the term "sakhī," for example, she told me, "Sakhī means that there is a lot of love (prema) among the sakhīs. All of us are going to the Ganges, both younger and older women. Sitting together, talking together, and doing pūjā together, we all become sakhī."

But what, exactly, does love entail in this instance? In an Indian context, love tends to mean something different from what it means in an American context. Romantic love in Western culture, for example, tends to entail an intense emotion directed toward a unique other person whose particular qualities one finds attractive; Indians tend to consider such an emotion dangerous and overly individualistic. Instead, Indians tend to associate love with feelings of interdependence, social attachment, and mutual obligation. Susan Seymour observes that in Indian families "love is not so much an emotion generated by a specific individual as it is a deep sense of emotional connectedness with the members of one's extended family" (Seymour 1999, 85; cf. Derné 1995, 73–74). While she focuses on family dynamics, she also notes that such "relational love," as she calls it, is "extended to nonfamily members as well—to friends, spouses, and other affinal kin" (73–74).

In Benares, as throughout India, people tend not to refer to one another by name, invoking instead relational terms, especially kinships terms. Margaret Trawick (1990, 152) observes that "the selective use of kin terms is a powerful way of conveying, igniting, or engendering certain sentiments" associated with that term; that is, if a person refers to an unrelated male as "brother," the use of that term evokes the feelings that one associates with one's real brother. When participants in Kārtik pūjā refer to one another as "sakhī" and speak of love among the sakhīs, they evoke feelings of "relational love" that they associate with human friendship. Love among friends, as among family members and between spouses, connotes feelings of connectedness and interdependence. Two particular characteristics pertaining to the meaning of the term "sakhī" in the context of this pūjā, however, came to the fore among the participants with whom I spoke: equality, and mutual assistance in conducting the pūjā.

"Sakhī means that we are equal." This is how one participant, Usha, described to me the importance of using the term "sakhī" in the pūjā. Several of the women whom I interviewed gave me similar explanations. As another put it: "All the women, all the girls in the circle, they are all equal. They are all in the same group, they all tell the same stories. That is why (they call each other sakhī); they consider everyone to be equal." Indeed, the ideal of equality among women means that they should refer to one another only as sakhī during the course of Kārtik worship. Ordinarily, women address one another in a variety of ways that often signal relational hierarchy. Young women, for example, generally would address older women by using a kinship term like "older sister" (*didi*) or "paternal grandmother" (*dādī*). In the pūjā circle, participants are supposed to abandon all ordinary terms of address in favor of the universal use of the term "sakhī," which signals a lack of hierarchy. As one informant, Taradevi, noted: "If you call me 'Auntie' or 'Mother' or 'Mother-in-Law,' a mother-daughter relationship entails difference. But sakhīs are equal. So if you are my sakhī, you will sit next to me and you will be equal to me."

In many contexts, Hindu devotional traditions have tended to stress the equality of all worshipers before the Divine. Gender and caste distinctions that mark bodies, and class distinctions that mark social status, should be irrelevant to God, who cares only about the quality of one's devotion. Kārtik pūjā participates to some extent in this emphasis. However, it is notable that women stressed to me the equality of all worshipers not just before God, but especially before one another. Friends should treat one another as equals. This value is reflected in the physical construction of the worship space as a circle, which grants all participants equal access to the icons used in worship regardless of their social context. It is also facilitated by a pattern of informal leadership, which affords all worshipers the opportunity to participate in construction of the icons and narration of religious stories.

In fact, however, women did not actually abandon all hierarchy in the worship circle. For one thing, I did not observe any participation on the part of low-caste or Untouchable women, suggesting that they might not be welcome in the pūjā circle. Among the women who did participate, however, caste and class, two of the most important markers of social hierarchy in daily life, did not figure prominently as important markers of status within the context of the pūjā. Instead, women tended to grant special honor to age, piety, and religious expertise. In particular, older women whom other participants recognized as religiously knowledgeable and highly devout were accorded great respect, and on many occasions I saw other women touch their feet in the widespread Hindu gesture of reverence to a superior.[12] While some elements of hierarchy persist, however, the aspiration toward equality that several participants clearly identified as an important dimension of being a sakhī in this pūjā remains a central ideal of the tradition.

To be a sakhī also entails ideals pertaining to mutual assistance in conducting the pūjā, most conspicuously by sharing one's pūjā items with other participants. Indeed, many women brought extra pūjā supplies with them to the worship circle, and I was struck by how self-consciously these supplies, including flowers, rice, *ārati* wicks, and so forth, were continuously passed around and around the worship circle. Even if a participant was holding the item to be offered at that moment in her hands, others would still offer extras to her, communicating a spirit of sharing that permeated the pūjā. One informant, Savita, commented on this practice, noting, "Sakhīs help each other, and in the month of Kārtik, when we sit in the pūjā, when one of us runs out of something, the others help. In the month of Kārtik, if you help someone with the pūjā things, this is considered very auspicious." Another participant, Mainadevi, made special note of the importance of mutual assistance in promoting equal access and feelings of love (prema) among participants, remarking, "If one (of the participants) is poor, another one helps. If I don't have enough to offer, then my sakhīs will give materials to me. So this is love (prema); you give to me, and I give to you. If someone is running out of pūjā items, we share." While some participants commented on sharing as a manifestation of prema, some also associated such sharing with the attainment of religious merit. In her comments on the self-conscious sharing of pūjā items, for example, Mainadevi noted, "By helping one another, you obtain more religious merit (*punya*)." In a similar vein, still another participant commented, "By doing pūjā and offering things and giving things to other people, that makes someone earn great merit. And that is why people give to one another."

An emphasis on sharing and helping, both as an expression of love (prema) for one's fellow worshipers and as a vehicle for attaining religious merit, suggests an ethical valorization of giving and sharing one's resources with others. One of the functions of ritual is to instantiate ethical social relations (Collins 1997, 173–76), although what is meant by "ethical" is, of course, conditioned by context. In this context, women ascribe positive moral value to concrete acts that express care for one's fellow worshipers.

To be a sakhī in the pūjā also has implications about the stance of the "ritual body" in the course of this tradition of worship in a way that reinforces a stress on interpersonal relationship. Catherine Bell has stressed the role of the body in the analysis of ritual practices, noting that ritual practices entail performing specific actions with one's body, which in turn impress upon bodies schemas and values fundamental to the ritual situation. (Bell 1992, 100). In Kartik pūjā, conventions concerning the use of one's body reproduce a stress on interrelationship. The continual passing around of worship items throughout the course of the pūjā obligates one to constantly touch and direct one's attention toward other participants. I was struck by the amount of chatting, joking, helping, adjusting of other women's clothing, and so forth that continually occurs throughout the pūjā, constantly directing one's attention away from the ostensible focus of worship, the icons of Krishna and the other deities who occupy the space at the center of the circle. Indeed, one of the male Benarsi mocked what he perceived to be women's lack of focus in performing pūjā, imitating the stance of a woman leaning over a religious icon and carelessly tossing pūjā items on it while gossiping loudly with someone else. But the constant physical and verbal interaction with other women that generally takes place throughout the course of this pūjā communicates a particular moral stance. It acts to constantly direct one's attention not only inward, toward the icons, but also outward, toward other worshipers, producing and reproducing an emphasis on the collective nature of this form of worship and one's relationship to one's fellow participants.

In Benares, as in many other contexts, women's lives are more likely than men's to revolve around caring for others. In her study of female-dominated religions, Susan Starr Sered argues that women's rituals and beliefs in such contexts tend to reflect strongly the interpersonal orientation of women's familial lives (Sered 1994, 121, 138). Lesley A. Northrup observes that the theme of "community" is a central aspect of women's worship in many contexts, although she qualifies her observation with the caution that a "stress on community must be balanced against a recognition of diversity, difference, and individual experience" (1997, 34). In the practice of Kārtik pūjā, participants clearly emphasize mutual dependence and interrelationship among women as coworshipers, not only in terms of the ideals participants express, but also the actions they perform. Small acts of caretaking within the pūjā circle, such as assisting another worshiper with pūjā items, function as a female idiom for communicating relational love (prema) and reinforce social patterns that encourage women to express love through such acts of caretaking. The term "sakhī" as it is deployed in this context embodies these emphases.

Hence when women participate in Kārtik pūjā, they interpret what it means to be a sakhī in this context in both religious and social terms, that are, as Sered puts it, "meaningful to and consistent with their perceptions, roles, identities, needs, and experience" as women. Devotionally, being a sakhī entails worshiping Krishna in ways that parallel women's own values and experiences. Socially, being a sakhī entails engaging in acts of caretaking and mutual assistance that the term itself, as a term of friendship, implies.

Krishna's Marriage to Tulsi

Women's Kārtik traditions entail an understanding of Krishna and his carnal nature that does not necessarily deny familiar images of Krishna as promiscuous lover of Rādhā and the gopīs but supplements them with a domesticated vision of Krisha as Tulsi's proper husband. Kirin Narayan (1997, 37) observes that in Kangra, where women also perform Tulsi's wedding, some women make an explicit link between Tulsi's life and the lives of human women, identifying

Tulsi's marriage and subsequent uprooting with human women's marriage and departure for the in-law's house. In Benares, too, women tend to experience Tulsi's life, especially her relationship with Krishna, as continuous with their own lives, reflecting their values and aspirations as well as their fears and concerns.

In addition to being a goddess and a plant with religious associations, Tulsi is also an herb, basil, with decidedly domestic connotations. In Indian Hindu households, women often use Tulsi in cooking and food preparation. Many home cures that women take or give to family members involve Tulsi. But Kārtik pūjā participants adamantly describe Tulsi also as the quintessential devoted and chaste wife, a *pativratā*, embodying Lakshmī's qualities of wifely auspiciousness. On many occasions, Kārtik pūjā participants stressed to me how completely devoted Krishna and Tulsi remain to one another as husband and wife, bound together by the profound love that each holds for the other.

Tulsi is considered to be a form of Vrindā, the devoted wife of the demon Jalandhara, whose dramatic battle with the gods is recounted in both *Kārtik Māhātmyas*. Jalandhara is a formidable foe, and Vishnu comes to realize that Jalandhara cannot be killed because his wife, Vrindā, is a pativratā. The spiritual powers attained by a pativratā are capable of increasing her husband's lifespan, and Vrindā's powers are considerable. To conquer and kill Jalandhara, Vishnu breaks Vrindā's chastity by disguising himself as Jalandhara and sleeping with Jalandhara's beloved wife. When Vrindā finds out what has happened, she immolates herself. Vishnu has become infatuated with Vrindā and is devastated by her death. Vrindā is then reborn as Tulsi, in which form she weds Vishnu (see also Pintchman 1999).

The *Devī-Bhāgavata Purāṇa* (9.17–25) tells a slightly different version of this story, describing Tulsi not as Vishnu's bride, but Krishna's. In this account, Tulsi is explicitly identified as a form of Lakshmī, born in a fully mature form on the night of Kārtik's full moon. Although she is married to a demon, here named Shankhacuda, we are told that she is destined to attain Krishna as her husband in the next life. In this account, too, Vishnu deceives Tulsi in order to conquer her demon-husband, assuming her husband's form and sleeping with her. Tulsi curses Vishnu to become a stone, which results in his manifestation as the *śālagrāma*, a type of stone found in the Gaṇḍaki River and considered a natural form of Vishnu. Vishnu proclaims that Tulsi's body will become the Gaṇḍaki River itself, with her hair becoming sacred trees. Since he is infatuated with Tulsi, he invites her to marry him, proclaiming that she will remain in Krishna's heaven as Krishna's wife (Krishna being a form of Vishnu) but will remain on earth in the form of a Tulsi plant.

While Kārtik pūjā participants sometimes conflate Rādhā and Tulsi as Krishna's blushing bride, the structure of the pūjā clearly distinguishes one from the other. Songs and stories associated with the pūjā paint a picture of irreconcilable tension between Rādhā and Tulsi and describe their competition over Krishna. In a song that I recorded from the pūjā in 1997, for example, Krishna appears wearing the garb and ornaments of a groom, and Rādhā becomes suspicious. When she discovers that he has married Tulsi, she is furious and locks Krishna out of the house. Krishna tries to appease Rādhā by assuring her that Tulsi will be her servant. In yet another song, Tulsi assumes her plant form, and Rādhā threatens to pull her up by the roots and destroy her. In exchange, Tulsi taunts Rādhā, claiming that no matter what Rādhā does, Tulsi will always remain with Krishna and serve him (see Pintchman, 2003 and forthcoming).

What are we to make of these accounts of rivalry between the two goddesses in the context of this devotional tradition? Some of the Kārtik pūjā participants with whom I spoke drew explicit comparisons between these songs and the practice of polygamy, once legal but now outlawed for Indian Hindus. In his exploration of marriage songs from this part of India, Edward Henry notes that while some marriage songs still refer to cowives, it is rare for a contemporary man to take a cowife (Henry 1988, 27). The few women in Benares with whom I discussed the issue, however, claimed that it is not all that uncommon for a Hindu man, especially a man of means, to take more than one wife or to keep a mistress on the side, sometimes with his wife's knowledge, although rarely with her consent. One high-caste, middle-class informant told me the following story:

> My sister's elder brother-in-law, he took two wives. He married for the first time when he was a student. Then he became an engineer in the navy and went abroad. When he came back, he was no longer happy with his first wife, so he married a second time, but he did not leave the first one. The first one had a girl, and the second one had a boy. And then he had an operation because he thought, "I have a girl and a boy; that is enough." In the end, something bad happened, and the younger wife stopped talking to the elder one. One wife lives in the village, and the second wife lives in Lucknow in a big bungalow. So if there are two wives, they don't ever get along.

When I mentioned the issue of cowives and mistresses to one of my close friends in Benares, a middle-class Brahmin woman, she confessed to me that her brother has two wives, one in his natal village and one in an apartment in Benares. She also commented that women of all classes and castes might worry when their husbands go out without telling their wives where they are going, fearing that a husband might be cultivating a relationship with another woman.

Hence on one level, songs and stories that describe Rādhā and Tulsi competing for Krishna's attentions resonate with women's experiences and fears concerning male infidelity, signaling anxiety that wives may have about husbands' capacities for engaging in sustained extramarital relationships with other women. But the tension between Tulsi and Rādhā that pervades these materials has larger symbolic resonance as well.

Krishna's proper marital relationship to Tulsi, culminating in their departure for Vaikuṇṭha, forms a counterpoint to the relationship between Krishna and Rādhā, whose love play in Vrindāvana is widely understood in contemporary Hinduism as always remaining outside the bounds of marriage. Indeed, Krishna devotional traditions throughout North India portray the relationship that Krishna shares with both Rādhā and the gopīs as tumultuous, passionate, intense, and illicit. Predominant religious interpretations of these materials understand the adulterous nature of their love to be symbolic of human passion for God, "the overwhelming moment that denies world and society, transcending the profanity of everyday convention, as it forges an unconditional (and unruly) relationship with god as the lover" (Kakar 1986, 88). In Vrindāvana, where Krishna is eternally at play, his erotic sport is not bound by *dharmic* conventions. Vaikuṇṭha, on the other hand, where Krishna and Tulsi are said to go when they leave the earthly realm at the end of Kārtik to take up residence as husband and wife, is the domain of Vaishnava kingship and marriage, both of which are subject to the demands of *dharma*.

I have noted that Kārtik pūjā participants tend to employ the term "prema" in the pūjā to refer to the friendly affection participants are supposed to feel for and express to one another. In the context of Krishna devotion, the term "prema" has other connotations as well. Krishna's relationship with Rādhā and the gopīs has been characterized as one that shuns the form of love known as *kāma* in favor of the more spiritually pure form of love known as prema.[13] Kāma is love tinged with personal desire, including desire for family and children. Prema, on the other hand, is selfless, desireless love that is aimed only at pleasing the loved one and does not aim to attain anything for oneself. When participants model themselves on the gopīs, they understand the pūjā as an expression of their desireless love for each other and for God. But the extraordinary nature of Krishna's relationships with his rāsa-līlā partners makes them unlikely models for conjugal relationships confined uniquely to the human realm. In this regard, informants tended to emphasize Krishna's union with Tulsi as one that parallels human marriage and is equally characterized by values generally associated with kāma. As one participant put it,

"Just as God gets married, I got married in the same way. It is the same. God's janeū took place, and then his marriage took place. We do the same things." In stressing Krishna's proper marital relationship to Tulsi as one that parallels human marriage, women's Kārtik pūjā traditions reflect values that are grounded not only in devotional ideals, as Krishna's relationships with Rādhā and the gopīs are often understood to be, but also in women's social realities, which lie outside the pūjā circle and hence are subject to the pull of kāma and all that it represents.

The women with whom I spoke rarely drew explicit comparisons between Krishna and human men, but when they did, the comparisons tended to focus on Krishna's antinomian behavior with Rādhā and the gopīs, and they were not favorable. In the course of discussing the song mentioned above in which Krishna marries Tulsi on the sly, for example, one informant complained, "God has lied, and that is why men lie. They don't lie? They say, 'I went here'; then they say, 'No, I didn't go here, I really went there.' It is like that in every house." Another noted that since God took many lovers, so do human men. Yet she also lamented, "It was important for God, but when men do this, there is no importance to it." For these women, the frolicking rogue Krishna is certainly not a male that human males should emulate. But what about Krishna the groom? His marriage to Tulsi, celebrated so enthusiastically on the banks of the Ganges, reflects the world of values and conventions that shape and inform human conjugal relations.

The privileging in Kārtik pūjā of the dharmic but staid conjugal bond between Tulsi and Krishna over the sexually passionate but tumultuous one shared by Rādhā and Krishna may reflect particular tendencies in women's romantic longing in traditional Hindu culture. Kakar (1990, 83–84) notes the centrality in Hinduism of imagery surrounding the unified male-female pair or couple, the *joṛi*, as two persons joined together in a harmonious, interdependent, and mutually fulfilling oneness. This ideal of a "single two-person entity" is captured in the image of Ardhanarīśvara, Śiva in his form as half-male, half-female. Kakar contends that this "wished-for oneness of the divine couple" is especially important to Indian Hindu women and represents their idealized image of marriage. The desired intimacy implied in the joṛi remains for women a romantic longing that, says Kakar, tends to manifest itself less as yearning for "the depths of erotic passion" such as we find in so many of the stories of Rādhā-Krishna, but for the "much quieter affair" of husband-wife intimacy, affection, and fidelity. This, contends Kakar, "is the real *sasurāl*—the husband's home—to which a girl looks forward after marriage" (1990, 23). Kakar downplays female sexual desire here in ways that are probably not accurate. But my own work among Benarsi women leads me to agree with Kakar that emotional intimacy, mutual affection, and fidelity are certainly qualities that many Indian women, like many of their counterparts in the United States and elsewhere, desire strongly in marriage.

As Tulsi departs for her own sasurāl on the night of Kārtik's full moon, she and Krishna become that perfect joṛi, the seamlessly harmonious couple forever joined in a blissful heaven that is the idealized sasurāl. Or do they? Most of my informants were quite clear that at the end of the month of Kārtik, Krishna leaves Tulsi, despite the love and devotion he supposedly feels for her, to return to his beloved Rādhā. Do Tulsi and Krishna live happily ever after in harmonious oneness, or does Krishna return to his beloved mistress, interrupting the blissful harmony of the conjugal bond? The ending is ambiguous, as is the "ending" of human marriages. Tulsi's marital fate, like that of human brides, is not entirely in her control. In Kārtik pūjā, the complex, ambiguous, and frankly contradictory nature of marital and sexual imagery functions as a vehicle for women to experience collectively the wishes, desires, and hopes, but also fears, anxieties, and disappointments surrounding the conjugal bond.

Marriage entails a monumental transition for a traditional Hindu bride, who leaves her own home for a new one, exchanging her natal family for her husband's family. Men do not move or leave their families behind, nor is male identity marked by marriage in the same way that female identity is. Marriage is not nearly as transformative for men as it is for women. As marriage is the focus of many Hindu women's lives, in Kārtik pūjā Tulsi's marriage becomes the focus of the entire month. Krishna is raised to be married, and his wedding to Tulsi, followed by their return to the sasurāl, is the goal toward which the entire tradition is directed. Such a teleology helps reproduce cultural norms that place marriage at the center of women's lives. Simultaneously, however, the focus on marriage reflects women's active appropriation and reshaping of Sanskritic Krishna traditions in ways that highlight their own values, experiences, and concerns.

Notes

1. E.g., Edward C. Dimock (1966a), (1966b); David L. Haberman (1988); John Stratton Hawley (1981), (1983); David R. Kinsley (1979).

2. The traditional Hindu calendar consists of twelve lunar months. In Benares, as in most of North India, these months are measured from full moon to full moon. When measured against the solar calendar commonly used in the West, the first day of Kārtik usually falls sometime in mid-October, although this varies from year to year. Normal discrepancies between lunar and solar cal-

endars mean that dates calculated by the solar calendar will not consistently correspond year after year to particular dates calculated by the lunar calendar. In addition, since the lunar year is about ten days shorter than the solar year, an intercalary month is inserted into the lunar year every two to three years to correct the discrepancy. When this happens the month of Kārtik can fall quite a bit later than it does in years that are not intercalated.

3. This chapter is based on field research that I conducted in India between 1995 and 1998 and is part of a forthcoming book. Support for this project was supplied by the American Institute of Indian Studies, the National Endowment of the Humanities, the American Academy of Religion, Loyola University of Chicago, and Harvard University, which granted me a position as research associate and visiting lecturer in the Women's Studies in Religion Program in 2000–2001 so that I could work intensively on this project. I am very grateful to all these organizations and institutions for their support.

Very special thanks to Sunita Singh, friend and research associate, without whom I could not have conducted the research on which this chapter is based. Very special thanks as well to my husband, William C. French, who helped me conduct interviews and collect film footage about Kārtik and Kārtik pūjā in autumn of 1998.

4. For a fuller treatment of these topics, see Tracy Pintchman (1999), (2003), and (forthcoming).

5. Mary McGee (1987), 124–25, outlines the major constituent parts of vrats as including a declaration of intention (*saṅkalpa*), ritual bathing (*snāna*), some form of worship (pūjā), the recitation of some kind of mantra (*japa*), an all-night vigil (*jāgaraṇa*), the sacrifice of oblations into a fire (*homa*), observation of a fast (*upavāsa*) and breaking of the fast (*pāraṇa*), "gifting" or giving donations (*dāna*), performance of a concluding rite (*udyāpana*), and the telling or hearing of a vrat story (*kathāśrāvana*). She also notes that for any given vrat one, or sometimes two, of these rites is designated as the principal rite, the *pradhāna*, whose performance is central to the vrat, while the less critical elements are considered subsidiary rites, the *aṅgas*, of the vrat.

6. "Fasting" in Hinduism encompasses a wide variety of food abstention practices, from complete abstention from all food and drink, to abstention from a single type of edible product.

7. Krishna's union with Rādhā during the pūjā raises interesting questions about how Krishna can be Rādhā's lover and Tulsi's groom simultaneously. Narrative logic informed by the constraints that govern earthly human experience might insist on relegating Rādhā and Tulsi to different times and places, refusing them shared space, but such logic does not hold in the devotional context. Religious traditions often embrace logical inconsistencies when it comes to representations of the Divine, often by invoking the claim that the Divine realm transcends mortal rules and mortal comprehension.

8. In John Stratton Hawley's research on rāsa-līlā performances in Braj, the term "rāsa-līlā" is also used to indicate both the rāsa-līlā episode itself and the entire līlā of Krishna's life enacted in liturgical drama. See John Stratton Hawley (1981) and (1983), chapters 6 and 7.

9. Theologian Rūpa Goswāmin details two ways that one might experience the amorous sentiment: one grounded in desire for direct sexual enjoyment of Krishna, and the other grounded instead in vicarious sexual enjoyment of Krishna. In the first case emphasis is placed on the sexual nature of the relationship between Krishna and the sakhīs. Their bond is illicit, for both Rādhā and the gopīs are married to other men; this makes the gopīs' love for Krishna more intense, as this love is characterized only by desire and not by duty (the *parakīya* doctrine). In the second case, vicarious sexual enjoyment of Krishna, emphasis is on the sakhīs as Rādhā's attendants; the sakhīs accompany the divine couple and serve them, facilitating their love play. See David L. Haberman (1994), 81.

10. I am grateful to Professor Richard Wolf of Harvard University for this insight.

11. John Stratton Hawley (1983) also notes in the devotional poems of Sūr Dās, a sixteenth-century Vaishnava poet, permeability between the parental and amorous sentiments concerning Krishna.

12. Demonstration of high regard for characteristics that suggest wisdom, depth of experience, and spiritual maturity is not unusual in female-dominated religious contexts. Cf. Susan Starr Sered (1994), 217.

13. Edward C. Dimock (1966a), 161–64; John Stratton Hawley (1981), 158–62; (1983), 275–78; Frederique Marglin (1985), 201–06.

References

Bell, Catherine. *Ritual Theory, Ritual Practice.* New York: Oxford University Press, 1992.

Bynum, Caroline Walker. "Women's Stories, Women's Symbols: A Critique of Victor Turner's Theory of Liminality." Reprinted in *Readings in Ritual Studies.* Ronald L. Grimes, ed. Upper Saddle River, NJ: Prentice Hall, 1996, 71–86.

Collins, Elizabeth Fuller. *Pierced by Murugan's Lance: Ritual, Power, and Moral Redemption among Malaysian Hindus.* DeKalb: Northern Illinois University Press, 1997.

Derné, Steve. *Culture in Action: Family Life, Emotion, and Male Dominance in Banaras, India.* Albany: State University of New York Press, 1995.

Dimock, Edward C. *The Place of the Hidden Moon: Erotic Mysticism in the Vaiṣṇava-sahajiyā Cult of Bengal.* Chicago: University of Chicago Press, 1966a.

———. "Doctrine and Practice among the Vaiṣṇavas of Bengal." In *Krishna: Myths, Rites, and Attitudes.* Milton Singer, ed. Chicago: University of Chicago Press, 1966b, 41–63.

Haberman, David L. *Acting as a Way of Salvation: A Study of Rāgānugā Bhakti Sādhana.* New York: Oxford University Press, 1988.

———. *Journey through the Twelve Forests: An Encounter with Krishna.* New York: Oxford University Press, 1994.

Hawley, John Stratton. *At Play with Krishna: Pilgrimage Dramas from Brindavan*. Princeton, NJ: Princeton University Press, 1981.

______. *Krishna, the Butter Thief*. Princeton, NJ: Princeton University Press, 1983.

Henry, Edward O. *Chant the Names of God: Music and Culture in Bhojpuri-Speaking India*. San Diego: San Diego State University Press, 1988.

Kakar, Sudhir. "Erotic Fantasy: The Secret Passion of Rādhā and Krishna." In *The Word and the World: Fantasy, Symbol, and Record*. Veena Das, ed. Beverly Hills: Sage, 1986, 75–94.

———. *Intimate Relations: Exploring Indian Sexuality*. New Delhi: Penguin, 1990.

Kinsley, David R. *The Sword and the Flute*. Berkeley: University of California Press, 1975.

———. *The Divine Player: A Study of Kṛṣṇa Līlā*. Delhi: Motilal Banarsidass, 1979.

Marglin, Frederique. *Wives of the God King: The Rituals of the Devadasis of Puri*. Delhi: Oxford University Press, 1985.

McGee, Mary. "Feasting and Fasting: The *Vrata* Tradition and Its Significance for Hindu Women." Th.D. Dissertation, Harvard University Divinity School, 1987.

Narayan, Kirin. "Sprouting and Uprooting of Saili: The Story of the Sacred Tulsi in Kangra." *Manushi* 102 (1997): 30–38.

Northrup, Lesley A. *Ritualizing Women*. Cleveland, OH: Pilgrim, 1997.

Pintchman, Tracy. "Kārttik as a Vaiṣṇava *Mahotsav*: Mythic Themes and the Ocean of Milk." *Journal of Vaiṣṇava Studies* 7/2 (1999): 65–92.

———. "The Month of Kārtik and Women Ritual Devotions to Krishna in Benares." In *The Blackwell Companion to Hinduism*. Gavin Flood, ed. Oxford: Blackwell, 2003, 327–42.

———. *Guests at God's Wedding: Celebrating Kārtik among the Women of Benares*. Albany: State University of New York Press, forthcoming.

Sered, Susan Starr. *Women as Ritual Experts*. New York: Oxford University Press, 1992.

———. *Priestess, Mother, Sacred Sister: Religions Dominated by Women*. New York: Oxford University Press, 1994.

Seymour, Susan C. *Women, Family, and Child Care in India: A World in Transition*. Cambridge: Cambridge University Press, 1999.

Trawick, Margaret. *Notes on Love in a Tamil Family*. Berkeley: University of California Press, 1990.

Chapter 5

Krishna as Loving Husband of God
The Alternative Krishnology of the Rādhāvallabha Sampradāya

GUY L. BECK

The broad category suggested by the term "Vaishnava" has been acknowledged by most scholars to encompass the majority of Hindu believers. This includes the veneration of Vishnu, Nārāyaṇa, Lakshmī, Krishna, Rādhā, Rāma, Sītā, and the remaining *avatāras* (incarnations) with their female consorts, saints, and sectarian leaders and followers. A very important division within Vaishnavism is comprised of the mythology and worship of Krishna, one of Hinduism's most beloved deities. Yet the "Krishna" traditions themselves are by no means uniform regarding the nature of the personality of Krishna nor the methods of worship. Divided into "normative" and "alternative," the normative Krishna tradition is based primarily on a canon of early Sanskrit texts, while so-called alternative Krishna traditions may or may not include these along with regional or vernacular sources.

One of the least recognized yet most unique of the alternative Krishna subdivisions is the Rādhāvallabha Sampradāya (RVS), a medieval Vaishnava sect that stands alone among the various Krishna traditions of Vaishnavism in North India that flourished from about 1400 CE. Despite its own singular characteristics and influence, the RVS has been neither adequately studied in academic circles nor fully appreciated within the Hindu public domain. The deity of Krishna looms very large in this sect, and on the surface even bears some family resemblances to the type of normative, pan-Indian Krishna that was based on older Sanskrit sources. Yet the actual composite is more complex and radically different from the normative tradition. Within the theology of RVS, Krishna is approached, not as the consummate Godhead, but as the penultimate step toward the supreme Deity which is not Krishna alone but primarily Rādhā, his spouse and only female companion. The alternative or "unorthodox" Krishnology that places Krishna subordinate to Rādhā, while not totally without precedent in Vaishnava literature, is firmly located within the literature and tradition of the RVS, beginning with the works of the founder.

Based on field research at the Braj headquarters of the RVS in Vrindaban, India, just South of New Delhi in Uttar Pradesh, this chapter will illuminate some historical and theological issues associated with this alternative Krishna tradition, and conclude with translations for the first time of special poems known as *Vyāhulau Utsav ke Pad* or "Marriage Festival Songs," composed by Dhruva Dās and Rūplāljī, celebrated Rādhāvallabhite poets. As part of the divine play (*līlā*) of God, these poems describe the eternal wedding of Rādhā and Krishna with praise and adulation. The devotional images conjured through these poems portray an ideal panorama of great joy and celebration for the Rādhāvallabha devotees.

The Rādhāvallabha Sampradāya was founded in the sixteenth century (1535 CE) by Śrī Hita Harivaṁśa (1502–52 CE) in the town of Vrindaban in North India. Vrindaban (cf. Vrindāvana) is believed to be the most important geographical location of the childhood activities of the incarnation of Krishna who appeared, according to pious tradition, in roughly 3000 BCE. Śrī Harivaṁśa was an important name in the early history of the medieval revival of the town of Vrindaban as a major pilgrimage center for Hindus, along with Caitanya and the Six Goswamis of the Gauḍīya tradition, Śrī Vallabha and the Aṣṭachāp poets, Śrī Bhaṭṭa and Śrī Harivyāsadeva from the Nimbārka Sampradāya, and Swāmī Haridās of the Haridāsī Sampradāya. All of these saints are recognized by historians as pioneers in reestablishing Vrindaban as the center of the *bhakti* tradition in North India, yet Śrī Harivaṁśa is much neglected for his pivotal role in elevating Rādhā to Supreme status, a theological move that nonetheless influenced the other sects in various degrees.

The standard account of the life of Śrī Hita Harivaṁśa, citing all of the original sources, is presented and commented upon by Rupert Snell. The following is a brief summary of the life of Hita Harivaṁśa from the account of Uttamadāsa, an eighteenth-century disciple of the Rādhāvallabha tradition. Hita Harivaṁśa's family was from the town of Deoband in Uttar Pradesh. His father, Vyāsa Miśra, was a wealthy Brahmin astrologer who served at the royal court but was at first unable to conceive a child. However, Vyāsa rejoiced at his brother's dream of a son who would soon be born to his family as a joint incarnation of Hari (Krishna) and *vaṁśa* (Krishna's flute). Since the Miśra family was often in transit, Harivaṁśa took birth in the small village of Bāḍa near Mathurā, Krishna's own birthplace. From an early age the child was obsessed with the name and form of the Goddess Rādhā, often receiving communication from her in dreams. Rādhā had told him to make known a special mantra of her name to the world, and to rescue a Krishna deity from a well in his father's garden. Harivaṁśa took these commands seriously by establishing this deity in a temple in his hometown. After marrying and raising three children, Harivaṁśa was further ordered by Rādhā to leave his family behind and proceed to Vrindaban, but only after going to another village and accepting two daughters in marriage from a Brahmin as well as another image of Krishna to be installed there. This deity was known as Rādhāvallabha and was installed in a new temple in Vrindaban in the year 1535. The name Rādhā-vallabha refers to Krishna as "the dearest of Rādhā," as she is the principal figure in the theological hierarchy, with Krishna always at her side. According to the record, "He [Harivaṁśa] established the service of the deity with seven food offerings (*bhoga*) through the eight periods of the day (*yama*), according to the season."[1] Also, it is held by their present members that their unique tradition of Samāj-Gāyan singing began with the inauguration of this temple and *sampradāya* (lineage), drawing first upon the early poems of Hita Harivaṁśa himself in the language of Braj Bhāshā. Samāj-Gāyan is a collective style of vernacular hymn singing resembling the Hindustani classical forms of Dhrupad and Dhamār.

The Rādhāvallabha scriptural canon is almost entirely in the vernacular dialect of Hindi known as Braj Bhāshā. This special language is believed to be the speech of the intimate associates of Rādhā and Krishna in both the earthly Vrindaban and in the corresponding eternal spiritual abode. Braj Bhāshā is also said to provide access to a more profound level of spiritual experience than that represented by the Sanskrit "canon." The canonical literature is thought to be inferior and even mundane since it is believed to be spoken only in the heavens by the various gods and goddesses, and nowhere discusses Rādhā as the highest truth. Though there are a few works in Sanskrit by members of the RVS, these texts sought to create a new theological understanding of Rādhā and Krishna rather than build upon standard themes of Vedānta, Mīmāṁsā, Yoga, Nyāya, or Vaiśeṣika philosophies. Moreover, the new theology did not align itself with classical philosophical positions such as nondualism, dualism, and so forth.

Śrī Hita Harivaṁśa's principal work in Braj Bhāshā is the *Hita-Caurāsī* (HC), eighty-four verses covering themes of *nikuñja-vihāra* (the intimate love pastimes of Rādhā and Krishna taking place in eternal time), the *rāsa* dance, Rādhā's *māna*, or pride, and descriptions of the spring and autumn scenery of Vrindaban. There are no theological assertions herein as such, since the work is meant to be a poetical description of love situations between Rādhā and Krishna. Rupert Snell has shown in his research that, while there are verses describing Krishna alone, "the protracted thematic sequence CP [HC verses] 37–42 introduces themes in which Krishna is dependent on Rādhā and suffering in her absence."[2]

More distinct placement of Rādhā as supreme is visible in his other major work, the Sanskrit *Śrī-Rādhā-Sudhā-Nidhi-Stotram* (RSNS), "The Treasury of Rādhā's Nectar." In this text, the supreme divinity of Rādhā is irrefutable. But while the authorship of this work is disputed by the Gauḍīya Vaishnava Sampradāya, it is claimed by Rādhāvallabhites to be authored by Śrī Harivaṁśa since there are over sixteen commentaries on it written by disciples in the Rādhāvallabha lineage.[3] Since the theology in RSNS complies more with the Rādhāvallabha perspective, we will also consider it as such. The RSNS of 270 verses gives some of the most direct evidence of the Rādhāvallabha theology. For instance, in this text devotion to Rādhā is eulogized in the following verses (in brackets) as "the secret of the Upanishads" [204], "the quintessence of all human attainments (*artha* [wealth], *dharma* [religiosity], *kāma* [sense pleasure], and *moksha* [liberation])" [2], that which surpasses all other religious acts including communion with Krishna: "If anyhow we get the sole privilege to serve Śrī Rādhā . . . What have we to do then with religions [*dharma*], multitude of Gods, Brahmā, Shiva, and even the efforts to meet Shri Shyām Sundar (Krishna)?" [115]. Krishna even chants the name of Rādhā, that wisdom which is beyond the Vedas, as his favorite mantra: "May the Supreme Knowledge—beyond the scope of the Vedas—in the form of two letters—Rā and Dhā, dawn upon my mind! This name—Rādhā—is incessantly muttered by Hari (Śrī Krishna) with tearful eyes, and He is extremely charmed by the rapture of love" [15].[4]

Beside the above two works of Śrī Hita Harivaṁśa, there is only a short work in Braj Bhāshā called *Sphuṭa-Vāṇī* and a prayer in Sanskrit to the Goddess Yamunā. In the *Sphuṭa-Vāṇī* there is additional support for the supremacy of Rādhā.[5]

The Rādhāvallabha tradition maintains a Krishnology that is complex, and believed to represent the highest and truest culmination of centuries of Vaishnavism and Krishna worship. In order to understand and appreciate this consummation of devotion, we need to briefly trace the development of Vaishnavism from the initial stages of Vedic religion that gives reference to the deity of Vishnu to the ultimate supremacy of Rādhā over Krishna. This will be followed by further discussion of the distinguishing characteristics of the Rādhāvallabha tradition of Krishna theology and worship.

The earliest literary sources of Vaishnava religion include the Vedas and several of the appended Brāhmaṇa texts. Vishnu appears in the *Rig-Veda* as an important solar deity included within a pantheon of Vedic gods and goddesses. He gained wider significance when later combined or identified with the gods Nārāyaṇa and Prajāpati of the *Śaṭapatha-Brāhmaṇa*. In further combination with the Rig Vedic Purusha (Primal Man) and the Bhagavān of the Bhāgavata sect, Vishnu as Krishna later becomes the principal hero and deity of the *Mahābhārata*. While pious tradition places the historical Krishna at the beginning of the Kali Age around 3000 BCE, from the point of view of the appearance of written texts he may not be earlier than 400 BCE. In any case, Vishnu was by then assimilated with Nārāyaṇa and Vāsudeva-Krishna to bear the title of Bhagavān, as in the Bhagavad Gītā and the later *Bhāgavata Purāṇa*. With the advent and final acceptance of the historical Krishna in the *Mahābhārata*, the normative Krishna tradition assumed the mantle of one of the most important divisions of theistic Hinduism. The Sanskrit canon of Krishna thus comprises the texts and learned commentaries on the *Mahābhārata* (including Bhagavad Gītā), *Harivaṁśa* (attached to *Mahābhārata*), *Vishnu Purāṇa*, *Brahma Purāṇa*, and the slightly later *Bhāgavata Purāṇa* (see introduction). Strong textual support in Sanskrit for Vaishnavism was also evident in the growing Pāñcarātra and Vaikhānasa literature primarily of South India.

The bhakti devotional movements that took form in rural areas of India after the fifth century CE were comprised of poet-saints who broke away from this Sanskrit canon by composing verses in vernacular languages, sometimes referred to as Prakrit or Apabhraṁśa. The Āḷvār saints of South India composed songs in the Tamil and Telugu languages, the Haridāsa Kuṭa saints of Karnataka composed songs in Kannada, and the Northern saints wrote in Marāṭhī, Gujarati, Braj Bhāshā, and Bengali. In this emerging literary corpus the childhood images of Krishna took precedence over the mature adult forms mostly found in the Sanskrit literature. This included especially the forms of Mākhan Chor (butter thief), Veṇu Gopāla (flute player), and Govinda (cowherd boy), which came to more prominence than, for example, Krishna as charioteer on the battlefield or as King of Dvārakā. While Krishna's childhood was not neglected in the early canonical texts, the credit for the wider dissemination of specific childhood pastimes and images is given by historians to these new bhakti poets and artisans who regaled in the youthful Krishna. As noted by J. S. Hawley with regard to Krishna as butter thief, one of the most enduring aspects of Krishna's personality: "In the oldest sources, in fact—the Harivaṁśa and the Vishnu and Brahma Purāṇas—we hear nothing at all of the butter thief. . . . The legacy of the butter thief is ancient indeed . . . but it was a popular legacy, so it came to expression primarily in vernacular and nonbrahminical texts and in the eloquent realm of art."[6]

In support of this devotional trend toward the childhood Krishna, a new "orthodoxy" was created during the early medieval period (900–1300 CE) in South India by renowned Vaishnava saints (*ācāryas*) who established sampradāyas or scholastic lineages in formal opposition to the nondualist Advaita Vedānta school of Shaṅkarācārya (ca. 800 CE). These theistic schools, founded by Rāmānuja, Madhva, Nimbārka, and Vishnuswāmī, were generally dualist or modified nondualist in philosophical outlook. From about the eleventh century CE, they built up a considerable literature in Sanskrit in combination with the received Sanskrit canon of the normative Krishna tradition and the developing vernacular corpus. Known as the Catuḥ-Vaishnava Sampradāya, "Four Authorized Vaishnava Schools," they boasted disciplic lineages that stretched back all the way to distinguished ancient Vedic sages and gods, yet also grew forward into formidable bureaucratic organizations with large temple compounds and thousands of followers. The general theological trend in this new orthodoxy was to treat Krishna as the avatāra of Vishnu or else equivalent to Vishnu.

Between 1500–1600 CE, a number of newer but smaller Vaishnava sampradāyas were founded or modified from previous sampradāyas in the late medieval or Mughal period in which the status of Krishna was elevated further. These new movements generally favored Krishna as the Supreme Being, over and above Vishnu, and drew even more exclusively on vernacular poetry from within their respective traditions that exalted Krishna's childhood pastimes. And instead of selecting an important site associated with Vishnu mythology or the adult life of Krishna as their base, they established headquarters in the rural vicinity of Braj in North India, the specific geographical region of Krishna's birth, infancy, and childhood activities according to pious tradition. These newer groups primarily included the Vallabha Sampradāya founded by Śrī Vallabhācārya, the Rādhāvallabha Sampradāya founded by Śrī Hita Harivaṁśa, a revived Nimbārka Sampradāya, the Haridāsī Sampradāya founded by Swāmī Haridās, and the Gauḍīya Sampradāya of Bengal inaugurated by Śrī Caitanya Mahāprabhu.

Shifting attention further away from the standard heroic images of Krishna found in the *Mahābhārata* and the Bhagavad Gītā, these new Braj sects cultivated fervent devotion to the childhood Krishna for its own sake, exploring the emotional experiences between Krishna and the various associates that he had lived with in Braj. This type of bhakti was a spiritual exercise in which disciples in these movements directed their religious devotions toward attaining various emotional states of intimate love of Krishna that were reported to have been savored by the founders, who themselves had originally savored the emotional states, called *rasas*, experienced by the living residents of the Braj area during the actual advent of Krishna roughly five thousand years ago. The young cowherd women of the rustic region of Braj became special targets of devotional focus, as they were purported to have ascended to the highest stages of intimacy and love of Krishna, the supreme goal of bhakti.

Most of the new Braj sects distinguished themselves by spotlighting the personality of one of Krishna's favorite female consorts, Rādhā, said to be the ultimate object of his enduring love and affection in Braj. Rādhā, while not mentioned in the normative canon and virtually unknown in Vaishnava lore before the seventh century CE, had gradually become an important goddess or divine *śakti* after being equated with Lakshmī, Vishnu's wife, and other Vaishnava consorts in the developing vernacular literature as well as in Tantric circles. Rādhā was originally described as simply one of the *gopīs* or cowherd maidens in Braj, but then, as she conquers Krishna with her beauty and love, she ascends to the level of the supreme devotee of Krishna in all of Vaishnavism.

While the name of Rādhā is mentioned in various places throughout the medieval period, her rise to prominence as an important goddess alongside Krishna is actually a comparatively recent phenomenon. According to Charlotte Vaudeville, "her [Rādhā's] emergence in the cultic and devotional sphere of Vaiṣṇavism as Krishna Gopāla's beloved and śakti is known to have taken place rather late, certainly not much earlier than the sixteenth century."[7] Within the entire Sanskrit canon that is accepted by normative Vaishnava traditions, Rādhā is actually never mentioned by name. In the earlier canonical texts there is only the suggestion of Rādhā's character, not her actual name, as one of Krishna's favorites among a number of "unmarried" (*Harivaṁśa*) or "already married" (*Bhāgavata Purāṇa*) cowherd girls (gopīs) who nonetheless seek his attentions during his childhood life in Braj. But even in these texts and other literatures the relation between Rādhā as "favorite" and Krishna is a tentative one of lover and paramour, not of husband and wife. In the vernacular Bengali poems of Chaṇḍīdās, for example, Rādhā is already married to someone named Āyana, and in Bengali *kīrtan* singing that name is completed as Āyana Ghosh. In the Sanskrit plays of Rūpa Goswāmin, Rādhā is already married to Abhimanyu, heightening the intensity of their illicit connection.

While there is brief mention of Rādhā in the *Padma Purāṇa*, and even a long discussion of her in the *Brahmavaivarta Purāṇa*, the antiquity and authenticity of these texts is highly contested. The *Brahmavaivarta Purāṇa*, a "Tantric" Purāṇa probably dating from the fifteenth to the sixteenth centuries CE, "attempted a thoroughgoing synthesis of Krishnaite and Śākta ideas, fitting Rādhā into the outlines of Hindu feminine theology so as to accommodate important devotional-theological movements in North India during the fifteenth and sixteenth centuries." On the other hand, "this same synthetic impetus led to an emphasis on Rādhā's maternal role that was largely peculiar to the Brahmavaivarta and was not acknowledged for the most part by the later Rādhā cults. To be sure, various notions about Rādhā in the Brahmavaivarta came to be widely accepted, such as the identification of Rādhā and Krishna with prakṛti and puruṣa. And such sects as the Rādhāvallabhis, who worship Rādhā above Krishna, may be especially indebted to the Brahmavaivarta."[8] However, this text does not really describe Rādhā as a sovereign deity. C. Mackenzie Brown explains that "Ontologically, it is true, she never rises above Krishna . . . in the Brahmavaivarta; for she arises out of Krishna and ultimately will dissolve back into him."[9]

With regard to the notions of divine śakti, or female energy, there was a surge of Tantric writings[10] during the late medieval period. In the Tantric tradition, according to Vaudeville, "Every Hindu male god has a distinct relation with at least one female deity, a devī, who usually stands as his wife or consort. If the male god is conceived as powerful, the consort goddess tends to be conceived as the embodiment of the god's power or energy, his śakti."[11] Vaudeville argues that at some point Krishna was connected to the Goddess Kālī, then Durgā, who was finally replaced by Rādhā. Rādhā is also sometimes described as an incarnation of Lakshmī, or one of her two forms. According to Ramakanta Chakravarti, "The Vaishnava emphasis on the Śakti aspect of Lakshmī, Kamalā, or Rādhā might have stemmed from the worship of the female principle by the Tantrikas."[12] As such, the religious writings of the Bengali Vaishnavas were deeply imbued with Tantric thought and practice, wherein Rādhā becomes theologized as Ādyaśakti (*hlādinī śakti*), the cosmic energy, the primeval mother of the world, a metamorphoses of the great goddess Durgā, whom Krishna had once known as his sister, Subhadrā, Yogamāyā.

In their pious veneration of Rādhā alongside Krishna as a dual divinity superior to Vishnu, however, most of these new groups preferred to distance themselves from Śākta and Tantric traditions that were receiving social disapproval for unsavory and unorthodox practices. Instead, they preferred to follow in the wake of the Vaishnava developments indicated by the twelfth-century Sanskrit text, *Gītagovinda*, by Jayadeva in Bengal. In this work the youthful Krishna is consistently paired with his lover and consort Rādhā. The verses of the *Gītagovinda* had showcased the pure relationship between Krishna and Rādhā as above all others, and while these themes were already present in vernacular poetry, according to Ramakanta Chakravarti, the popularity of this text throughout India made it "evident that the Rādhā-Krishna legend had become universally popular in the twelfth century."[13]

In the *Gītagovinda* the former avatāra of Vishnu known as Krishna, along with his consort Rādhā, had fully usurped the primacy of Vishnu as the Supreme Being ("Jagadīśa"), becoming the *avatārin*, or source of the avatāras. According to Barbara Miller, "The compounding of Krishna with Rādhā into a dual divinity is central to Jayadeva's conception of Krishna, not as an incarnation (avatāra) of Vishnu, but as the source (avatārin, daśavidharūpa, daśakṛtikṛt) of all the incarnate forms he himself assumes in order to save the world. Jayadeva's Krishna is addressed as Jagadīśa, the loving compassionate 'Lord of the World,' a title that must be a variant of Jagannātha, the name of the complex composite Buddhist-Śaiva-Vaiṣṇava god of Puri." Krishna's former normative title of Bhagavān, Lord, which is everywhere in the *Mahābhārata*, the *Harivaṁśa*, and various Purāṇas, and which is the title of the Bhagavad Gītā, "is notably absent from Jayadeva's poem. Its absence, along with that of such basic Bhāgavata terms as dharma, karma, and bhakti, distinguishes Jayadeva's conception of Krishna from that of the divine object of the orthodox Bhāgavata cult."[14] The rise of Rādhā and Krishna into theological prominence in the bhakti traditions of Vaishnavism was thus observed "officially" by her presence in this work, which was enormously influential. For example, under the influence of the *Gītagovinda* the Bengali and Maithili poets Chaṇḍīdās and Vidyāpati molded the character of Rādhā in East India and set the stage for the Bengal Vaishnavism of Caitanya.

Krishna as a childhood deity enwrapped with love for Rādhā as outlined in *Gītagovinda* was, understandably, not acceptable to the orthodox or normative tradition. According to Barbara Miller, "The orthodox cult was basically antithetical to Jayadeva's notion of Krishna's exclusive, erotic relationship with a single consort as the supreme expression of his love and as a model for the relation between Krishna and his devotee."[15] The full implications of this new image were not developed until the newer sects of Braj four hundred years later.

As one of these newer sects, the Rādhāvallabha Sampradāya flourished and sustained its very unique religious perspective for more than five hundred years from its base at the Braj center of Krishna worship and devotion, Vrindaban. It was generally compatible with most of the post-Jayadeva bhakti movements that were established during the Moghul period throughout India, and several external features of this group even appeared harmonious with those of other Vaishnava and mainstream Hindu traditions, such as temple worship, male hereditary priesthood, seasonal festivals, religious hymns, musical instruments, vegetarianism, ritual purity, bodily markings of sandal paste, and initiation with mantras. Yet despite these apparent similarities, there were more profound differences in theology and practice that clearly set the RVS apart from all other Vaishnava and Hindu traditions and thus squarely within the "alternative" domain. A brief discussion of four aspects of difference follows.[16]

First, for purposes of authenticity and continuity, it was deemed necessary by the founders of Vaishnava communities in medieval times to align themselves with one of the four major sampradāyas mentioned above. The new Gauḍīya Sampradāya of Bengal was said to be linked to the earlier Madhva Sampradāya, the Vallabha Sampradāya to the Vishnuswāmī lineage, and the Haridāsī Sampradāya to the Nimbārka Sampradāya. The RVS, however, resisted affiliation with any of these four so-called orthodox Vaishnava sampradāyas—Rāmānuja, Madhva, Nimbārka, and Vishnuswāmī. While the other sects founded in Braj at this time made concerted efforts to align themselves with one of these, the RVS preferred to remain autonomous and unaffiliated. As explained by Rupert Snell, "The Rādhāvallabha Sampradāya does not claim affiliation to the 'classical' Vaishnava Catuḥ-sampradāya [Four Sampradāyas], nor does it specifically profess any one of the major philosophical positions of classical Hinduism. Its claim to autonomy as a sampradāya in its own right rests on its following a particular mode or style of bhakti, and in the maintaining of distinct lines of authority descending from Hita Harivaṁśa himself."[17] Moreover, while a religious conference was held at Jaipur in Rajasthan during the early eighteenth century for purposes of affirming affiliation, according to A. W. Entwistle, "Followers of the Rādhāvallabha Sampradāya say that their leading teachers declined to send a representative, produce a theological commentary, or align themselves with one of the four Sampradāyas. This was because they regarded their devotional practices as being based on divine love."[18]

The issue of direct connection with earlier lineages was not uncontested, however. For example, with regard to the Gauḍīya order, "The Madhva affiliation of the Caitanya order [Gauḍīya Vaishnavism], first propounded by Baladeva Vidyābhūshaṇa in the eighteenth century is a . . . debatable point." There is also no mention of Caitanya in the annals of the Madhva Sampradāya to this day, such that "The Gauḍīya Vaiṣṇava affiliation with the Madhva Sampradāya was merely a matter of form. The Gauḍīya Vaishnava order was for all practical purposes a new Vaishnava order."[19] The alleged Nimbārka affiliation of Swāmī Haridās as well as the Vishnuswāmī connection of Vallabha was equally tenuous at best.

Perhaps foreseeing inevitable and unwelcome controversies, the RVS simply abstained from affiliation with a former Vaishnava lineage. One of the principal reasons for this was that the "Krishnology" (cf. Christology, "the nature of the person of Christ, including the union in him of the human and divine natures"), the nature and divine status of Krishna, espoused by the RVS was at variance with that of the earlier orthodox Vaishnava lineages and the normative or traditional Krishnas endorsed by them. And while there were indeed many localized folk traditions of Krishna worship throughout India that also differed from these orthodox groups, the Rādhāvallabha situation was distinctive since this particular Krishna tradition had purposely and knowingly distanced itself from the normative tradition and even established itself as a formalized alternative "church" in which there was a strong ecclesiastical center and lineage with a new "orthodox" theology of its own, directing thousands of initiated disciples and followers all over India.

Second, in the RVS many of the otherwise normative concepts and practices of orthodox Vaishnavism and Hinduism were either rejected as distractions or kept at a distance. In relation to Vaishnavism, these included most of the canonical Sanskrit literatures, avatāra mythology and worship, Vishnu forms, Vishnu's spouse Lakshmī, *vyūha* expansions, Vedānta philosophy, and observances like fasting on Ekādaśī and so forth. Moreover, much of what passed as mainstream Hindu practice, including caste duties, life-cycle rituals, Vedic fire sacrifices, and the like, were viewed as extraneous and even held with a certain disdain. According to Vaishnava literary scholar Rupert Snell, "The use of Vedic ritual, and the observance of certain generally accepted Vaishnava practices such as the ekādaśī vrata, are spurned as irrelevancies."[20] These depictions corresponded with my own observations of the RVS during the years 1988 and 1992 to 1993, and consultation with members. While the sect did not dispute the authenticity of the Veda as in some heterodox communities, the point is that the central focus of the tradition lay elsewhere, in the eternal love play between Krishna and Rādhā.

From within the tradition itself, there is the following statement made by Uttamadāsa, a Rādhāvallabha disciple, as cited by Jan Brzezinski: "He [Hita Harivaṁśa] rejected all orthodox precepts and prohibitions in favor of pure devotion, and renounced fast-days because they denied him the consumption of *prasāda* [food sacraments]. He ignored the ten rites of passage (*saṁskāra*) and defeated ceremonialists, Śaivas, Śāktas and the followers of other doctrines."[21]

Third, the RVS venerated the householder stage of life as ideal, and did not endorse renunciation of world and family in any form, as found in the normative Hindu tradition of *sannyāsa*. Even within sectarian Vaishnavism, upholding solely the married life is strikingly at odds with other Krishna traditions such as the Haridāsī Sampradāya and the Gauḍīya Sampradāya. In both of these groups, as well as in some branches of the Rāmānuja, Madhva, and Nimbārka Sampradāyas, renunciation is idealized and sannyāsa is praised among its members and especially its leaders. In contrast with Hita Harivaṁśa who lived and died as a householder, the Gauḍīya founder Śrī Caitanya and his most important followers the Six Goswāmins of Vrindaban including Rūpa Goswāmin all practiced a severe form of renunciation and detachment from the world: "The goswāmins were unquestionably celibate and ascetical. With meticulous care they practiced strict self-denial as religious discipline. They lived in poverty like their leader Caitanya."[22] In this respect the RVS resembled only the Vallabha Sampradāya, in which sannyāsa was also discouraged.

Fourth, Rādhāvallabha Krishnology posed striking differences from normative Krishna perspectives found in other sampradāyas. Most of the other Vaishnava theological traditions or sampradāyas placed Krishna firmly on the throne of Īśvara, or Supreme Being. While keeping the figure of Krishna close in proximity to the center of their cultic life, Rādhāvallabhites nonetheless depicted Krishna not as the ultimate Supreme Being in the ordinary sense but as the most intimate servant of God, in this case the Goddess Rādhā. While the normative tradition generally claims Rādhā as the dearest servant and mistress of Krishna, the RVS claimed that Rādhā was the Supreme Being, Brahman, and Krishna's eternal divine spouse. Some of the Vaishnava sects in Vrindaban that were contemporary with Hita Harivaṁśa placed Rādhā in positions of mistress or spouse, and were similar in their approach in venerating Rādhā as united with Krishna. Yet, as also discerned by White, "Hari Vaṁś is closely allied to the Vaiṣṇava schools that have Krishna as the chief deity—the difference being that Hari Vaṁś extols Rādhā above Krishna."[23] And this simply reaffirms the prior testimony recorded by one of the earliest Westerners to interview a member of this sect, J. N. Farquhar in 1917: "Krishna is the servant of Rādhā. He may do the coolie-work of building the world, but Rādhā sits as Queen. He is at best but her Secretary of State. We win the favor of Krishna by worshipping Rādhā."[24]

As an interesting precursor to the RVS Krishnology, there is a reference by Jayadeva in the *Gītagovinda* (twelfth century CE) regarding the placing of Krishna beneath Rādhā. The "submission" of Krishna to Rādhā is suggested in *Gītagovinda* (10.9), where Krishna implores

Rādhā to place her feet on his head. The orthodox Vaishnava insists on the ultimate superiority of the Lord, but Krishna submits to Rādhā according to a verse believed to have been interpolated by Krishna himself into the text. Jayadeva justifies Krishna's submission to Rādhā at the end of the *Gītagovinda*: "When Jayadeva conceived the climax of Krishna's supplication to Rādhā as a command for Rādhā to place her foot on Krishna's head in a symbolic gesture of victory, the poet hesitated to compose the verse, in deference to Krishna. Jayadeva went to bathe and in his absence Krishna himself appeared in the poet's guise to write the couplet; then Krishna ate the food that Padmāvatī had prepared for Jayadeva and left. When the poet returned he realized that he had received divine sanction to sing about his vision of Krishna's relation to Rādhā."[25] The *Gītagovinda* 10.9 (10.8) thus states, *dehi pada pallavam udaram*, "Now like a diadem, crown this my head with the tender petals of your feet, a pleasurable balm for the venom of desire. And let it cure my suffering from the burning fire of desire."[26] Is this simply a gesture of humility by Krishna, or a harbinger regarding the superiority of Rādhā to Krishna as exemplified in the RVS? Nonetheless, the placement of Rādhā alongside Krishna as his only consort was an important first step made by the *Gītagovinda*, and was controversial and "alternative" in its time. The RVS took a further step and placed her as the Supreme Being over and above Krishna who was never merely a paramour but always her husband.

Krishna as the husband of Rādhā is also an important dimension of RVS Krishnology, yet one which has also sparked controversy. Their permanent married state diverges from the normative relationship between Krishna and Rādhā, which is adulterous. In keeping with the atmosphere of the *Gītagovinda*, most of the newer Vaishnava sects in Braj had placed Rādhā alongside Krishna as his loving devotee and mistress without compromising his status as Supreme Lord. Though there are theological works explaining her as the śakti, or energy, of Krishna in these sects, David Kinsley describes her general social relationship with Krishna as adulterous and thus controversial: "Although she is married to another, she is passionately attracted to Krishna. Rādhā's illicit relationship with Krishna breaks all social norms and casts her in the role of one who willfully steps outside the realm of dharma to pursue her love."[27] What is interesting here is that this adulterous relationship became a kind of normative tradition within the new Vaishnavism, and so to describe Rādhā as the spouse of Krishna was viewed as going against the grain. After all, while Krishna was unmarried during his sojourn in Vrindaban, according to the normative account, he went on to marry over sixteen thousand wives throughout his adult life, and sire quite a number of sons through at least eight of them (see introduction).

In other parts of India, Krishna is worshiped with Rukmiṇī, his first and most important wife who was queen of Dvārakā where he ruled as king. Krishna fathered no children through Rādhā in any of the Vaishnava traditions, whether married to her or not, yet in the Braj sects she is the primary female companion of Krishna.

The issue of the spiritual superiority of union versus separation (*milana* versus *viraha*), or the married state versus unmarried state (*svakīya* versus *parakīya*), in the relationship between Rādhā and Krishna has occupied the attention of Vaishnava theologians for generations. Including confrontations and rebuttles, according to Chakravarti, "The subject of Krishna's marriage with Rādhā and other Gopinīs or milkmaids became a highly debatable one."[28] Large segments of conservative Hindu society were hesitant about the so-called scandalous affair between Rādhā and Krishna. As noted by White: "Because their code of morals usually was family-oriented, the Vaishnavas would have to find ways and means to avoid being drawn into the erotic attitudes and behavior of the Tantrics and others whom they did not wish to emulate. We find in the history of Krishna Bhakti that a considerable theological effort has been made to determine whether Rādhā was Krishna's wife or his mistress. For a large number of Vaishnavas, including the followers of Harivaṁś, the erotic descriptions were no doubt acceptable only if they were thought to derive from the married state."[29] The so-called Tantric traditions had developed a reputation for unorthodox social behavior and were generally avoided by mainstream Vaishnavas. The opposing side, such as the Gauḍīya school, while not explicitly Tantric, had argued that love which is free from the restrictions of married life was somehow higher or purer in substance. Within the Gauḍīya Sampradāya of Bengal, after years of debate the parakīya (unmarried) state was declared orthodoxy in 1717. Several factions within this group had been influenced by the svakīya (married) position but to no avail.

In a very clever theological sleight of hand, the RVS claimed that all the possibilities of union and separation were experienced within the married state, and were ultimately reconciled in the eternal sport of Rādhā and Krishna. For example, many of the poems in the RVS liturgical hymnal describe at length the blinking of the eyes of Rādhā and Krishna as moments of intense union and separation. As explained by White: "The experience of the union of Rādhā and Krishna is a very rapid and completely fulfilling alternation of these states. Hence Krishna experiences viraha in the most minute instances of separation—when he closes his eyes for a brief second and loses sight of Rādhā; whereas, the experience of milana is almost constant, and, moreover, it is without beginning and will be without end." Moreover, the eternal reconciliation is transcendental to mundane distinctions and temporal history: "The bliss of love-in-separation and love-in-union is transcended in their nitya-vihāra."[30]

The Rādhāvallabha experience of *śṛṅgāra rasa* (conjugal love) in the form of the eternal *nitya-vihāra* pastimes of Rādhā and Krishna was also believed to transcend all other known experiences of bhakti, including those outlined by the normative and orthodox traditions. The normative scriptures like *Bhāgavata Purāṇa* and *Vishnu Purāṇa* were upheld and strongly emphasized in the teachings of Caitanya, Vallabha, Nimbārka, and other Vaishnava saints, which held that "Rādhā and Krishna experience the polarities of separation, *viraha*, and union, *milana*; they are tormented by the experience of love under the guise of *parakīya* (illicit heterosexual love) and its alternative *svakīya* (licit heterosexual love)."[31] Yet the RVS believed that this represented a lower form of bhakti in which it was difficult to savor the fullness of śṛṅgāra rasa. The true experience of bhakti in the form of śṛṅgāra rasa was said for the Rādhāvallabhites to exist in the constant and simultaneous presence of both meeting and separation. And this could only be sustained in the married or svakīya state of conjugal union.

The precise theological teachings of the Rādhāvallabha Sampradāya have been explained by historian of religions Charles S. J. White. Regarding the centrality of Rādhā, he says: "Rādhā is the very ground of being. She is eternal power and the giver of bliss in the universe. Being absolute she is without form and qualities, and yet her devotees are her companions (*sakhī* or *sahacarī*) who adore her while she is amorously sporting with Krishna. It is through Rādhā's physical manifestations and the grasp of her psychological character that a devotee at length finds the route to her eternal aspect. The love play and the granting of all wishes and desires for the devotees are merely aids to that discovery. Rādhā is without equal in the universe for beauty, and her power constantly defeats the god of love, Kāmadeva [cf. Cupid]. There are no negative emotions appropriate to her; hence she is without the characteristics of Devī or Śakti. Simply put, she is the goddess of love to Krishna."[32]

In terms of the particular position of Krishna, White explains: "Krishna, the eternal young lover deity, enjoys rasa—the ecstasy of love—forever and is the only male participating in the love sport of Vrindavan. He, too, is the supreme Lord but functions as the sexual companion to Rādhā. In these amorous actions he arouses Rādhā who then releases the *śṛṅgāra rasa* [conjugal love experience] to the devotees and to the world through the *rāsa līlā* [dance] and the bower sport. Krishna has become incarnate in order to love Rādhā."[33]

Hence the substance of Rādhāvallabha theology revolves around the eternal love shared between Rādhā and Krishna in the form of divine conjugal union, which for the human devotees is the most sought-after spiritual attainment, experienced as sublime bliss. And while the poetic descriptions of these conjugal postures appear to delve deeply into erotic themes of an almost carnal nature, the approach of the devout is nonliteral and meant to reflect a lofty realization of eternal *prema*, or intense spiritual love. Salvation for the Rādhāvallabha devotees consists of permanent mystical participation in that divine romantic love which is also the topmost secret.

An understanding of the actual practices associated with emotional bhakti within the boundaries of the Braj area, including Mathurā (Krishna's birthplace) and the village of Vrindaban, provides additional context for this theological development. The extreme forms of bhakti practiced here by ascetics and devotees were of the *rasika* variety; that is, the cultivation of specific emotional states for their own sake rather than for liberation (moksha) or some other benefit in the postmortem realm. The area of Vrindaban was a fertile region for the appropriate spiritual practices that involved intense *sādhanas* or routines of chanting, musical performance, hearing, devotional worship, meditation, bathing, and especially *sādhu saṅga*, association of like-minded devotees. Various groups fostered these practices, including the Sakhī or Haridāsī Sampradāya founded by Swāmī Haridās (ca. 1500–95 CE) and the local exponents of the earlier Nimbārka Sampradāya founded by Nimbārka (ca. 1200), all of which also drew upon local folk expressions found only in the Braj area. The Gauḍīya Sampradāya and the Puṣṭimārg tradition (Vallabha Sampradāya) were also central to this development.

As a Rasika Sampradāya, the Rādhāvallabha Sampradāya stressed almost exclusively the *nikuñja-vihāra*, or private love play dimension of the Krishna story, adopting *mādhurya bhāva* or conjugal love as its preferred devotional approach. This aspect was thus singled out from the extraordinarily diverse types of images and pastimes associated with Krishna. Rādhā and Krishna are married yet continue to engage in conjugal activities wherever they find intimate pleasure, preferring the *nikuñja*, or sacred grove. Rupert Snell explains further by referring to the distinction that was maintained between "*nikuñja līlā* [private intimate relations in a secluded bower], in which the sublimated passion of Rādhā and Krishna provided the focus of the devotee's attention, and *vraja līlā*, the generality of Purāṇic Krishna mythology, regarded as inferior as a source of *rasa* since its diversity is detrimental to the experiencing of single-minded absorption (*ananya bhāva*) in the sport of the joint deity." Yet the full experience of the divine union of Rādhā and Krishna of course could not be experienced by the devotee through imitation or other participation, but was only approximated by a kind of spiritual voyeurism that satiated the devotee in the form of a spectating sakhī or handmaiden to the couple: "The role of the *sakhī* in promoting (but not participating in) the *nikuñja-vihāra* is emulated by the devotee, whose highest aim is to achieve the vicarious delight of being an onlooker in the *nikuñja*. An *alaukika* Vrindāvana [other-worldly Vrindaban] is the setting for this divine activity, and takes the place of other Vaishnava conceptions of paradise such as Vaikuṇṭha and Goloka [the abodes of Vishnu and the normative Krishna]."[34] The actual attention of the sakhīs (handmaiden devotees) is firmly fixed upon the sexual congress of the divine lovers, such that "for the female companions it is the source of sublime religious delight. In a sense there is nothing else of value in their world—Vrindavan, where the cool, gentle, sweet-smelling wind ever blows, has none of the distraction of what could be called historical change. The sakhīs live in the eternal present, the now of the consummate erotic experience wherein what they experience approaches the level of the bliss of Rādhā and Krishna."[35]

For Rādhāvallabha devotees, the uniting of Rādhā and Krishna takes place both in the terrestrial Vrindaban, a place the human devotee can aspire to visit, and at the highest levels of the cosmos in the eternal Vrindāvana. This is where "Rādhā's function transverses and transcends all known and unknown dimensions of reality. It is no more impossible for Rādhā to assume the functions of such a universal deity and yet remain in her basic ideological expression within the Vaishnava mode than it is for Vishnu himself to function as a universal deity without losing his distinctiveness, vis-à-vis Śiva, or as an avatāra."[36]

The late arrival of the actual deity representation of Rādhā with Krishna on center stage of the Vaishnava temple altars took place in Vrindaban under the influence of the Bengal school of Vaishnavism founded by Caitanya Mahāprabhu (1485–1534 CE). Caitanya himself did not devote himself to the form of the Divine Couple, since he "does not seem to have made the Rādhā-Krishna couple the special object of his devotion,"[37] preferring the Jagannāth image. Yet it was his followers who established Rādhā-Krishna worship in full detail and regalia in Vrindaban. According to Vaudeville, "It was in Brindavan (Skt Vṛndāvana), in the heart of the Braj country, that the gopī Rādhā, Krishna's sweetheart in popular tradition and the very embodiment of pure love (*mahābhāva*) for Krishna, came to be established as the latter's Śakti and consort in the theological and cultic sphere."[38] The intense focus of the RVS on Rādhā thus makes sense in light of this and also the fact that Śrī Hita Harivaṁśa was a Gauḍa Brahmin, son of Vyāsa Miśra, originally perhaps of Bengali descent. Caitanya was the son of Jagannāth Miśra, another Gauḍa Brahmin.

However, while most of the other Vaishnava temples in Vrindaban have deity forms of Rādhā on their altar, most of the shrines in the numerous temples of Śrī Rādhāvallabha in Vrindaban do not contain anthropomorphic representations or statues of Rādhā. She, high above physical representation, is worshiped in the form of a small tablet inscribed with her name and placed, suitably adorned and garlanded with flowers, on Krishna's left side. According to White, "In the main temple of the sect in Vrindavan the image of Śrī Krishna, as Rādhāvallabha, was installed but with no corresponding image of Śrī Rādhā. Instead, the goddess is represented by the throne cushion or gaddī, an object regarded throughout Hinduism as a surrogate, nonliteral, image of a revered person or deity." As explained further with reference to the work of Rādhāvallabha scholar Vijayendra Snātak: "the *gaddī* [throne cushion], placed alongside the *mūrti* [statue] of Rādhāvallabha, has a golden leaf suspended over it upon which is written the name of Śrī Rādhā. Several reasons are given for service to Rādhā as the throne (*gaddī-sevā*). First, Rādhā's beauty is indescribable (she is the Absolute and beyond all forms). Thus no icon would be suitable to represent her. Second, Rādhā is a teacher; because the symbol of the teacher is the *gaddī*, the mind of the devotee should be fixed upon it. Third, because Rādhā and Krishna are engaged in eternal bower sport, if they are depicted together, this would have to be the main subject of the icon. It would be improper to depict them so, and it has been avoided; the devotee is enjoined to fix his attention mentally upon Rādhā through contemplating the *gaddī*. Devotion to Rādhā is further shown through writing her name on creepers, stones, and pieces of wood . . . in various sacred places."[39]

We have argued thus far that the RVS promoted an alternative Krishnology by establishing and sustaining the supremacy of Rādhā over Krishna in Vaishnavism. As Rasika Sampradāyas, most of the newer Braj sects venerated Rādhā in some fashion, yet it was the RVS that became exclusively associated with Rādhā. In a comparative study of the RVS with the Haridāsī Sampradāya, the sect closest to RVS in devotional understanding, Vaishnava scholar Lucy Rosenstein found that "whereas Hita Harivaṁśa's name is specifically bonded to Rādhā, that of Haridāsa is not; if there is any imbalance it is in favor of Krishna."[40]

The strong emphasis of RVS on Rādhā was influential nevertheless in elevating the status of Rādhā among the Braj movements that had originally revered primarily Krishna or the divine couple of Rādhā-Krishna. Regarding the Haridāsī Sampradāya, Rosenstein observed: "Whereas *Kelimāl* [work by Swāmī Haridās] clearly suggests that Rādhā is equal to Krishna and part of the joint form, in later developments she is elevated to a position higher than Krishna's."[41] In Gauḍīya Vaishnavism Rādhā is the energy of God and was never placed above Krishna theologically, yet, "by the sixteenth century Rādhā holds a central position in the theology of Bengali Vaishnavism."[42] According to Rosenstein, a similar increase in the importance of Rādhā can be viewed in the history of the Vallabha Sampradāya: "Whereas the founder of the sect, Vallabhācārya, gives no place to Rādhā in his compositions, his son Viṭṭhalnāth dedicates two of his works . . . to Rādhā."[43] John S. Hawley[44] also traces the increased importance of Rādhā in the poems attributed to Sūr Dās, a famous Hindi poet often associated with the Vallabha Sampradāya, over several centuries. Since Vrindaban is the place where Rādhā and Krishna engaged in their love play, it was perhaps inevitable that Rādhā would assume greater importance, such that today the standard greeting in Vrindaban among devotees is not "Jai Krishna" (Hail Krishna!) but "Jai Rādhe" (Glories to Rādhā!). The RVS was at the very helm in spearheading this trend toward complete elevation of Rādhā above Krishna since the very beginning of the re-founding of Vrindaban.

The figure of Krishna in the Rādhāvallabha tradition thus differs significantly from the "canonical" Krishna found in the epics and Purāṇas and in each of the orthodox Vaishnava sampradāyas. Krishna is worshiped in this sect due to his eternal connection with Rādhā, who is showcased in all her beauty and splendor as the Supreme Godhead. Their Krishnology was a clean departure from the normative tradition, yet one which has influenced other groups and continues to flourish today. While not very well known outside of the Braj area, the RVS nonetheless remains an active sampradāya, with temples and centers throughout Braj as well as in Rajasthan, Uttar Pradesh, and even Calcutta.

Notes

1. Rupert Snell (1991), 20. Cited from the account of Uttamadasa.
2. Rupert Snell (1991), 329.
3. See Jan K. Brzezinski (1998), 19–61.
4. Lalitā Caraṇ Goswami, trans. (1991), 109, 1, 62, 50.
5. Aside from these two works, there is an immense body of poetic literature of succeeding members of the Rādhāvallabha Sampradāya that is unfortunately mostly unedited and unpublished. However, many of the existing writings and manuscripts attributed to members of the various RVS disciplic lineages, with dates, have been tabulated by Śrī Kiśorī Śaraṇ Alī in *Śrī Hita Rādhāvallabhīya Sāhitya Ratnāvali* (1950).
6. John Stratton Hawley (1983), 30, 22.
7. Charlotte Vaudeville (1982), 1.
8. C. Mackenzie Brown (1982), 71.

9. C. Mackenzie Brown (1982), 70.

10. In Tantric traditions, the nonmarried state is viewed as superior to the married. Tantrics practiced forms of sexual yoga, and viewed Rādhā as a human incarnation that taught yoga and meditation. She is also believed to have taught goddess worship to Krishna, who is popular today due to the grace of the goddess Kālī. See June McDaniel (2000), 133–46.

11. Charlotte Vaudeville (1982), 1.

12. Ramakanta Chakravarti (1985), 19.

13. Ramakanta Chakravarti (1985), 9.

14. Barbara Stoler Miller (1982), 18.

15. Barbara Stoler Miller (1982), 19.

16. Vijayendra Snatak (1968), 97–98, recounted four great differences between the RVS and the Gauḍīya Vaishnavas as noted by Gopāla Bhaṭṭa Goswamin: (1) Hita Harivaṁśa had faith in the primacy of Rādhā; (2) Hita Harivaṁśa worshiped Rādhā as *svakīya* (Krishna's own wife), while the Gauḍīyas preferred *parakīya* (Rādhā as the wife of another cowherd); (3) Hita Harivaṁśa worshiped Rādhā in *nitya-vihāra* (heavenly pastimes), while Gauḍīyas preferred the *prakaṭa-līlā* (earthly pastimes) in which separation between Rādhā and Krishna was manifest; and (4) the external rites, deity service, *ekādaśī* fasting, etc., of the Gauḍīyas was not accepted by the RVS.

17. Rupert Snell (1991), 3.

18. A. W. Entwistle (1987), 194. Entwistle draws from the account in Lalitā Caraṇ Goswami (1957), 70–72.

19. Ramakanta Chakravarti (1985), 67.

20. Rupert Snell (1991), 5.

21. Jan Brzezinski (1998), 22.

22. Ramakanta Chakravarti (1985), 116.

23. Charles S. J. White (1977), 35.

24. J. N. Farquhar (1920), 318.

25. Barbara Stoler Miller (1982), 23.

26. Durgadas Mukhopadhyay, ed. and trans. (1990), 89.

27. David Kinsley (1986), 81.

28. Ramakanta Chakravarti (1985), 110.

29. Charles S. J. White (1977), 33.

30. Charles S. J. White (1977), 30.

31. Charles S. J. White (1977), 30.

32. Charles S. J. White (1977), 28–29.

33. Charles S. J. White (1977), 29.

34. Rupert Snell (1991), 3.

35. Charles S. J. White (1977), 30.

36. Charles S. J. White (1977), 30–31.

37. Charlotte Vaudeville (1982), 10.

38. Charlotte Vaudeville (1982), 11.

39. Charles S. J. White (1977), 32.

40. Lucy Rosenstein (1998), 8.

41. Lucy Rosenstein (2000), 122.
42. Lucy Rosenstein (2000), 120.
43. Lucy Rosenstein (2000), 123.
44. See John Stratton Hawley (1982).

References

Alī, Śrī Kiśorī Śaraṇ. *Śrī Hita Radhavallabhiya Sāhitya Ratnāvali*. Bombay: Bombay Nivasi Katipaya Radhavallabhiya Vaisnava, 1950.

———. *Śrī Hita Caturāsī (Śaṭikā)*. Vrindaban: Madan Mohanlal Gupta, 1965. Hita Caurasi with Hindi commentary by Śrī Kiśorī Śaraṇ Alī.

Beck, Guy L. *Sonic Theology: Hinduism and Sacred Sound*. Columbia: University of South Carolina Press, 1993.

———. "Vaiṣṇava Music in the Braj Region of North India." *Journal of Vaiṣṇava Studies* 4.2 (spring 1996): 115–47.

Brown, C. Mackenzie. "The Theology of Rādhā in the Purāṇas." In John Stratton Hawley and Donna Marie Wulff, eds. (1982), 57–71.

Brzezinski, Jan K. "Prabodhānanda, Hit Harivaṁśa and the Rādhā-rasa-sudhā-nidhi." *Journal of Vaiṣṇava Studies* 7.1 (fall 1998): 19–61.

Chakravarti, Ramakanta. *Vaiṣṇavism in Bengal: 1486–1900*. Calcutta: Sanskrit Pustak Bhandar, 1985.

Farquhar, J. N. *An Outline of the Religious Literature of India* London: Oxford UP, 1920.

Goswami, Lalitā Caraṇ. *Śrī Hita Harivaṁśa Goswami: Sampradāya aura Sāhitya*. Vrindaban: Venu Prakashan, 1957.

———, ed. *Śrī Hita Caurāsī evam Sphuṭa Vānī [of Śrī Hita Hari Vaṁśa]*. Vrindaban: Venu Prakashan, 1972.

———, ed. *Śrī Rādhāvallabhajī kā Vārṣotsava*. Vrindaban: Srī Radhavallabha Mandira Vaisnava Committee, v. 1, 1978, v. 2, 1979, v. 3, 1980. Based on *Śṛṅgāra Rasa Sāgara* in 4 volumes, 1956–62, edited and published by Tulsidas Baba in Vrindaban.

———, trans. *Śrī Rādhā Sudhā Nidhi Stotram*. Bombay: Bharatiya Vidya Bhavan, 1991.

Gupta, Motilal. *Braj: The Centrum of Indian Culture*. Delhi: Agam Kala Prakashan, 1982.

Hawley, John Stratton. *Krishna, the Butter Thief*. Princeton, NJ: Princeton University Press, 1983.

———. "A Vernacular Portrait: Rādhā in the Sūr Sāgar." In John Stratton Hawley and Donna Marie Wulff, eds. (1982), 42–56.

Hawley, John Stratton, and Donna Marie Wulff, eds. *The Divine Consort: Rādhā and the Goddesses of India*. Berkeley, CA: Graduate Theological Union, 1982.

Kinsley, David. *Hindu Goddesses: Visions of the Divine Feminine in the Hindu Religious Tradition*. Berkeley: University of California Press, 1986.

McDaniel, June. "The Tantric Rādhā." *Journal of Vaiṣṇava Studies* 8.2 (spring 2000): 131–46.

Miller, Barbara Stoler. "The Divine Duality of Rādhā an Krishna." In John Stratton Hawley and Donna Marie Wulff, eds. (1982), 13–41.

Mukhopadhyay, Durgadas, ed. and trans. *In Praise of Krishna: Translation of Gīta-Govinda of Jayadeva*. Delhi: B.R. Publishing, 1990.

Rosenstein, Lucy. "Rādhā in the Haridāsī Sampradāya." *Journal of Vaiṣṇava Studies* 8.2 (spring 2000): 119–29.

———. "The Rādhāvallabha and the Haridāsī Sampradāyas: A Comparison." *Journal of Vaiṣṇava Studies* 7.1 (fall 1998): 5–18.

Snātak, Vijayendra. *Rādhāvallabha Sampradāya Siddhānta aur Sāhitya*. Delhi: National Publishing House, 1957, 1968.

Snell, Rupert. *The Caurāsī Pada: A Rādhāvallabhī Text in Medieval Hindi*. Ph.D. Thesis, University of London, 1984.

———. *The Eighty-Four Hymns of Hita Harivaṁśa: An Edition of the Caurāsī Pada*. Delhi: Motilal Banarsidass, and London: School of Oriental and African Studies, 1991.

———. "Metrical Forms in Braj Bhāṣā Verse: The Caurāsī Pada in Performance." In *Bhakti in Current Research 1979–1982*. Monika Theil-Horstmann, ed. Berlin: Dietrich Reimar Verlag, 1983, 353–83.

Vaudeville, Charlotte. "Krishna Gopāla, Rādhā, and the Great Goddess." In John Stratton Hawley and Donna Marie Wulff, eds. (1982), 1–12.

White, Charles S. J. *The Caurāsī Pad of Śrī Hit Harivaṁś*. Hawaii: University Press of Hawaii, 1977.

Appendix: Wedding Hymns of Rādhā and Krishna *(Vyāhulau Utsav ke Pad)*

In the Rādhāvallabha Sampradāya, Rādhā and Krishna are viewed as eternally married in the spiritual realm of *nitya-vihāra*. Yet the devotees reimagine and reexperience the wedding of the divine couple in their poetry and music as part of their calendrical religious discipline. The Braj Bhāshā hymns below represent a very intimate part of the Rādhāvallabha worship tradition and are available here in English translation for the first time. These hymns are sung annually at Rādhāvallabha temples during the festival of Vyāhula (Wedding of Rādhā and Krishna), which is held on the first day of the bright half of the month (*śūkla-pakṣa*) of Kārtik (fall season), just after the new moon (*āmāvasya*) which is otherwise celebrated as Diwali in Hindu traditions. The songtexts are from the Rādhāvallabha liturgical hymnal known as the *Śrī Rādhāvallabhjī kā Vārṣotsava*, 3d volume, 164–67 (Vrindaban: Sri Radhavallabha Mandira Vaiṣnava Committee, 1980), compiled by Śrī Lalitā Caraṇ Goswami, with English translation in 2000 by Śrī Harishankar Mathur of Baton Rouge, Louisiana, former manager of Śrī Raṅganāth Temple, Vrindaban, India.

I. Two Hymns Describing the Marriage Ceremony of Rādhā and Krishna, by Śrī Dhruva Dās

A. First Hymn:

1. Rādhā's girlfriends think of arranging a cheerful marriage ceremony. The idea is appreciated by everyone, and it greatly enhances their joy. They are drenched in the colors of divine love. Being immersed in the joy of serving the couple—Rādhā and Krishna—they cannot relish any other worldly object. Being absorbed in this single thought they lose all sense of time, and the *gopas* and *gopīs* (cowherd men and women) enjoy this unattainable bliss everyday.

2. The new bride (Rādhā) is very tender, and Bihārilāl (Krishna) is the newlywed groom. Dearest to the hearts of each other, they are both colorful, and their bodies are decorated with sixteen kinds of embellishments. Thus the beauty of their forms increases immensely. They are wearing wedding crowns with radiant faces. The veil (*sehra*) of garlands worn by the groom is made of lotus flowers with jewels and diamonds shining through it. Thousands of Kāmadevas and Ratīs (gods and goddesses of love) feel vanquished at their wondrous beauty.

3. The gate of the lovely canopy in the grove is adorned with buntings tied around. The inner courtyard is painted with red powder (*kuṁkum*) and is decorated with designs of pearls, with many paintings having been made on it. When the couple (Rādhā and Krishna) arrives, everyone is wonderstruck. Their feet and palms are beautifully and artfully colored with *hina*

(*mehandi*). The trinkets on their waists and feet are producing varied musical sounds.

4. The platform (vedi) for the marriage ceremony looks lovely. The hearts, eyes, and ends of clothing of the couple are "tied together." All the marriage ceremonials are performed properly with the worship of the goddess of love. After this worship, the couple is engrossed in amorous play. At this time the girlfriend Lalitā and others fervently wish for the couple's welfare. The couple appears so natural, being of the same age and temperament. Rādhā and Krishna are tied to each other with an eternal cord of love.

B. Second Hymn:

1. Vrindaban captivates the hearts of all aesthetic connoisseurs, and is the natural site for performance of the wedding ceremony of the couple—Śrī Rādhā and Śrī Krishna.

2. Every day they are adorned with new garments and ornaments and, being of the same age and tastes, they are drawn to each other.

3. The headgear of Krishna made of peacock feathers is the acme of loveliness, and the grace of Krishna (Navala Kishora) is beyond description.

4. The red powder (sindura) in the parting of Radha's hair is an emblem of love, and the brilliance of the crown on her head is a token of the auspicious marriage.

5. The new grove is shining with jewels, and the canopy is permeated with loveliness all around.

6. The wedding platform has been designed very artfully with various types of flowers.

7. Even the peacocks and swans are singing merrily. Girlfriends have been joyously performing all the ceremonial rites.

8. The graceful couple has been wandering together. Like the ends of the marriage ceremony clothes, their eyes are fixed on each other and their hearts are thumping with joy.

9. Their bangles, strengthened with unique love and entwined with the thread of love, will never break.

10. Their tender feet and palms are painted with beautiful colors, and Krishna has a natural grace with a perfect figure.

11. The small bells of their ornaments, on their feet, waists, and arms, are jingling, and it appears that thousands of Kāmadevas (gods of love) have been dancing there, making all the women feel shy.

12. His heart is full of great joy, and Krishna, the glory of Vrindaban, roams full with extreme delight.

13. The girlfriends arranged many plays for fun, and the ceremony of the couple feeding milk and rice to each other greatly enhanced their joy.

14. When the girlfriends conveyed messages from Krishna, Rādhā concealed her face behind the veil because of shyness.

15. With her neck bent in shyness, Rādhā does not speak and the girlfriends try all their wits so that she may remove her veil.

16. With his bluish hands Krishna is struggling to hold the golden and tender hands of Rādhā, and the friends have been enjoying this lovely scene.

17. They make Krishna bend his head at Rādhā's feet, and make him drink the sacrificial water given first to Rādhā.

18. They offer Krishna scented betel leaf to eat, and Rādhā smiles at this action.

19. There is much more frolic and fun, but only a fraction of the eternal pleasure and play can be described here.

20. All the girlfriends bless the couple behind the veil and view the ever increasing good fortune with gladness.

21. Both Rādhā and Krishna, with knowledge of their mutual tastes and likings, make newer and newer plays of love.

22. Extremely lovely Rādhā, with dazzling and indescribable beauty, is sitting in her bower.

23. The great connoisseur Krishna admires her beauty again and again. His eyes are filled up and he is drawn into himself.

24. He is unable to contain his great effusion of pleasure. Being submerged in the waves of enchantment, he gives himself to Rādhā.

25. With intense enchantment of mutual love, their hearts and eyes are entangled as if the lover and beloved have two bodies but one soul.

26. Both of them smile and laugh and never feel satiated watching each other's beauty.

27. The girlfriends are also fully submerged in their joys and do not relish anything else.

28. Everyone is drowning in the sea of love, and such pleasure is unavailable even to Lord Vishnu.

29. Śrī Dhruva Dās says that one who sings about this auspicious ceremony every day, obtains the supreme nectar of love.

II. A Hymn of Blessing for the Divine Couple, by Śrī Rūplāl

Dear Rādhā! May your marriage bond (*suhāg*) last forever. May your love for playful Krishna with curly hair ever increase. May you enjoy the groves of Vrindaban with your Sakhīs Lalitā and others. Śrī Rūplāl, who witnesses the mutual affection and love of Rādhā and Krishna, considers himself to be very fortunate.

Chapter 6

Holī through Daūjī's Eyes

Alternate Views of Krishna and Balarāma in Daūjī

A. WHITNEY SANFORD

Every year, on the second day after the full moon of Caitra, busloads of pilgrims arrive at the Daūjī Temple in Baldeo, Uttar Pradesh. Daūjī (or Daūbābā), meaning elder brother in Braj Bhāshā, is both the local popular address for Balarāma and his *dhāma,* or place.[1] Although Braj is primarily known for its emphasis on Krishna devotion, Balarāma reigns supreme during the spring festival of Holī. The Holī season officially lasts for approximately six weeks, and many devotees have been playing Holī with Daūjī every day and now sport a conspicuous (and possibly permanent) yellow tint. For the previous week, devotees have traveled throughout Braj to play Holī in famous villages such as Barsana, Rādhā's village, and Nandagaon, Krishna's village. But, today they will play a form of Holī that is unique to Baldeo, and this festival, I argue, encapsulates creative tensions in the relationship between Balarāma and Krishna.

Most of these devotees will be intimately familiar with almost every detail of Krishna's life, but they know little about Balarāma outside of his association with Krishna. In fact, although Holī is one of the most important and enthusiastically celebrated festivals in Braj, few outside of Baldeo know why Holī is such a special festival for Balarāma. Holī is the most significant festival for Balarāma who is the *kūl-devatā* for the Ahivāsī Gauṛ Brahmans of Daūjī. At this time, according to the *Bhāgavata Purāṇa*, Balarāma returned to Braj (without Krishna) and had his own *rāsa-līlā* with the *gopīs*. So, Holī provides an opportunity to examine the complex character of Balarāma and, in doing so, to reevaluate our notions about the relationship between Balarāma and Krishna.

Balarāma, or Daūjī, has long been eclipsed by his more popular younger brother, Krishna. Indeed, the pastoral Krishna-Gopāl tradition appears to dominate Braj practice, and most scholarly and devotional accounts implicitly plot Krishna at the center and relegate Balarāma—and related local traditions, that is, *Nāga*, *Yakṣa* and Goddess worship—to peripheral status. Yet, if we view the Braj panorama from Daūjī's perspective, we might remap the paths and relationships of the Braj religious landscape and ultimately destabilize Krishna's (hegemonic) occupation of the center. I argue that by locating Balarāma at the center of this inquiry, that is, in his village (Daūjī) on his festival (Holī), we reconfigure our understanding of Balarāma's relationship with Krishna and of Balarāma's role in Braj practice.

Devotees of Balarāma, particularly those at the Daūjī Temple, elevate him to a position of centrality, a practice which contradicts textual accounts and challenges assessments of Balarāma as subordinate to Krishna. This elevation—which reflects his pride of place as the elder—is most evident during the (approximately) six weeks of the Holī season when devotees crowd the small village of Baldeo, or Daūjī, to play Holī with Balarāma.

The Daūjī we meet at Holī challenges the pastoral characterization of Balarāma promulgated by the sixteenth-century Vaishnava devotional movements. As the kūl-devatā and elder brother of Krishna, Daūjī is merciful, protective and one who fulfills desires; he embodies the *maryādā* persona depicted (at times) in both the *Mahābhārata* and the *Bhāgavata Purāṇa*. As *maryādā-puruṣa,* Balarāma is known for his attention to propriety and social decorum—virtues typically associated with Rāma. Devotees point to an episode in the *Mahābhārata* (92–3) as illustrative: Toward the end of the great war between the Pāṇḍavas and Kauravas, mortal enemies and cousins Bhīma and Duryodhana (Balarāma's student) were engaged in battle. By recalling Bhīma's previous oath to break Duryodhana's thighs, Krishna incited Bhīma's rage so that he smashed his *gadā* (mace) down upon Duryodhana's thighs and shattered them. Balarāma saw this illegal blow and censured Bhīma and Krishna for breaking the rules of fair combat. According to notions of martial propriety, the mace should never be struck below the waist. Residents of Daūjī note Balarāma is known for his *bala* (strength) while Krishna is known for his *cala* (cunning).

At the same time, Daūjī is fond of intoxicants and (sexually) aggressive—qualities that are also deemed to be maryādā in Balarāma's case because Balarāma uses them in the service of righteousness. Similarly, Harlan notes the connection between lust, wine, and strength in the Rajputs. Meat and wine are important for Rajputs because they build lust and strength, important traits for professional warriors and kings.[2] Every day, at 3 PM Daūjī (and the [male] *Paṇḍās* who serve him) receive *bhāng prasāda*, and, at no other time of the year than Holī does this intoxicant flow freer in Daūjī's temple in Baldeo. And, at this time, while intoxicated, Balarāma forcibly relocated the Yamunā with the edge of his plow—an act which bears multiple interpretations.

Balarāma's aggressive characteristics recapitulate his associations with Nāgas (semidivine serpentlike beings); that is, his irascibility, fondness of drink, and connections to water, agriculture, and fertility, in relation to Krishna's tame pastoral image, have determined both Balarāma's elevation and subordination. Devotees of Balarāma interpret these characteristics as existing to benefit his devotees and as maryādā. However, both Gauḍīya Vaishnavism and the Vallabha Sampradāya utilize these characteristics and the attribute maryādā to establish a hierarchy with Krishna as dominant. For righteousness and propriety have no role in the pastoral landscape wherein Krishna is lauded for his irreverence and capriciousness. Balarāma's maryādā persona contradicts the pastoral images of Balarāma and Krishna popularized by the sixteenth-century devotional movements which elevated emotion (*bhāva*) toward Krishna over social decorum.

The traditional images of Balarāma and Krishna—both in scholarship and in their religions depictions—are routinely portrayed as pastoral, that is, simple boys and girls populating an idealized rural landscape. These images embody a set of conflicts in Braj pastoralism, chiefly the disjuncture created by Balarāma's (anomalous) rusticity in relation to Krishna's rural persona that masks an urbane sophistication. Balarāma's earthy image conveniently frees Krishna to exist in that pastoral ideal in which nature never presents danger and erotic dalliances have no unwanted consequences. The pastoralization process of the sixteenth-century Braj seems to have concentrated in Balarāma those elements that do not easily fit into the pastoral ideal. After all, Balarāma is Haladhar, the one carrying the plow, the deity of agriculture, and farmers rarely have idealized notions about a cooperative nature. Entwistle has observed that "pastoralization more adequately describes the dialectic between elite and folk cultures than Sanskritization or Brahmanization," and this raises questions about the relationship of Balarāma to Krishna.[3]

That Balarāma and Krishna appear in a familial relationship is significant because the extended (and possibly dysfunctional) family structure provides a flexible structure through which divergent groups and practices can be related to the center, inevitably a form of Krishna. The Nāga traditions, for example, powerful in the Mathurā region could be integrated to the increasingly powerful Vaishnava movement by incorporating the serpent Śeṣa as the *avatāra* of Balarāma. Local goddess traditions can be related in this extended family metaphor through the figure of Krishna's consort, Rādhā, or—briefly—through Krishna's sister Subhadrā. The flexibility inherent in this family relationship which appears in multiple dimensions (e.g., theological, iconographic, and communal) allows familial connections to be maintained, yet with shifting meaning—just as the roles and meanings of relationships within biological families are consistently (re)negotiated.

A Brief History of Balarāma Devotion

Let us step back and examine Balarāma's relationship to the Nāga tradition because this conflation determines Balarāma's role within Vaishnavism and Braj practice. The qualities of Balarāma (who first appears in the *Arthaśāstra*) have historically been conflated with those of the Nāga traditions that have been active in the Braj region since at least the fourth century BCE. Balarāma's association with the Nāga cult is well represented in text and practice by his irascible temper, fondness of drink, and palmyra leaf emblem—all Nāga traits. Like Nāgas, Balarāma is closely associated with fertility and agriculture and is usually depicted carrying a *mūsala* (pestle) and a *hala* (plow).[4] Popular iconography depicts Balarāma with right hand upraised, *madirā* (wine) in the left, and frequently with a hooded Nāga canopy.[5]

The popular images of both Balarāma and Krishna are largely derived from the tenth-century Sanskrit text, the *Bhāgavata Purāṇa*. The *Bhāgavata Purāṇa* situates Balarāma in his connection to the following: (1) the *Pañcarātra* Bhāgavata doctrine of Saṃkarṣaṇa (another name of Balarāma indicating plowing) as *vyūha* (emanation); (2) the Brahmanical doctrine of Balarāma as the avatāra (incarnation) of Śeṣanāga, the serpent upon which Vishnu rests; (3) Balarāma as heroic *vīra* of the Vṛṣṇis; and (4) Balarāma as brother and playmate of Krishna-Gopāl.[6] In the following centuries, this representation of Balarāma spreads from the south to the north with the ecstatic Krishna devotion influenced by the Āḷvār saints, although north Indian devotion develops independently of that in the South.

Although Sanskritic and other Brahmanic sources inform much of Braj devotion, local pre- and non-Āryan influences, such as the Nāga and Yakṣa influences, are incorporated into Brahmanical Vaishnavism, a historical process possibly beginning as early as the Kuṣāṇa period (first century CE).[7] In the period prior to the sixteenth century, Śiva, Balarāma, Yakṣas, and forms of the Goddess were important deities, and Nāga worship and wandering ascetics had greater influence on local peasants than did Vaishnava orthodoxy. Vaishnava worship focused on four-armed representations of Vishnu/Vāsudeva resting upon the serpent Śeṣa rather than the two-armed images of Krishna seen later.[8] Local traditions such as Nāga, Yakṣa, and Goddess worship continue to exist in Braj but are overshadowed by the hegemonic Krishna-Gopāl tradition.

In the sixteenth century this pastoral Krishna-Gopāl Vaishnavism flourished in the Braj region, particularly among urban elite newcomers, and incorporated local Braj traditions. This urban elite imposed an idealized notion of nature upon a noncooperative reality, setting up privileged hierarchies between urban and rural, sophisticate and rustic. Though the pastoralization process radically transformed Braj devotion, Balarāma retains many of his pre-Vaishnava associations. While Krishna largely reflects the concerns of an urban elite—for example, the Bengali and South Indian presence of the sixteenth century in Braj—Balarāma maintains his archaic Nāga associations and reflects the concerns of a rural and agrarian populace.

Balarāma's habits such as drinking and wrestling render him the embodiment of aggression and sexuality. Balarāma mediates the Nāga affinity for wine, a multivalent symbol in sectarian concerns. Saṃkarṣaṇa, the second of the *Pañcavyūha*, represents the inebriation, or self-delusion, similar to the role of Yogamāyā, a role necessary for creation to unfold from divinity.[9] The *Pañcarātra* literature depicts the vyūha Saṃkarṣaṇa as the *tāmasik* form of Vishnu (Kāla, or the destroyer), an essential component of the cycle of existence. Balarāma's association with intoxication is also expressed through Nityānanda (Caitanya's disciple) and embodied by the Chaubes of Mathura.[10]

After the wave of Krishna-Gopāl devotion in the sixteenth century, devotion to Daūjī (re)emerged in several centers in Braj, but Baldeo, or Daūjī, today is the center of Balarāma devotion in Braj. Daūjī is a small village approximately fifteen kilometers from Gokula, Balarāma's birthplace. Both Gokula and Daūjī are on Daūjī's side of the Yamunā. Although Daūjī is the king of Braj, Braj is divided into two halves with the Yamunā as the dividing line. Krishna reigns supreme in his half, which includes Mathurā and Vrindāvan, while the other side of the Yamunā belongs to Daūjī.

Prior to the manifestation of Daūjī's *svarūpa* (1638), what is now the village Baldeo was simply the Vidrumaban forest, used primarily for grazing cattle. According to Baldeo tradition, Daūjī appeared to the Ahivāsī Braj cowherd Kalyāṇadeva in a dream in his *yugal* (joined) form, both as Revatī, Balarāma's wife, and Balarāma. Balarāma told him that his and Revatī's images were hidden under the banyan tree where Kalyāṇadeva had been doing penance. While on a pilgrimage to Braj shortly after the *Mahābhārata* war, Krishna's grandson, Vajranabha, had installed these images, yet, in the intervening years, they were buried and forgotten. On *Mārgaśīrṣa Pūrṇimā*, Kalyāṇadeva unearthed these images, installed them under the tree and built a small temple. Gokulanātha, Vallabha's grandson, attempted to relocate the Daūjī image to Gokula: After all, Gokula is both Balarāma's birthplace and an important seat for the Vallabha Sampradāya. However, Daūjī tradition states that not even "one hundred fifty men or twenty-four oxen" could dislodge it from the site under the tree—a clear statement of Daūjī's preferences.[11] Since that night, the full moon of Aghan (December), Daūjī has remained in Daūjī served by the lineage of Kalyāṇadeva, the Ahivāsī Gauṛ Brahmans, also known as the Paṇḍās, or Pandeys, of Daūjī. These traditions are documented in the *Balabhadra Mahātmya*, a section of the Sanskrit text *Gargasaṁhitā,* the biography of Krishna and Balarāma traditionally ascribed to Garga, the family priest for Krishna and Balarāma. These *sevakas* note that Daūjī instructed Kalyāṇadeva himself about his preferences for sevā, and the daily (*nitya*) and yearly (*utsava*) sevā patterns reflect his wishes.

Daūjī's Nāga heritage is underscored by the curious lineage of the Ahivāsī Gauṛ Brahmans of Daūjī: The Ahivāsī Gauṛ Brahmans of Daūjī embody their connections to the Nāgas by tracing their ancestry from the serpent Vāsuki.[12] Kalyāṇadeva's heirs trace their lineage back to the sage Saubhari.[13] Saubhari had a small ashram on the Yamunā River, in what today is the tiny village Sunrakh. Saubhari offered refuge to the serpent Kālīya from Garūḍa. Every day the eagle Garūḍa ate a snake, the natural prey of an eagle, and Kālīya wanted to escape this fate. Therefore Ahivās, or residence of serpents, became the name of Saubhari's place.[14] The serpent then gave a boon to Saubhari: "Just as you have protected my lineage, in the Kāliyuga, my birth Śeṣāvatāra Baladeva will become the *kūl-devatā* of your lineage and will protect you."

The Ahivāsī Gauṛ Brahmans of Daūjī descend from Saubhari through Kalyāṇadeva and collectively own the temple and serve the svarūpa of Daūjī. These families share the daily and seasonal sevā of Daūjī and Revatī, and many of these families are employed as traditional Paṇḍās, or temple guides, for visiting pilgrims. They know the songs, rituals, and the stories—local and *Purāṇic*—about Daūjī, and these families play a predominant role in all Daūjī festivals.

Textual Sources for Balarāma s Holī: Bhāgavata Purāṇa, the Balabhadra Mahātmya of the Gargasaṁhitā and Sixteenth-Century Braj Poetry

Although the Paṇḍās of Daūjī are steeped in lore about Balarāma and his Holī, few outside of Daūjī know why Holī is such a special festival for Balarāma. Once, in Vrindāvan I had a revealing conversation with Srivatsa Goswami regarding Balarāma. Srivatsa and his brother, Venugopal, travel throughout India and abroad giving *Bhāgavata Kathās,* discourses on the *Bhāgavata Purāṇa.* He mentioned that most devotees—even those relatively knowledgeable about the *Bhāgavata Purāṇa*—not only do not know that Balarāma had his own rāsa dance with the gopīs, but, in fact, would be shocked if they found out.[15] I casually asked some representative devotees and found this to be so.

Certainly every devotee knows of Krishna's *Mahārāsalīlā* under the romantic full moon of October. Krishna fulfilled the desires of the gopīs that night while Daūjī—not invited to the party—watched the games while hiding behind a rock.[16] The next day, Krishna and Balarāma left for Mathurā to slay the demon Kaṁsa and promised to return in a week's time. Krishna never returned to Braj, and the trope of this lengthened separation from Krishna is the basis for many devotees' emotional stance toward Krishna.[17]

Balarāma—the king of Braj and the elder brother—returned to Braj, and the fact that Balarāma returns to his childhood home is critical to his devotees. Devotees in Daūjī note that Balarāma's homecoming reflects his protection of and commitment to Braj. According to the *Balabhadra Mahātmya,* Daūjī's return satisfied a promise he made as the serpent Lord Ananta in a previous life. The serpent Śeṣa appeared as the serpent Lord Ānanta and announced that he would take birth as Balarāma to assist Krishna in liberating the earth. The Nāga princesses who served in his underworld court were eager to join him in Braj (as were all those attending in the court), so he promised that they had earned birth in the homes of the gopīs through their devout asceticism. So, the gopīs, the cowherding girls of Braj, are incarnations of these Nāga princesses. He proclaimed that at that time "I will dance the *rāsa* with you on the banks of the Kālindī and fulfill your desires." The *Balabhadra Mahātmya* emphasizes Balarāma's rāsa-līlā as the chief desire of the gopīs (via the Nāga princesses) so obviously places less emphasis on the gopīs' desire to meet Krishna than does the *Bhāgavata Purāṇa.*

The *Bhāgavata Purāṇa* states that Balarāma missed his friends and family and decided to return to Gokula. His family and friends were overjoyed and greeted him with tears of joy and warm embraces. As etiquette required, the villagers asked about the health of their relatives in Dvārakā and wondered if he ever remembered them. The gopīs, of course, had the hardest task: although they felt honored by Balarāma's visit, they desperately yearned for their lover Krishna. Bravely, they smiled and asked if Krishna was happy. Questions flowed: Does he remember us? Will he visit his mother even just once? Does he remember all we've done for him? They reminded Balarāma of their great sacrifice in abandoning their husbands, brothers, and fathers on his last night in Braj. Questions turned to complaints as they recalled Krishna's fickle nature, and Balarāma consoled them as best he could.

Balarāma remained for the two spring months in Braj—Caitra and Vaiśākha—and frolicked with the gopīs every night. Interestingly, while the *Bhāgavata Purāṇa* simply notes that Balarāma's rāsa-līlā occurred on the night of the full moon, the *Balabhadra Mahātmya* names *Caitra Pūrṇimā* as the date of Balarāma's rāsa-līlā. On this night, fragrant breezes redolent of the scent of night lotuses wafted over the banks of the Yamunā, and the full moon's rays bathed the revelers. Varuṇā, sovereign of all waters, dispatched his wife Varuṇī, the goddess of wine, to Braj, and this ambrosia flowed from the hollow of a kadamba tree, filling the forest with its fragrance. Enticed by the scent, Balarāma and the gopīs found the honey beverage and drank.

After drinking his fill, Balarāma regaled the gopīs with song and frolicked with these devoted women. The beauty of this sight captivated the deities who gazed, rapt from their sky vehicles and joyfully sang of his wondrous exploits. Intoxicated, Balarāma staggered from forest to forest; his eyes rolled, unable to focus. Yet, despite (or due to) this condition, this handsome youth appeared resplendent, wearing his wreath of five flowers and only a single earring.

After the rāsa-līlā, Balarāma and the gopīs wanted to play in the waters, as *jala-krīḍā* (water play) usually follows the rāsa. The Yamunā River—a goddess herself—had not come near or watched Balarāma's rāsa, so he demanded that she approach him so he could play in her waters. She demurred, and he became enraged. In his intoxicated state, he saw her hesitation as contempt. He thrust the pointed edge of his plow into the earth and dragged her to his feet. He rebuked her: "Oh you sinner! You scorned me. I called you, and you delayed. Now you will flow in one hundred directions!" The terrified Yamunā lay prostrate at his feet and implored him to show mercy. She praised his majesty and his immense strength and begged him to free her. Satisfied, he released her. These permanent changes to the Yamunā's flow attest to Balarāma's infinite potency.

Balarāma entered into her waters, sporting like an elephant in rut with the gopīs. When Balarāma emerged, the goddess Kānti gave him the blue clothes he traditionally wears. She further adorned him with precious jewels and a dazzling golden necklace. Balarāma was so infatuated with the charms of the gopīs that the two months of his visit seemed as if one long night.

Sixteenth-century vernacular Braj poetry and local lore adopts the story as told in the *Bhāgavata Purāṇa.* As in the *Bhāgavata Purāṇa*, the tropes applied to Krishna and Balarāma are evident. Paramānand, a sixteenth-century Braj poet, composed lyrics that describe his own vision of Holī.

Rāga Sārang[18]
She cries for the mercy of Gopāl.
The one who carries a plow is intoxicated and speaks to none.
He has diverted the Yamunā's flow.
Eyes rolling, he staggers, swaying as if at the peak of a mountain.
As if confused, he donned blue clothes and swallowed from a gold cup.
He roams from forest to forest with a thousand maidens, singing songs.
The pure hand of Balabhadra killed the demon Dvivid, the kin of Kaṁsa.
Long live Rāma, cheer the gods! They shower him with countless Kusum blossoms.
He is the brother of Paramānand's lord, the diadem of the serpents, the limitless support. (*Sāgar* 1162)

Rāga Basant
Hey, it's Holī. Haladhar is coming.
Such love of the beautiful dark one. He sings of Hari's play with his own mouth.
Saṃkarṣaṇa has drunk the wine and become intoxicated.
His eyes are full of passion, and his loosened hair dangles.
His eyebrows are raised, and his turban hangs from his head.
With slurred speech, his lower lip is wet and heavy.
With his beautiful blue clothes and staggering footsteps, the body of Rohiṇī's son is radiant.
Paramānand says, Rāma, the young beloved, wears one earring smeared with sandal-paste. (*Sāgar* 1210)

While Krishna might be lusty and intoxicated with love, he is usually seen as articulate and able to spar with the gopīs, but intoxicated Haladhar, the one who carries the plow, staggers and slurs his speech. Contrast this depiction of Balarāma's lower lip to that of Krishna's. Krishna's lower lip is the site of bliss, with nectar falling from it, not wine, while Balarāma's lower lip is wet and heavy. According to one story, once after seeing Krishna play Holī with Rādhā, Balarāma approached Rādhā afterward in a lustful manner. Rādhā, however, loved only Krishna, so after she danced for Balarāma, she and the gopīs "stripped him and flogged him with his own lust."[19] Hearing of

Balarāma's rather demanding form of Yamunā worship, one might be struck by the apparently pervasive themes of aggression and sexuality. Balarāma's intoxication, for example, and his dragging of the Yamunā reflect his Nāga connections to liquor and fertility and render him antithetical to his and Krishna's pastoral representations.[20] (Although residents note that Balarāma drinks liquor or bhāng for (mostly) the same reasons anyone does, his propensity for drink (or bhāng) endows him with the strength and power to fight enemies.) Daūjī Paṇḍās, however, read this episode as manifesting Balarāma's embodiment of maryādā propriety: The importance of this act to Daūjī devotion cannot be overstated: Daūjī's *mūl-mantra* is

> *Om, klīm kālindī bhedanāya Sankarṣaṇāya svāhā*
> Om, the Kālindī which is split by Saṃkarṣaṇa, *svāhā!*

This mantra is recited in every ritual for Daūjī and specifically uses an epithet that refers to the act of creating a furrow, or plowing. Balarāma's relationship with the goddess is integral to his persona and his worship.

After his rāsa dance, Balarāma—like Krishna—wanted to worship the Yamunā, or the Kālindī, who, like him, embodies propriety. After all, Kālindī (or the Yamunā) is Balarāma's family goddess, and, by worshiping her, he observes his familial duty. As in any pūjā ceremony, one invokes a god or goddess, and the deity responds to the devotee's summons. Balarāma assumed that the Kālindī would respond to his invocation. The Yamunā river as goddess has obvious connections to Vaishnavism—the Yamunā is at times understood to be Krishna's wife. But Balarāma has an even closer relationship with the goddess: Mahāsarasvatī bestowed upon him—as Baladeva, one of the *Bhāgavata vyūhas* (emanations)—his strength in the *Dvāpara Yuga*; her *śakti* has the greatest bala (strength), and this wisdom and strength helps Balarāma fight evil.

These texts and stories are the backdrop against which Holī is played in Daūjī. Holī is a particularly joyous time, for Balarāma—the king of Braj—has returned home. The themes of aggression, intoxication, and sexuality also manifest in Daūjī practice yet appear as the means by which Daūjī, the elder brother, can best serve and protect his devotees.

Daūjī s Holī

> The Full Moon of Holī
> The boy Balarāma plays Holī.
> Revatī sits radiant with her friends, Balarāma with his friends. It
> is Holī.

The lord and his friends are helpless and are forced to jump.
Revatī hits them with powder. It's Holī.
Drums beat out a rhythm, the raised mallet strikes the gong. It is Holī.
Śrī Vāsudeva and Mother Rohiṇī were amazed, seeing his strength. It is Holī.
Those living in Braj forget all their wisdom and learning;
Enemies are broken and defeated. It is Holī.
The gods rejoice. Daū is tired.
They watch the spectacle of this Holī. It is Holī.
Sanaka and the other sages eternally sit in meditation.
He makes all of Braj prosperous. It is Holī.
Lord Jagannāth, your infinite beauty increases and awes your servant.
The boy Balarāma plays Holī.[21]

The Paṇḍās sang this poem daily in *samāja* (group singing), and echoes of it refrained in the markets and streets of Daūjī. Balarāma has returned from Dvārakā and is reunited with his friends. Even Revatī—who is rarely mentioned in Braj poetry—plays Holī and renders the powerful Balarāma helpless. Ironically, it was for Balarāma's strength that Revatī, or Jyotiṣmati (her proper name), meditated so that she might gain Balarāma as her husband. After all, Balarāma is the incarnation of Śeṣa, the cosmic serpent who holds the entire world upon his head just as if it were a tiny mustard seed. Such is the reversal of Holī: the weak become strong. Normally she must show respect to her husband. In the Daūjī temple, she is positioned directly across from him so she might continually perform *carana-sevā*. (Revatī is nothing like the saucy Rādhā of Krishna and Balarāma's youth.)

Holī is officially played on the full-moon day of Phālguna (February–March), but devotees play over approximately a week-long period so they can travel throughout Braj to enjoy Holī on different days in villages particularly significant to Krishna, Balarāma, and Rādhā, such as Nandagaon and Barsana, their respective hometowns. The Holī season officially lasts for an entire season, starting on *Vasant Pañcamī,* the fifth day of the bright half of Māgh. From this day on, the temperature begins to rise and heralds the coming of spring. The Daūjī temple in Baithain, for example (named for the fact that Daūjī and his friends once rested there), inaugurates Holī on Vasant Pañcamī with a processional samāja of Holī and Vasant (spring) songs as well as the throwing of color. The season ends with a final blast of color on *Raṅg Pañcamī,* the fifth day of the dark half of Caitra (March–April).

Residents of Daūjī stressed repeatedly that Daūjī's Holī is different from the rest of Braj, that Holī in Daūjī is played with love. (Of course, residents of other Braj villages might take exception to that distinction.) Ravi Pandey, the youngest of the Pandey brothers, explained that Holī is a game of love, or *prema*. Not only do friends renew bonds, but it is a time to make amends and let bygones be bygones. After all, Holī is the time when Balarāma came home to Braj and met his friends and family for the first time since leaving for Mathurā long ago.

Throwing of color is but one aspect of Holī which, both in text and practice, displays strong aggressive and sexual undercurrents. Pranks and outlandish behavior are common, for this is a time when the strictures of normal society are loosened—to a point anyway. Women tease men; younger people gang up on elders, and lower castes wreak havoc on the upper castes. However, one should not overstate this reversal. Certainly everybody has more license than normal, yet, despite claims to the contrary, those wielding power—that is, men, higher castes—have considerably more license to violate social boundaries. The phrase on everyone's lips in Daūjī at this time was *buṛa na māno, Holī hai,* or don't take it badly, it's Holī. It is considered poor sportsmanship to complain about rough behavior at this time.

Typically, and when I observed Holī in Daūjī, the Paṇḍās and residents of Daūjī played Holī for the entire season, though the most significant days are those surrounding the full moon of Phālguna, the actual night of Balarāma's rāsa play. As this day approached, the number of pilgrims increased, and a palpable sense of excitement grew. Crowds thronged the daily samāja prior to the midmorning *darśana* period during which the Paṇḍās sang Holī *bhajanas* (devotional lyrics), accompanied by a large drum. The Paṇḍās sang for Daūjī, sitting in two long rows facing each other on the platform immediately in front of the temple, surrounded on all three sides by onlookers. Most of the Paṇḍās—particularly the older ones—knew the words, but the lines were sung and repeated for the benefit of those who did not. The Paṇḍās performed the bhajanas energetically, with animated gestures and enthusiastic repetition of the repeated lines.

It was impossible to confuse the Paṇḍās with the crowds of pilgrims. The Paṇḍās wore their trademark *tilaka* of saffron, sandalwood and turmeric smeared across their foreheads. Their white or yellow cloths, partially dyed safflower yellow, bore witness to days of playing Holī. Safflower garlands, received as prasāda from Daūjī, were draped around their necks and wound about their heads like headbands. Almost everyone wore at least one item of silk cloth, a tunic or perhaps even a headband, which was once worn by Daūjī. The outfits given to Daūjī are divided by and distributed to the Paṇḍās once yearly.

As darśana time approached, the singing and gesturing became more and more animated. At 10:30 AM, temple *pūjāris* pulled back the curtain, offering darśana of Daūjī and Revatī to the crowds. This darśana was special because it was the only period of the day in which Daūjī played *pani Holī* (wet Holī); at all other times, he played dry Holī. The color used comes from safflowers *(ṭesū)* and was stored in the gullies alongside the courtyard. During the entire Holī season, thousands of gallons of color were thrown. This dye, which needs at least a twenty-four-hour lead time for preparation, is considered medicinal, particularly for skin diseases such as scabies. Some devotees came for the curative aspect of this festival.

When darśana opened, the crowds drove forward with handfuls of *makkhan-misarī*, Daūjī's favorite food. Devotees hurled this hard substance—something like rock candy smeared with butter—over the railing toward the svarūpa of Daūjī. As the pūjāris dodged the hail of makkhan-misarī and coins, they filled buckets and clay cups full of yellow color and spilled their contents over the crowd. The shoving intensified as each devotee wanted to play Holī with Daūjī and receive prasāda. The younger Paṇḍās climbed over the railing, while the guard ineffectively beat them back with a stick. The Paṇḍās guiding devotees propelled them to the front of the railing. Those so favored received a full dousing of "Daūjī kī prasāda." After darśana, the crowd was clearly divided in two: those who played Holī and those who did not. The yellow and petal-drenched minority laughed at themselves and the spectacle, while the remainder appeared a bit puzzled and headed for their busses.

All of this was merely prologue: the real Holī revelry in Daūjī began on the late afternoon of the full moon. On this afternoon, the residents of Daūjī process in groups through town, winding through the village to the bonfire site. First, the Paṇḍās, the largest group, next the Sanāḍhya Brahmins, and later the Baniyās and others have far smaller processions. The Paṇḍās proceeded through town, singing and throwing powder. They carried the temple's large red anthology of devotional poetry—it leaves the temple only on this day each year. One older man with a tricolor beard danced suggestively with a pole; others carried halas, or plows, Daūjī's trademark item. They also carried a *jhaṇḍā*, a pole with mango buds (*baur*) and leaves and *aśoka* leaves attached to it. Balloons (and possibly condoms) and safflowers adorned it further. Mango buds are important because not only do they remind one of spring and Holī, but they have medicinal value as antisnake venom.[22] This jhaṇḍā reappeared in Daūjī's official Holī celebration in the temple several days later. Approximately thirty minutes later, the Sanāḍhya Brahmans paraded through town, also carrying a jhaṇḍā. Their numbers were smaller, and some danced. In the latter processions, I saw the first real evidence of the carnival aspect of Holī. Men wore fake beards and funny hats, several rode backward on an ass and one danced in a stuffed bra, encouraged by the crowd.

The procession led to the Holikā bonfire, which would be lit later that night when devotees throughout Braj burned bonfires commemorating Prahlād's devotion to Vishnu. Prahlād was a young boy who devoted himself to Vishnu against his father's wishes. This devotion infuriated his father Hiraṇyakaśipu who ordered the boy killed, but nothing would kill the boy, not even fire. Devotees commemorate Prahlād's survival by placing Prahlād's image in a large bonfire. Just when the flames reach the image, a young man leaps into the fire and snatches the statue from certain immolation.

While the men paraded, the women did pūjā in their homes and offered *govar, ghee,* wheat, and rice, as well as barley, which was later roasted. Barley was the crucial ingredient in this offering, indicating Holī's origins as a springtime agricultural festival. The branches of the bonfire were draped with strings of govar; this govar was shaped into small round balls and strung together as necklaces. Many people had worn those necklaces all day and then placed them on the bonfire. The bonfire itself was lit at midnight, and men retrieved coals from the bonfire for the home fire at around 4:30 AM. The barley then was roasted and distributed to family and friends on the morning of Holī to show friendship and intimacy.

At 11 AM, the morning's Holī festivities concluded, and everyone returned home to bathe and don new clothes for the afternoon's mahārāsa dance in the temple. Most of the Paṇḍā families have silk cloths—mostly yellow and pink scarves—once worn by Daūjī. Many dressed as gopīs, with green for Rukmiṇī, Krishna's wife, and yellow for Rādhā and Revatī. At 2 PM, the temple opened for a special darśana before the dance. Traditionally, only the Paṇḍā families could participate in this dance (and the next day's Hurangā), although this rule is less strictly observed today. The dance itself highlighted the *devar-bhābhī* relationship, that is, the younger brother and his elder brother's wife. Traditionally, a joking, if not implicitly sexualized, relationship exists between these two. According to Krishna's familial structure, Revatī and Krishna are the devar and bhābhī. Technically, Balarāma, as Daūjī, or elder brother, cannot play—although devotees note that all of Balarāma's family plays Holī. Pairs and, in some cases, threesomes, danced in the temple courtyard, holding a sash between them, so the men and women did not directly touch. After the dance, they performed a *parikrama* around the temple tank, following Daūjī's blue flag, which comes out once a year for this occasion.

The following morning (Caitra Krishna 2), Daūjī prepared for its big event: Hurangā. Ghanashyam Pandey, current head of the *Śrīhaladhar Samagradarśana Śodh-Samsthān,* stressed that the Hurangā, which indicates the throwing of color, is unique to Daūjī. Holī, on the other hand, includes playing with sticks—that is, *lāthī-Holī*—as is done in Barsana or Nandagaon.[23] Krishna, he said, plays Holī with sticks, while Daūjī plays only with color, that is Hurangā. Holī and Hurangā are joined though: Holī is the *patnī,* or wife; while Hurangā is the *pati,* for men. The pair are husband and wife. Several lines of a poem sung (and composed) by Raghubir, a ninety-two-year-old pūjāri, echoed this concept.

> Let's watch the Holī of Braj.
> She's come to the Braj-*maṇḍala;* the wheat-complexioned one
> resides here.
> My heroine is Holī; her lover is Hurangā.
> Golden liquid rains down.

By 11 AM, the courtyard and the rooftop were filled to capacity in anticipation of the Hurangā. Small boys dressed as Krishna and Balarāma sat on a raised platform facing the image of Daūjī; the VIPs sat under a canopy on the roof overlooking the courtyard. Others (including myself) sat on the ledge just below the temple roof with large bags full of colored powders. Sprinklers were attached to this ledge, and, although they were not yet turned on, the courtyard floor was flooded with several inches of water. The Paṇḍās in the courtyard below wore their silks, and many were dressed as gopīs. They began to dance, and revelers below threw buckets of color and water-filled condoms at the watching crowd. I was seated on the ledge just in front of the VIPs. After about twenty minutes of play, the VIPs realized the effect of my presence: they got doused with all the color aimed at me—a natural target. The mood in the courtyard below reflected the vast quantities of bhāng-laced *ṭhaṇḍhāī* (a cooling drink) offered as prasāda in the morning. After the dancing had begun, an engineer sitting next to me leaned over and told me that it would start soon. It looked to me as if something had already begun: I wondered what more would start?

The Paṇḍās stood in front of Daūjī singing *samāja* to invite Daūjī to play. Two *jhaṇḍās* (poles) appeared in the courtyard, signaling the start of the Hurangā; the play continues until both jhaṇḍās have fallen over. Then they will be ripped up, the pieces taken for prasāda. The jhaṇḍā was placed before Daūjī, and there was a brief darśana. In the courtyard, the devar-bhābhī pairs danced, and soon the women began to rip off the men's shirts. They twisted the shirts, dipped them in the water on the floor and beat the men with their own wet clothing. No boy or man on the courtyard floor was exempt.

Then the play began: everyone (but me) knew it was time. Those sitting on the ledges threw the powder on those dancing below. Those not dancing below threw buckets of color. The air was full of flying power of red, yellow, and silver, and it was almost impossible to see through the cloud. Below, some Paṇḍās paraded the jhaṇḍās around the courtyard, while others danced or beat someone or tried to avoid being beaten. Some men were raised overhead and carried about. On and off, the cloud of color thinned and rendered visible the frenzied activity below. The water on the courtyard floor was almost four inches deep, and wet, colored powder stuck to everything. After forty-five minutes, the jhaṇḍā*s* fell, and prasāda was distributed. Everyone returned home to share a traditional meal of *pūrīs* and *khīr*, two of Daūjī's favorite foods.

The temple meanwhile was strewn with prasāda and flooded with color; clumps of soggy powder covered the ground. The following day, the onerous job of cleaning the temple courtyard began in earnest. Piles of powder-covered *misarī* and coconut lay in large piles. The Paṇḍās weighed and distributed this prasāda to all the Paṇḍā families. The gutters, which had been full of the safflower color, were emptied and cleaned. The Holī season was almost over. Holī, though, was still played at the temple for the few remaining days, but with significantly reduced numbers.

The final throwing of color occurred on *Raṅg Pañcamī*, the fifth day of the bright half of Caitra, and afterward, the devar-bhābhī relationship was highlighted once again. On this day, the devar must give his bhābhī a sarī, and the bhābhī offers the devar a sweet rice dish. This final day resembled less the daily samāja and throwing of color than the large Hurangā. The younger Paṇḍās sat in front of the temple door, mock-wrestling and jostling each other; They mobbed those who carried prasāda to distribute to the crowd. The gentle restraint of most of Daūjī's Holī was gone; today's Holī seemed significantly rougher than that of the previous days. When the darśana opened at 1 PM, an hour late, the crowds rushed forward. Pūjāris soaked devotees from the four waist-high vats of color. Others threw colored powders. The sprinklers again flooded the courtyard. To conclude the Holī samāja, the Paṇḍās sang a poem attributed to Sūr Dās that is sung only on this day. Sūr Dās watches the antics of Rādhā and Krishna playing Holī and pleads to live to have this darśana again.

Ḍol Raṅg Pañcamī Poem
Let's play, let's play on the banks of the Yamunā, on the banks of
the Kālindī.

Singing and playing with Hari.
Whoever is the bridegroom of the beloved Rādhikā?
Who is the bride of Ghanaśyām?
Wheat-complexioned, the beloved Rādhikā.
Ghanaśyām, the color of a rain cloud, singing and playing with Hari.
At whom did they smear the fragrant paste; at whom did they throw the colored powder?
The beloved smeared paste on his garland; he turned and threw powder.
Singing and playing with Hari.
Sūr Dās pleads, let me live to play again.
Singing and playing with Hari.

Conclusion

The Holī festival in Daūjī evokes different nuances of Balarāma's character, particularly those of intoxication, sexuality, and aggression—qualities he inherits from his Nāga associations. Nonetheless, these qualities underscore his status as protector and elder brother. Certainly Holī manifests tensions of sexuality and aggression, in the general teasing and prank playing and, particularly, in the devar-bhābhī actions that characterize Holī. While these pairs dance together in the temple on one day, during the Hurangā, when the bhābhīs thrash their devars, their actions look like nothing less than a war. (This is, after all, a ritual space in which women vent their frustrations with men.)

In fact, a pair of Canadian reporters had observed the Hurangā from the temple roof. Afterward, they told me they thought this was a festival of revenge, a time for people to get back at one another. This theme of revenge also emerges in Marriott's observation of Holī in Kishan Garhi, a village in Aligarh district; he notes that many of the pranks were based on retaliation for previous injustices. Yet, like me, he too was told repeatedly that Holī is a festival of love.[24] These themes echo Balarāma's Holī as depicted in the *Bhāgavata Purāṇa*.

The familial trope shifts once again when we interrogate Daūjī's role in terms of the devar-bhābhī emphasis seen in Daūjī's Holī. The *Bhāgavata Purāṇa* emphasizes Balarāma's return to Braj alone: Neither Krishna nor Revatī have a role in this text. Yet, according to Balarāma's family structure, the devar-bhābhī relationship denotes Krishna and Revatī. Balarāma, Daūjī residents say, as the elder brother, does not participate in the devar-bhābhī activities, although all festivities in Daūjī are conducted in Daūjī's sight and for his benefit. The ambiguities of the devar-bhābhī relationship parallel that of the Hurangā-Holī pairing. Holī and Hurangā are wife and husband, respectively, or at least a couple. In this sense, it parallels the devar-bhābhī relationship in both the pairing aspect and in terms of a sexualized/teasing relationship, although, in this case, husband and wife do not play Holī together. This ambiguity seems reminiscent of the ambivalence regarding Krishna and Rādhā's relationship—that is, are they married or lovers? In practice, the devar-bhābhī pairing embodies Holī-Hurangī, complete with all of its ambivalences.

In Daūjī's Holī, Daūjī embodies the standard of maryādā, of propriety and decorum, and devotees look to Daūjī for healing, protection, and agricultural benefits, among other things.[25] Daūjī is the kūl-devatā, the elder brother who is the center—if not always a direct participant—of all activities, and local practice in Daūjī firmly places Krishna in a familial—and subordinate—role, a role the text does not emphasize.

Prem Pandey, a Pāṇḍā at Daūjī, said that "Daūjī lets Krishna be Krishna," a sentiment echoed by other devotees. While Krishna might be the *rasa-rāja* and fulfill devotees' emotional needs, Daūjī stands guard and fulfills devotees' essential, worldly needs. Devotees of Daūjī assess Balarāma's maryādā characteristics as above, if not equal to, Krishna's qualities of love. Such a ranking exists in opposition to both major sixteenth-century devotional movements who ranked *puṣṭi/anurāga* over *maryādā/vaidhi* devotion.

Indeed, the sixteenth-century Braj devotional movements institutionalize both Balarāma's propensity for aggression and maryādā by seeing their leaders as incarnations of Krishna and Balarāma. The concept of maryādā becomes a trope that is applied and ranked differently by the Vallabha Sampradāya, Gauḍīya Vaishnavas, and Daūjī devotees. For examples, devotees of Balarāma see him as a maryāda-puruṣa, one who maintains propriety at all times—as opposed to Krishna. For devotees of Daūjī, maryādā has positive connotations, whereas in the Vallabha Sampradāya, it connotes a lesser stage of devotion, one bound more by rules of society than the heart.

In the centuries after the growth of devotional Vaishnavism in the sixteenth century, Balarāma emerged within sectarian Vaishnavism as Krishna's supporter. Empirical evidence of Balarāma's continued Nāga associations in relation to the theme of hierarchical pairings is provided by sectarian groups (with radically different organizational structures) who see their leaders in these same terms of the brothers Krishna and Balarāma. In the Vallabha Sampradāya, Balarāma is identified with Gopīnātha, Viṭṭhalanātha's eclipsed elder brother.[26] In the Gauḍīya Vaishnava tradition, Balarāma is regressively understood through Nityānanda, Caitanya's disciple who is assigned the role of Caitanya's elder brother and the incarnation of Balarāma.[27] In both sectarian traditions, the subordinate as Balarāma is assigned those qualities deemed inappropriate, a narrative strategy that allows the leader as Krishna to operate free of contention.

The trope of the complementary pair reflects (and reaffirms) hierarchies and is a fluid structure by which qualities associated with Balarāma can be assigned to a figure who is incorporated into the structure as subordinate—by groups who see Krishna as central. In Bengal, for example, Nityānanda's activities, when understood as those of Balarāma, exemplify these patterns. By Caitanya's command, Nityānanda spread the doctrine to and is noted for "converting" the *tāntrikas*.[28] In his proselytizing, he consorted with prostitutes, drunkards, and others of dubious character, activities normally considered outside Brahmanical standards; yet these acts could be accommodated, if not sanctioned, by Nityānanda's association with Balarāma.

Nonetheless, Balarāma is an ironic character whose existence controverts categories and notions of propriety, for example, the bhāng alongside maryādā. Balarāma's Holī is carnivalesque, yet the undercurrents of aggression and sexuality ultimately strengthen Balarāma's protective role as the king of Braj. Balarāma's role does reaffirm hierarchies, to a point, but he also transforms hierarchies by reinterpreting some of the factors that have made him—in some eyes—subordinate. So, for example, in some Vaishnava eyes, māryadā is a subordinating element. Balarāma, however, redefines maryādā—and turns it upside down—by its linkage with bhang, sexuality and aggression. In this system, there is much less room for the capricious antics of Krishna.

Daūjī's Holī challenges our complacency regarding schemas that incontrovertibly locate Krishna as central to Braj tradition. It is certainly difficult to contest the importance of the pastoral Krishna tradition to Braj devotion, and I do not deny that it is a dominant motif of Braj. However, throughout Braj are sites wherein the Krishna tradition is adapted and (re)negotiated according to local hierarchies. While most Vaishnavas might accept the stories of Balarāma that appear in the *Bhāgavata Purāṇa,* interpretations of these stories differ. The characteristics applied to Krishna and Balarāma adapt to their environs and allow them to act as tropes in a complementary pairing—in which Daūjī supports and enables Krishna.

A visual analog for seeing Krishna solely as the center is the famous "map" that portrays the world from a Fifth Avenue New Yorker point of view: The center-standpoint is facing west from Fifth Avenue. The avenues that run the length of Manhattan loom large while the rest of the United States, particularly the Midwest, fade out and become increasingly insignificant. Often those at the center and the periphery continue to accept such a perspective. However, if one takes a point on the periphery as center and scans from that perspective, then this hegemony is challenged. And, the next step is to interrogate other Braj local traditions, such as Goddess and Yakṣa sites.[29] These traditions—as with Daūjī—are related to Krishna, yet marginalized and appear peripheral to the dominant tradition. Yet, understanding the dynamics of these local traditions in and of themselves and in relation to the Krishna traditions reveals not only a different understanding of Braj religious practice, but also the way different groups manipulate tropes in light of their own agendas.

Notes

1. The fieldwork portion of this work was enabled by fellowships from the American Institute of Indian Studies and the National Endowment for the Humanities. I would like to express my appreciation for their generous support.
2. Lindsay Harlan (1994), 127.
3. A. W. Entwistle (1991), 88.
4. A. W. Entwistle (1987), 121.
5. Charlotte Vaudeville (1991), 113.
6. Sudhir Jaiswal (1967), 58–59
7. N. P. Joshi (1979), 18; A. W. Entwistle (1987), 118.
8. A. W. Entwistle (1987), 136; Charlotte Vaudeville (1991), 113–14.
9. Dennis Hudson (1993), 151.
10. Owen Lynch (1990), 91–116.
11. This story and others reflect a contestation of power over the image between Gokulanātha and Kalyāṇadeva. Some versions of the story state that Gokulanātha himself unearthed the images. See A. Whitney Sanford (2002).
12. Charlotte Vaudeville (1991), 114.
13. See *Bhāgavata Purāṇa* 9.6. See Ganesh Tagare (1989).
14. The *Bhāgavata Purāṇa* uses the word *Ahivās*. In the *Brahma-Vaivartapurāṇa*, the word is *Sarpāvās*. See Ghanashyam Pandey (1998), 3.
15. Personal Communication with Srivatsa Goswami, February 1999.
16. *Bhāgavata Purāṇa* 10.33. See Ganesh Tagare (1989). See also *Śrīmad-Bhāgavata-Mahāpurāṇam: Sri Subodhini*. Jodhpur: Sri Subodhini Prakashak Mandal, ND.
17. *Bhāgavata Purāṇa* 65. Ganesh Tagare (1989).
18. *Paramānandasāgar*. (*Sāgar*).
19. David L. Haberman (1994), 211.
20. See A. Whitney Sanford (2000).
21. This poem comes from the poetry anthology owned by the temple. I found a similar version in Ghanashyam Pandey (1998).
22. Dr. Yogendra Pandey and his family (Ayurvedic doctors) run a clinic in Daūjī. As a service, on the morning of Holī, they offer an anti-snake-bite venom to the town's residents. The main ingredient is the baur, and a teaspoon

of the anti-snake-bite venom should last an entire year. Virtually all of Daūjī's residents appear and pay their respects to the Pandey family.

23. Each year, women from Barsana (Rādhā's village) travel to Nandagaon, Krishna's village, to protest of Krishna's heartless (as they see it) treatment of the gopīs. The women carry heavy sticks and beat the men who protect themselves with shields.

24. McKim Marriott (1966), 211. See also William Crooke (1968).

25. The hobby horse is a symbol of fertility as is the burning straw man, both typical of agricultural festivals. McKim Marriott notes that Holī must represent the assimilation of local festivals with sixteenth-century Vaishnavism. The forms of revelry that appear in Braj have no textual referents. See McKim Marriott (1966), 209–10.

26. Richard Barz (1976), 38, 222.

27. S. K. De (1961), 78, 565.

28. S. K. De (1961), 95, 447; Edward C. Dimock (1989), 91–95.

29. See A. Whitney Sanford (forthcoming).

References

Barz, Richard Barz. *The Bhakti Sect of Vallabhacarya*. Haryana: Thomson Press (India), 1976.

Crooke, William. *The Popular Religion and Folklore of Northern India*. 3d reprint. Delhi: Munshilal Manoharlal, 1968.

De, S. K. *Early History of the Vaishnava Faith and Movement in Bengal from Sanskrit and Bengali Sources*. 2d ed. Calcutta: K.L. Mukhopadhyaya, 1961.

Dimock, Edward C. *The Place of the Hidden Moon*. Chicago: University of Chicago Press, 1989.

Entwistle, A. W. *Braj: Centre of Krishna Pilgrimage*. Groningen: Egbert Forsten, 1987.

———. "The Cult of Krishna-Gopāl as a Version of Pastoral." In *Devotion Divine: Bhakti Traditions from the Regions of India, Studies in Honor of Charlotte Vaudeville*. Diana Eck and Francoise Mallison, eds. Groningen: Egbert Forsten, 1991, 73–90.

Haberman, David L. *Journey through the Twelve Forests: An Encounter with Krishna*. New York: Oxford University Press, 1994.

Harlan, Lindsay. *Religion and Rajput Women*. Delhi: Munshiram Manoharlal, 1994.

Hudson, Dennis. "Vāsudeva Krishna in Theology and Architecture: A Background in Śrīvaiṣṇavism." *Journal of Vaiṣṇava Studies* 2.1 (winter 1993): 139–70.

Jaiswal, Sudhir. *The Origin and Development of Vaiṣṇavism*. Delhi: Munshiram Manoharlal, 1967.

Joshi, N. P. *Iconography of Balarāma*. New Delhi: Abhinav Publications, ND, [E37 Haus Khas] 1979.

Lynch, Owen. "The Mastrām: Emotion and Person among Mathurā's Chaubes." In *Divine Passions*. Owen Lynch, ed. Delhi: Oxford University Press, 1990, 91–116.

Marriott, McKim. "The Feast of Love." In *Krishna: Myths, Rites and Attitudes*. Milton Singer, ed. Chicago: University of Chicago Press, 1966, 200–12.

Pandey, Ghanashyam. *Śrī Haladhara Nityārcana*. Baldeo: Sri Haladhar Samagradarsana Sodh-Samsthan, 1998.

Paramānandasāgar. (*Sāgar*). Sribrajbhushan Sharma, ed. Kankaroli: Vidyavibhag, ND.

Sanford, A. Whitney. "Painting Words, Tasting Sound: Visions of Krishna in Paramānand's Sixteenth-Century Devotional Poetry." *Journal of the American Academy of Religion* 70.1 (March 2002): 55–82.

———. "The Svarūpa's Desires: Legitimizing Narratives of Deity Manifestation's in Sixteenth-Century Braj Devotion." *International Journal of Hindu Studies* 6/1 (April 2002): 29–55.

________. "Uneasy Partners: Balarāma as Embodiment of Wilderness." In *The Banyan Tree: Essays on Early Literature in New Indo-Aryan Languages*. Vol. 2. Mariola Offredi, ed. New Delhi: Manohar, 2000, 363–87.

________. "Yakṣas on the Margins of Braj Practice." *Journal of the American Academy of Religion* (forthcoming).

Śrīmad-Bhāgavata-Mahāpurāṇa: Śrī Subhodhinī. Jodhpur: Sri Subodhini Prakashak Mandal, ND.

Tagare, Ganesh, trans. and annot. *Bhāgavata Purāṇa*. Delhi: Motilal Banarsidass, 1989.

Vaudeville, Charlotte. "The Lord of Govardhan Hill." In *Hinduism Reconsidered*. Gunther Sontheimer and Herman Kulke, eds. New Delhi: Manohar, 1991.

Chapter 7

A Family Affair
Krishna Comes to Paṇḍharpūr and Makes Himself at Home

CHRISTIAN LEE NOVETZKE

Krishna came to Paṇḍharpūr from Dvārakā to make amends with his wife, Rukmiṇī. Rukmiṇī had spied her rival Rādhā sitting on Krishna's lap and she was not happy. Rukmiṇī ran to what seemed to her a secure hiding place: the remote town of Paṇḍharpūr where the Bhīmā River curves into the shape of a crescent moon and is called the Candrabhāgā. Krishna pursued his wife with a contrite heart and a retinue of cows, cowboys, and cowgirls. But when he arrived in Paṇḍharpūr, he could not find Rukmiṇī. He did happen to meet the great sage and singer Nārada who suggested that Krishna inquire of Puṇḍalīk, another famous sage who lived nearby. Krishna arrived at Puṇḍalīk's door and found him selflessly doting upon his parents. Krishna was so impressed by Puṇḍalīk's filial devotion that he tried to interrupt the faithful son for a moment to express his admiration. Puṇḍalīk hardly looked up from where he was massaging his father's feet. Instead of greeting Krishna, Puṇḍalīk threw a brick to him and asked him to stand on it and wait until Puṇḍalīk's service to his parents was done. Krishna did so and is still standing in Paṇḍharpūr, waiting on the brick for Puṇḍalīk's eternal work to be finished. His devotees call him Viṭṭhal, a name many devotees interpret as "the one standing on the brick."

This folk story is attested to in several Marāṭhī and Sanskrit sources, in a number of oral traditions, and with a wide range of variation.[1] All versions explain how Krishna is moved to stay in Paṇḍharpūr as a kind of reward for Puṇḍalīk's devotion to his parents.

The legend also provides Krishna with the means to change his randy ways, which in the Marāṭhī tradition he does.[2] No longer is Krishna the absent lover of the *Gītāgovinda* or the flirtatious cowboy of Vrindāvan among his gopis. In Paṇḍharpūr, he becomes a responsible and faithful husband (for the most part).[3] His chief wife is Rukmiṇī, but he is also married to Satyabhāmā and Rādhā or Rādhikā.[4] However, to his devotees he is primarily seen as a loving father, or more often, a protective mother. In learning how to be a family man, Krishna takes a lesson from Puṇḍalīk: it is the need to resolve a fight with his wife over his infidelity to her that brings him to Paṇḍharpūr, but it is the wholehearted devotion of a son that convinces him to stay. Krishna comes to Paṇḍharpūr to see Puṇḍalīk but makes a home for himself as the years unfold a lineage of devotees who refer to one another as a family, and revere Krishna as their father—Viṭhobā—and as their mother—Viṭhāī.[5]

This chapter explores the architecture of Krishna worship among the Vārkarīs of Paṇḍharpūr and further elaborates on a theme first pointed out by Eleanor Zelliot in her work on "household *sants*" (saints) and especially the family life of the Vārkarī sants.[6] Following Zelliot, I take the theme of family values and domestic issues as a defining character of early Marāṭhī devotional literature. I further this thesis by examining a portion of one of their earliest statements of Marāṭhī devotion, the Marāṭhī *Tīrthāvaḻī* or "The Garland of Sacred Places," in order to show how the metaphor of family to express a love of god and others is centrally important.[7] The story of the *Tīrthāvaḻī* addresses themes similar to the Puṇḍalīk legend, but involves two other sants, Nāmdev (c. 1270–1350 CE) and Jñāndev (d.c. 1296 CE). Like Puṇḍalīk, Nāmdev is a simple devotee and a faithful son, but to Viṭṭhaḻ rather than to his own parents.[8] Jñāndev, on the other hand, is an accomplished yogi, orphaned at a young age, who lures Nāmdev away from "Mother Viṭṭhaḻ" and onto the pilgrimage trail of northern India. In a reversal of the story of Viṭṭhaḻ's arrival to Paṇḍharpūr, these two principal Vārkarī sants leave Paṇḍharpūr and travel to Dvārakā. The text ostensibly recounts this pilgrimage. However, the *Tīrthāvaḻī*, as it is remembered and performed today, is less a spiritual travelogue than an expression of the intimate relationship between Viṭṭhaḻ/Krishna and his devotees. The story serves several agendas. It dramatizes the separation anxiety both god and devotee undergo when apart, as well as the nature of their codependence, as a mother and a child, or a cow and her calf (*vātsalya*).[9] The friendship struck between Nāmdev and Jñāndev exemplifies a range of social and religious alliances: Nāmdev is an illiterate low-caste tailor and Jñāndev is a scholarly Brahmin and Nātha yogi master. The two represent early facets of the Vārkarī tradition, where the elite and scholarly strata of Krishna worship (and Śaiva worship) intermingled with "local" or "folk" practice and belief. The story also addresses a theological problem, especially in the remembrance of Nāmdev, whose hagiography in North Indian languages remembers him as a frequent traveler and resident of the North as far as Punjab. Why would a devotee, especially one as seminal to the Vārkarī tradition as Nāmdev, want to travel away from Paṇḍharpūr when Krishna himself came and stayed in Paṇḍharpūr for the sake of his followers? By reinforcing the importance of familial relationships and the centrality of Paṇḍharpūr, the text offers an early sketch of Marāṭhī ethnicity conceived through Vārkarī devotion to Krishna.

Today the Vārkarī tradition is perhaps best known outside India for its biannual pilgrimage to Paṇḍharpūr, documented in writing and film, and for its eloquent sant Tukarām (c. 1608–1650 CE).[10] The *Tīrthāvaḻī* is far less well known but has remained prominent in the discourse of the Vārkarī tradition as a fundamental narrative exemplifying the role of biography and commenting on Vārkarī and Marāṭhī identity in relation to larger religious contexts in India. The story is set in an early period of Vārkarī history when the role of pilgrimage and the nature of a devotee's relationship to Krishna apparently needed to be articulated. The *Tīrthāvaḻī* works out several issues within the framework of a story certainly famous by the sixteenth century, if not well before.

My use of the *Tīrthāvaḻī* as a central text in this chapter is not meant to endorse the idea that the Vārkarīs have a definitive transcript of belief; indeed, the religion has often deemphasized texts, evidenced by the lack of written sources for early Marāṭhī devotionalism.[11] It is probably for these reasons that European Indologists largely ignored the Vārkarīs.[12] My hope in using the text is to elucidate one statement in one medium—one among innumerable others—that has risen over several hundred years to a high level of popularity and adaptability. The text is therefore representative of Vārkarī belief and its historiographic self-understanding, but it is also misleading. The story of the *Tīrthāvaḻī* is just that, a story, told in many different ways, remembered orally, performatively, and literarily. I have selected what I consider the best known of various retellings. Any devotee of Viṭṭhaḻ's could supply you with many iterations more eloquent.

The One on the Brick, The Master Yogi, and Crazy Nāmā

The worship of Krishna as Viṭṭhaḻ was firmly settled in and around Paṇḍharpūr by the time the story of Nāmdev's pilgrimage through northern India became famous. The Vārkarī folk etymology of the name ascribed to Krishna, Viṭṭhaḻ, combines the Marāṭhī/Sanskrit word for brick, *viṭ*, and a word similar to the Sanskrit root *sthal* in this case, *thala*, to arrive at "the one who stands on a brick," a reference to Viṭṭhaḻ's rootedness in Paṇḍharpūr and his iconographic representation: a jet-black figure, he stands with his hands on his hips, he arms bowed, and his feet placed parallel on a square slab. Philologists reject this etymology, instead tracing the origin of Viṭṭhaḻ's name to the old Kannada word for Vishnu, *biṭṭa* or *biṭṭaga*, suggesting that the worship of Viṭṭhaḻ migrated from the Kannada-speaking region before 1000 CE.[13] Paṇḍharpūr was probably a center for the worship of Śiva but slowly transformed into a Vaishnava holy place, perhaps under the influence of another Krishnaite devotional tradition, the Mahānubhāv religion. An alternative name for Viṭṭhaḻ, Pāṇḍuraṅga, might refer to a Śaiva deity who remained the inspiration for the name of the town, Paṇḍharpūr. The word Pāṇḍuraṅga certainly implies a figure with "a white (*pāṇḍu*) color (*raṅga*)," rather than the usually black Viṭṭhaḻ or dark blue Krishna. The first reference to the city of Paṇḍharpūr occurs in a copperplate inscription dated 516 CE and calls the place "the village of Pāṇḍuraṇga."[14] However, by the Yādav rule of the twelfth century, Pāṇḍuraṇga became equated with Vishnu/Viṭṭhaḻ and Paṇḍharpūr became the home of Krishna as Viṭṭhaḻ.[15] There is quite a bit of evidence to suggest this mix of Śaiva worship within the early Vārkarī tradition. For example, before entering Viṭṭhaḻ's temple, Vārkarīs worship at Puṇḍalīk's memorial (*samādhi*), an ancient and simple Śiva-*liṅga* temple half submerged in the Bhīmā river. Vārkarīs, as well as some scholars, claim that the conical headdress Viṭṭhaḻ wears is a Śiva liṅga.[16] Śiva is certainly important to the Vārkarī tradition, as are other religious traditions, such as Buddhism, Jainism, and Sufism.[17]

Observing the eclectic nature of Viṭṭhaḻ worship, and in particular the intersection of Śaivism and Vaishnavism, Charlotte Vaudeville described the religion a "Śaiva-Vaishnava Synthesis" and as "nominal" Vaishnavism, containing a free mix of other religions (1996). However, the Vārkarī tradition in theology and practice is today predominantly Vaishnava.[18] The Puṇḍalīk story, as well as the folk etymology of Viṭṭhaḻ's name, survive as the definitive origin myths of the Vārkarī tradition and reinforce how completely the Vārkarīs bring Krishna into their theology, mythology, and history. In a sense, the Vārkarīs naturalize him, melding his character with folk or pastoral religion, matching his legend with the geography of Mahārāṣṭra[19] and incorporating him into their diverse religious history.

By the early thirteenth century, Viṭṭhaḻ as Krishna was popular in the Deccan region and had attracted the attention of powerful benefactors. An inscription found in Paṇḍharpūr dates the first recorded use of the title Viṭṭhal̲ for the god of the town in 1189 CE.[20] By 1277 CE copperplate inscriptions record that the Yādav King Rāmacandra, through his advisor Hemādri, made generous donations to the Viṭṭhal̲ temple, indicative of its rising importance. The inscription calls the town "Phagūṇipūr," which G. A. Deulery takes to be a corruption of "Phālgūṇipūr." He suggests the reference points to Phālgūṇi verses sung by the *gopī*s to their beloved Krishna. By the middle of the thirteenth century the Mahānubhāvs had produced hagiographies of their preeminent guru Cakradar, whom they considered to be the last of five *avatāras* of Krishna, the first of the five being Krishna himself.[21] A Mahānubhāv work from the early fourteenth century, the *Gādyarāja*, narrates the lives of all five Krishna avatāras, but focuses its attention on the Krishna of the *Māhābhārata* and *Bhāgavata Purāṇa*.[22] Though the Mahānubhāvs did not recognize Viṭṭhal̲ as an incarnation of Krishna, their frequent vilification of the Vārkarī's deity points toward Viṭṭhal̲'s established importance in the religious milieu of Mahārāṣṭra in that period and perhaps their attempt to discredit this "sixth" Krishna.[23] In any case, Krishna had become a stable and vital figure in Marāṭhī religious life in a variety of ways at least by the beginning of the thirteenth century.[24]

Jñāndev is remembered to have completed his translation and commentary on the Bhagavad Gītā by 1290 CE. The text is rich with *advaita vedānta*, Nātha philosophy, and Krishna *bhakti*. This work, the *Bhavārthadīpikā* or simply the *Jñāneśvarī*, links the Marāṭhī tradition with at least one classical source for Krishna's legacy at an early stage in the Vārkarī religion. Around this period, Jñāndev may also have written his *Haripaṭh* extolling the names of Vishnu.[25] Jñāndev is reputed to have lived a short life, completing his masterpieces by the age of twenty-two. His Brahmin father had renounced his caste and traveled to Vārānasī to live as renunciate. After the birth of his four children—Nivṛtti, Sopān, Jñāndev, and Muktābāī—he returned to society. In order to reinvest his children with social status and purify them of their inherited sins, Jñāndev's father and mother were instructed by the Brahmins of Paiṭhaṇ to commit suicide by drowning themselves in the Bhīmā river.[26] Jñāndev and his three siblings, now orphans but Brahmins again, were all initiated into the Nātha Śaiva sect and became famous yogis, but retained in their songs a skepticism and critique of ascetical religion and caste.[27] At twenty-two, Jñāndev ended his life by entering a state of deep meditation (*mahāsamādhi*) and enclosing himself in a tomb in Al̲andi.[28] But before ending his life, Jñāndev resolved to see the most famous Hindu pilgrimage sites of the North. He traveled to Paṇḍharpūr and, as the

Tīrthāvaḻī recalls, approached a well-known performer of devotional songs (*kīrtankār*) to Viṭṭhaḻ with his wanderlust.

Nāmdev, or Nāmā, is remembered to have lived sometime at the end of the thirteenth century or the beginning of the fourteenth century.[29] The Vārkarī tradition generally places the span of his life between 1270 and 1350 CE. He was a *śimpī* or tailor by caste, but lived as the archetypical Viṭṭhaḻ devotee (*bhakta*), who was childlike in his complete dedication to Krishna. The latter affectionately calls his devotee "slow, unworldly, and crazy," as we will see in the *Tīrthāvaḻī* (908:10). Nāmdev's songs range from the first Marāṭhī versions of Krishna's *bāla-krīḍā* episodes, to autobiography and biographies of his contemporary sants. The bāla-krīḍā collection provides a link to the larger classical Krishna tradition and sets a standard in Marāṭhī for the local performative art of *kīrtan* where the child-Krishna stories are an important basic text.[30] Nāmdev criticizes pompous religiosity in his songs (*abhaṅgs*, literally, "unbroken"),[31] advocates absorption in both singing God's name and retelling his legends, and pays explicit devotion to Viṭṭhaḻ's image in Paṇḍharpūr. Nāmdev is also remembered in North India, most notably among the Dādū Panthīs, Kabīr Panthīs, and Sikhs.[32] He is famous for spreading bhakti in the North at an early period, where his *pads* blurred the distinction between *nirguṇa* and *saguṇa* varieties of devotion. He is also remembered as a child bhakta who literally had Viṭṭhaḻ eating out of his hand.[33] By Nāmdev's early adulthood he had acquired a reputation as a great performer of Viṭṭhaḻ devotional material (songs, stories, *nāmasaṅkīrtana*), but also as being uncouth in his understanding of theology and philosophy. Viṭṭhaḻ himself directed Nāmdev to the Śaiva-Nātha guru, Visobā Khecar (fourteenth century), for more refined religious instruction. Khecar taught Nāmdev to accept the ubiquity of God—in this case, Śiva.[34] Despite the pervasive philosophy of nonduality in the *Tīrthāvaḻī*, Nāmdev and Viṭṭhaḻ experience tremendous separation anxiety. The resolution of this anxiety becomes a central theological issue played out in the narrative.

The Tempered Text

The *Tīrthāvaḻī* is a story with a diverse pedigree. Two distinct versions, with several variations, exist in old Marāṭhī manuscripts and modern anthologies (*gāthā*), and a third version is part of the quasi anthology of Vārkarī hagiography, the *Bhaktavijay* (Victory of the Devotees), composed in the mid-eighteenth century and attributed to Mahipati (c. 1715–90 CE). The oldest version attested in manuscripts is an autobiographical account of a pilgrimage to sites in North India, whereas the later two are biographical accounts of Jñāndev and Nāmdev traveling northward, performing miracles, and returning to Paṇḍharpūr to realize the futility of pilgrimage anywhere else. The latter two are by far the more famous; the first, autobiographical version, appears in the appendix of only a few anthologies.[35] The three versions each have their own significant variations found in manuscripts that stand one to two hundred years apart, and probably drew their source from a legend about Nāmdev's travels popular from his time in the thirteenth century until the late sixteenth century, when the story was written down. However, a parallel oral tradition of retelling the story of Nāmdev's travels, and his relationship to Krishna, is no doubt older than the written tradition and better known. The written tradition is likely a sort of still-shot, representing important moments of change and emendation of the oral story since the sixteenth century. An examination of the difference between and within the three major versions reveals a process of "authorizing" the Vārkarī tradition through the character of Nāmdev (and Jñāndev to some degree), setting the tradition against the politics and social trends of the sixteenth century to the late eighteenth century, and fixing certain beliefs within the framework of narrative, set to song, drama, and eventually to film in the twentieth century.

In this chapter, I use the biographical version of the *Tīrthāvaḻī*, attributed to Nāmdev, and found in all anthologies of Nāmdev's work. This version is the "standard" text, and forms the basis of Mahipati's eighteenth-century retelling. The biographical versions—both Nāmdev's and Mahipati's retelling—are the most widely read, recited, anthologized, performed, and accepted versions of the story of Jñāndev and Nāmdev's journey. Manuscripts containing the biographical version attributed to Nāmdev begin to appear in the early seventeenth century, shortly after the renaissance in Vārkarī and Bhāgavata religion in Mahārāṣṭra initiated by Eknāth (1532–99).[36] The language of the biographical *Tīrthāvaḻī* is a mixture of seventeenth-century Marāṭhī and much older Marāṭhī, akin to the language of the *Jñāneśvarī*. The text consists of fifty-eight to sixty-one highly poetical abhaṅgs that reveal the author's mastery of the form.[37] The story's structure is a dialogue (e.g., between Nāmdev and Jñāndev, Viṭṭhaḻ and Rukmiṇī, Jñāndev and Viṭṭhaḻ) and a third-person narrative. The text recounts miraculous events and presents Viṭṭhaḻ as a character who interacts in a human way with his devotees, in this case, primarily with Nāmdev. I refer to this version of the story as biographical because of the overarching third-person narrative. Nāmdev is praised in the text as the most exalted of all Krishna devotees, a characterization not found in his supposedly autobiographical songs.

The authorship of the *Tīrthāvaḻī* is sometimes attributed to Nāmdev and sometimes to Jñāndev. The oldest version of the text, dated to 1631 CE, credits authorship to Jñāndev, not to Nāmdev. However, the Vārkarī tradition and other Nāmdev followers attribute the story, as well as this very text, only to Nāmdev. That the text itself seems to be about both sants and, in a sense, by neither sant alone, lends credence to the idea that this is an older, famous legend probably recast by any number of kīrtankārs who remembered and passed on the story orally. As to authorship, I find it helpful to think of Nāmdev as the author of the story in as much as he is the principal actor in it and hence the progenitor of the narrative. In other words, he is the author of the life, if not the author of the life story. However, the story certainly has had a significant genealogy of producers who have embellished the storyline and eventually committed the legend to the medium of writing in the sixteenth and seventeenth centuries.

Since the biographical version of the *Tīrthāvaḻī* has received a consensus of approval from Vārkarīs (exhibited through more than two hundred years of anthologizing and performance), I take it to be representative—though not definitive—of their beliefs. All my translations and references to the *Tīrthāvaḻī* found in this chapter are drawn from the biographical version attributed to Nāmdev. I will examine only the first third of the text. I have chosen to focus on this portion of the story because it contains the complete account of the pilgrimage and how it affected all the primary characters: Viṭṭhaḻ/Krishna, Jñāndev, and Nāmdev. The second and third portions of the *Tīrthāvaḻī* take place after Nāmdev and Jñāndev have returned to Paṇḍharpūr. This subsequent narrative concerns an obligatory feast offered to Brahmins and critiques caste bias, commensality, and Brahminical religious practices, while accommodating Brahmins within the scope of the Vārkarī community.[38] These portions are fascinating, but do not directly reflect Vārkarī belief vis-à-vis Krishna and his followers as proficiently as the first portion does, and would lead the discussion away from Krishna bhakti and into intercaste rivalry and other murky waters. The first third of the *Tīrthāvaḻī* also reflects, in a skeletal form, the earliest strata of the legend itself, attested in manuscripts from 1581 CE.[39]

A Reluctant Pilgrim on an Antipilgrimage

The *Tīrthāvaḻī* opens to a great historical moment in Vārkarī religious history. Jñāndev travels from his home in Aḻandi and arrives at Paṇḍharpūr. He knocks on Nāmdev's front door and the two sants convene a meeting that has been incorporated into the Vārkarī pilgrimage and symbolically reenacted once a year, probably since the early fifteenth century, if not much earlier.[40] Their introductions are brief. Nāmdev immediately recognizes the great yogi and scholar, and Jñāndev has heard of Nāmdev's devotion; he has come specifically to lure Nāmdev away from Paṇḍharpūr and on to the pilgrimage trail. Nāmdev expresses his humility at meeting such a famous figure, claiming he is "dull, dumb, unintellectual, fit only for the smallest particles of dust kicked up by the feet of the *sants*" (904:4).[41] But he's not complaining. Nāmdev says, "Therefore, the Lord of Paṇḍharī[42] looks after me, and by god I've got a great life" (5). When Jñāndev discloses his intentions, however, Nāmdev's tone changes. He ponders the offer, "Mother Viṭṭhal̤ gives me everything I need. . . . Why would I want anything less than Viṭhobā's feet. . . . Life after life I've been raised by Viṭṭhal̤. . . . Why would I sell off all this to Jñāndev?" (905:8–10). Nāmdev tells his guest to ask Viṭṭhal̤ himself.

The ensuing encounter is the first of only two points in the biographical *Tīrthāval̤ī* when all three major figures—Nāmdev, Jñāndev, and Viṭṭhal̤/Krishna—gather together; the second time marks the end of the pilgrimage. Standing before Viṭṭhal̤, Jñāndev asks god to allow Nāmdev to join him on his voyage (*tīrthayātra*) because Nāmdev is the archetypical devotee and Jñāndev wants "to enjoy the sweetness of Nāmā's companionship" (907:11). Viṭṭhal̤ is both amused and saddened. It seems to please Viṭṭhal̤ that a great yogi and scholar would want to keep company with an illiterate tailor. He considers the coupling a "miracle," and gives his permission (908:1). Yet Viṭṭhal̤ does so reluctantly because he is afraid his beloved Nāmdev will forget him when they are separated. Viṭṭhal̤ makes Jñāndev promise to look after Nāmdev, saying, "My Nāmā is slow, unworldly, and crazy (*veḍa*). Keep an eye on him" (10). Viṭṭhal̤ passes on responsibility for Nāmdev by placing Nāmdev's hand into Jñāndev's hand (12). Before the two depart, they bathe in the Bhīmā River, worship at Puṇḍalīk's Śiva-liṅga temple near the water, and cross to the other side, setting out on their way northward.

We are then given a description of Viṭṭhal̤'s severe separation anxiety. Three long abhaṅgs detail his anguish as "a best friend, a brother, mother, and father" who has let Nāmdev out of his care (909:8). In a conversation with his wife, Rukmiṇī, who has found him in a disheveled state, Viṭṭhal̤ describes his love for his bhaktas:

> I keep my *bhakta*s close to my heart and to them there is none other as dear as me. I take the form of a human for their pleasure and from age to age continue parading this body around. I give them whatever they need because they are the greatest happiness of my life. They are my refuge and I am their rest. Their mouths invoke my name. I am their mistress (*soyarā*); they are my companions. It's a

> wonderful thing to be alone with them. Voice, mind, body, breath—they give it all to me. I please them by living among them. They make me happy; they're in charge. For them I made the dwellings of Heaven. Their secrets I alone know, and they can read my signs of love. They cool my mind by reciting my name. I take such pleasure in those moments. The sun shines with its own rays of light, and those rays are not different from the sun. That's the way it is with my servants and me: I am sad because we are of one essence, without division. They are constituted by their devotion to me and devotion produces my own form just as a flame and a lamp are the same. (910:1–12)

The language of dependence and separation is striking, almost reminiscent of the genre of love songs in Marāṭhī called *lāvaṇī* where a female narrator usually pines away for her absent lover. Even Rukmiṇī is taken aback, reminding Viṭṭhal̠ that his devotees are as close to him as they are to the sound of his name uttered in their throats (909:11). But Viṭṭhal̠ cannot be placated. His anxiety turns to guilt because he gave Nāmdev "no reason to love and work for me, and yet he has never asked anything of me. . . . I gave him neither morals, wealth, or love [*dharma artha kāma*]. I am the one who owes him a debt in this life" (911:6–7). The idea emerges that Krishna is indebted to Nāmdev, and not the other way around. This relationship is repeated throughout descriptions of Nāmdev's relationship to Viṭṭhal̠ in the poetry of other sants. Nāmdev is, in a manner of speaking, a self-made man, who nonetheless gives everything to his god. The situation is difficult for Viṭṭhal̠ to take and it compounds his sense of obligation to protect Nāmdev.

At this point, the attention of the narration leaves Viṭṭhal̠ and shifts to the two pilgrims walking down the road. We are given the image of Nāmdev reluctantly following Jñāndev, turning around frequently and looking back in the direction of Paṇḍharpūr, sometimes crying out, "O Mother . . . why have you sent me away? I'm nervous among all these foreigners . . . and I don't see anyone who is dear to me" (912:3). Away from Paṇḍharpūr, from his circle of fellow sants, he's like an abandoned child. He cries to Viṭṭhal̠:

> You're my mother and my father, my brother and my uncle, Lord of Paṇḍharī. You're my best friend; you're loved as the family god of my people. You're my vow; you're my holy place; you're my morals, wealth, and love, O god. You're my eye of wisdom; you're my aim in life; you're the witness to my deepest nature . . . protect your poor orphan. (912:6–11)

Jñāndev tries to console Nāmdev, but he has no experience as a parent and is, in any case, Nāmdev's junior. However, he is an accomplished yogi, a scholar of Sanskrit learning, and a dedicated nondualist, so he tries to put his knowledge to use in assuaging Nāmdev's suffering. He tells Nāmdev, "You've got to come to your senses and think rationally. . . . Viṭṭhaḻ is spread in every direction, so give up seeing things as divided and separated. Listen instead to the sound that is not sounded, that is without space and time. This is the knowledge that you ought to pursue with abandon" (913:3–11). But Nāmdev is not convinced, "You mean to say that god is like the sky, filling all space? It's not like that. To me god is about the body, voice, and mind. I feel happy and alive when I can sing songs to him, listen to those songs, and see him with my own eyes. In my heart I must reject what you've said, just like the Cataka bird drinks rain only from the clouds and rejects the water pooled and flowing on the Earth" (913:8–17). The great debater, Jñāndev, is not used to this strategy. When presented with reason, Nāmdev reacts with emotion; when offered philosophy Nāmdev replies with feelings. Frustrated, Jñāndev obliquely tells Nāmdev, "Your faith is certainly focused [*ekavidha*]." (913:19).

As they share the road further, Jñāndev's opinion begins to change. We are given the sense that Jñāndev has mulled over Nāmdev's simple way, and has come to second guess his own path of knowledge. He asks more questions as they walk, engaging Nāmdev's beliefs based on empiricism, evidence, and proof. And slowly he becomes convinced that Nāmdev may not be as simpleminded as he appears. He wants to learn more, so he implores Nāmdev:

> Nāmā, tell me how your Self became undifferentiated from god, who is the embodiment of love. Pleasure and devotion are unbreakably united in you. What are the details of your method? How do you practice it? Tell me. What rites do you observe? How do you maintain your intellectual activities? What is your way of stilling the mind through meditation? Give me some kind of answer to these questions. How does one hear about your way? How does one think about it? How do you become firm in your practice through concentrated effort? Who is the one that worships? Who is the one that teaches? Show me someone who takes up this occupation? I am giddy and impatient! I should get started fasting and practicing your method today! Tell me your experiences. (914:4–10)

But Nāmdev is reluctant to speak with authority because he feels he has none: "My knowledge is nothing without my teacher. I've never known the power of knowledge without first submitting humbly to Viṭṭhaḻ . . . like a babbling child in his mother's arms" (915:9–10). Despite Nāmdev's eloquent disavowal of any expertise, Jñāndev insists that he tell him everything. Futhermore, Jñāndev changes his strategy. As line 10 above indicates, Jñāndev stops asking Nāmdev about his knowledge, or *jñāna*, and instead inquires about Nāmdev's experience or *bhāva*. The former is accessible only by the privileged and educated; experience, however, comes to everyone.

Jñāndev's rhetorical maneuver works, and Nāmdev is moved to fulfill his friend's request. Nāmdev's response articulates a core of belief and practice:

> Hearing Jñāndev speak, a great love welled up inside Nāmā. He says, 'Listen to the story of my experience. Action, laws of religion, and the rest, they're all extraneous. Knowledge of these things will bore you. For people who follow this knowledge, meeting with the good people—those who have become detached from the world by becoming rooted in the highest love—and just being happy, are very rare events. All spiritual powers should be used for mercy for other beings and all faiths should be about compassion. Those aspects of *bhakti* diminish a sense of otherness. Singing god's name is, to me, the sweetest thing. I see no reason to labor away at religious austerities. I see no sin in bowing to the soft, blissful inner light. Know that the way of knowledge can be hypocritical and misleading. I put no faith in those things in my own life. Unfaltering meditation on god's Name is a good thing, which allows me to see everything through Viṭhobā's eyes. I endlessly remember him in my heart by imagining his beautiful feet together on the brick. Like a deer distracted by a sound, one should naturally forget the sensations of the body. On this subject, the mind should remain firmly intent, taking pleasure in hearing god's Name, just like business people who apply their minds in miserly ways, worrying about their profits all the time. Like them, one ought to continually think of ways to apply one's thoughts in the pursuit of self-virtue. Just as when a married woman goes to another man, she knows she deviates from the custom of monogamy. Or just as a bee flies to investigate other things, but remains intent on flowers, it's a good thing to focus your attention inwardly. Only one god, Viṭṭhaḻ, gives all existence life so one should see his form in all beings. We divide and categorize everything, but devotion to him transcends this and is simply the art of love in a state of bliss. One who intensely concentrates on indifference from the world, who stands apart and alone, such a person is called a warrior of the Self. This body does not remember the merit of past lives, but should be firmly and unceasingly fixed upon the present moment. Absent of desire, one should focus the mind completely on self-improvement, and harbor no doubts about one's own knowledge. In this state of personal reflection, Govinda [Krishna] will give you his love. Without doing this, there is no solace from suffering. These are my experiences with the body, speech, and mind, and I have told you all I know . . . all my words are directed by him, Pāṇḍuraṇga, who generously gives all wisdom." (917:1–23)

Jñāndev is stupefied: "There are many devotees of Vishnu, many have gone, many more will come, but Nāmdev's words are not like the ordinary poetry those others compose. His words are essential, fantastic, and unparalleled" (918:1–2). Jñāndev has been convinced that Nāmdev's way is superior to the way of knowledge that he himself maintains. He compares Nāmdev to those who practice jñāna, saying "there have been brilliant academics who have become famous for their intellects . . . those who observe rites perfectly, who have a vast knowledge of ritual, and they even have been worshipped by the people. There have been artists, poets, and entertainers . . . accomplished lecturers who produce brilliant books . . . masters of inner-concentration who sit in seats of authority . . . advanced yogīs liberated even in life . . . the lucky, rich, and smart, but I know of no one like you, O Slave of Vishnu" (918:2–10). Jñāndev compares all the gems of society to Nāmdev's devotion, and finds they are all dull. And he includes himself within this roster of lesser beings. Despite this, however, there is one thing Jñāndev has not yet been disabused of: the efficacy of pilgrimage and the superiority of his own yogic abilities. In this regard, Nāmdev has one more lesson to teach.

The two eventually arrive at Dvārakā, the former home of Nāmdev's beloved Krishna. In the autobiographical *Tīrthāvaḻī*, a version that may be older than the biographical one, Nāmdev continues on from Dvārakā to the Himālayas, Vārānasī, South India, and then homeward to Paṇḍharpūr. However, in the biographical version followed here, the companions go no further than Dvārakā and return to Paṇḍharpūr directly, visiting no holy sites of Śiva. On their return, as they pass through a dense forest, they are stricken with terrible, life-threatening thirst. The two search out a well, but find it is too deep to determine if water is at the bottom. Jñāndev uses his yogic powers to make himself very light. He then descends along the well's wall, finds water at the bottom, and when he's drunk all he can, he comes back up by the same method (919). Jñāndev offers to retrieve water for Nāmdev, who is obviously in dire need, but Nāmdev refuses, responding, "There is no space between my soul and Viṭṭhaḻ . . . if he gives the word, in a second I'll have water," and confidently adds, "Be patient for a minute, O Swami, and I'll show you a miracle" (919:13–15).

However confident Nāmdev appears to Jñāndev on the outside, he is panicking inside. Nāmdev summons Viṭṭhaḻ's image in his mind and addresses that image, "You are my best friend, my brother, my cousin, my mother, and my father . . . come quickly, come running, O Keśav, my Mother and Father" (920:2–3, 5). He reminds Viṭṭhaḻ of how he helped Gajendra and Draupadī in their time of need and that Viṭṭhaḻ himself is responsible for entrusting Nāmdev to Jñāndev's care. He appeals to Krishna, "Treat me like your little boy" (920:15). Back in Paṇḍharpūr, Viṭṭhaḻ gets an uneasy feeling. Though he lives in constant bliss, he knows something's not right with one of his devotees. Just then, Rukmiṇī hears a far-off cry and recognizes Nāmdev's voice. "Nāmā is dying of thirst! Run to him!" (921:9). Viṭṭhaḻ does just that, and within seconds the well begins to overflow with water, soaking Nāmdev and Jñāndev, and providing water for everyone who lives in the forest.

Jñāndev is impressed. It wasn't just that Nāmdev could get water from the well; Jñāndev himself had no problem doing the same. But Nāmdev's method also provided water for others, something Jñāndev did not do (though he offered). Jñāndev finally sees the limit of his own abilities, "I have known yogīs who can sit in the highest state of meditation, yet none of them can create peace in their own minds. I can't think of anyone else who can immediately indenture god to himself but you, Slave of Vishnu" (922:1–2). The play on servitude is intentional: Krishna is Nāmdev's slave, and Nāmdev is Vishnu's slave. Jñāndev concedes that Nāmdev's way is superior, and he also comes to regard pilgrimage as futile, saying, "I know now that pilgrimage to other holy places is pointless. Only hearing the perfect beauty of your songs means anything" (922:6). I have not noticed these sorts of pronouncements about pilgrimage and yoga in Jñāndev's other works, where knowledge and devotion are generally on an equal footing.[43] But here Jñāndev is unequivocal: "The practice of deep meditation detaches one, and keeps one from concentrating on one's home life. The sages, singing angels, and deities—we've all mistakenly set our attention on the Formless god. You have confronted us with our folly" (922:9–11). The abhaṅg ends with Jñāndev lying down at Nāmdev's feet, converted and convinced.

The duo returns to Paṇḍharpūr where Nāmdev is reunited with his beloved Viṭṭhal̠. The reluctant pilgrim reports to his Lord about the strangeness of the lands through which he traveled: "My eyes did not see the dwelling place of god in the pilgrimage sites, and no one there worshipped god. They did not follow the same tradition that I follow, as if they had never heard of the glorious stories of Viṭṭhal̠. They didn't worship the one on the riverbank, with his hands at his waist. I didn't see those feet on the brick . . . I didn't hear the Vaishnavas sing the songs that we sing, nor did I see the abundant stories of Hari" (923:8–12). Viṭṭhal̠ also shares his own distress when his bhakta was away from him, and vows never again to let his precious, crazy Nāmā out of his sight.

Śatapāūlī: One Hundred Steps

Every night in neighborhoods like the Deccan Gymkhana area of Pune, men, women, and children—entire families—come out of their homes after dinner for a walk, often led by the tug of a shaggy Pomeranian. My friend Tātyā Paranjpe says he has taken a "constitutional" nearly every day for most of his eighty-three years; he calls this *śatapāūlī* "one hundred steps." He walks fifty steps outside his front door, turns around, and then walks fifty more back home. Tātyā's daily practice reminds me of the *Tīrthāvaḻī* and the emphasis on returning home. Most Hindu pilgrimages are about arriving at the sacred place and returning home again, and nowhere is that more apparent than in the *Tīrthāvaḻī*.[44] The section of the text I have narrated above comprises barely one-third of the entire story. The remaining two-thirds takes place in Paṇḍharpūr, all in or around Viṭṭhaḻ's temple or *mandir*, a word interchangeable in Old Marāṭhī with "home."[45] The emphasis on coming back to and being in Paṇḍharpūr suggests that the *Tīrthāvaḻī* is more than an antipilgrimage account; it reinforces the importance of Paṇḍharpūr within the larger context of Krishna worship in India and delineates some of the terrain of the Vārkarī tradition. The text reflects an ethnic self-consciousness that underlines a shared geographic space, a common linguistic heritage, a central iconic figure, and a socioreligious structure constituted by familial metaphors.

The *Tīrthāvaḻī* serves to recognize the larger Krishna tradition in India and situates itself both within and outside that tradition, inscribing its own terrain. The text produces difference while expressing Marāṭhī ethnoreligious unity.[46] The two pilgrims go no further than Viṭṭhaḻ's former home, Dvārakā, and in essence retrace their god's path back to Paṇḍharpūr. The mimesis of Krishna's journey from Dvārakā to Paṇḍharpūr asserts a relationship, both geographic and historiographic, to a larger Krishna tradition, while exemplifying the "migration" and assimilation of Krishna.[47] The *Tīrthāvaḻī* focuses on Paṇḍharpūr as a home and gives expression to the relationship between god and devotee through familial metaphors. Nāmdev is a child to Viṭṭhaḻ; Viṭṭhaḻ is his mother, father, brother, and friend. When the two are separated, they suffer and yearn to be reunited, just as Krishna and Rādhā do elsewhere. However, the language used in the *Tīrthāvaḻī* is devoid of the eroticism commonly associated with the sentiment of *viraha* in other Krishna traditions.[48]

The term "*viraha*" denotes the agony of separation, especially that of parted lovers. However, the word "viraha" does not appear in the text of the *Tīrthāvaḻī*, and indeed is almost never used in any of Nāmdev's songs.[49] Instead, one finds *viyoga*, or "disjunction," and *bheda*, or "distinction," used to designate separation. Similarly, scholarship in Marāṭhī about the text infrequently uses the word "viraha" to explain the implications of the sentiment of separation.[50] The emotional vocabulary of separation found elsewhere in relation to Krishna—the agony of parting and the bliss of reunion—is present in this text but drained of any erotic content. The famous parlance of the lonesome lover, brought on by Krishna's truancy from the scene of love in such contexts as the *Gītāgovinda*, the poetry of the *aḷvārs*, the *pads* of Sūr Dās, and the *Bhāgavata Purāṇa*, is articulated in the *Tīrthāvaḻī* between Viṭṭhaḻ and Nāmdev, but not as a lover yearning for her absent Krishna. The choice of descriptive terminology both in the *Tīrthāvaḻī* and in scholarship about it might indicate a deliberate dissociation of the Vārkarī tradition from the erotic devotionalism or *madhura bhakti* of other Krishna traditions, while still aligning itself with the theology of separation.[51] Furthermore, the yearning to be reunited is not one-sided, as it is in the songs of the Āḷvārs, for instance, but rather is similar to the *Gītāgovinda*, where we hear of Krishna's yearning and his beloved Rādhā's, as well. Rather than the pain of two lovers, however, Viṭṭhaḻ and Nāmdev suffer from the separation of a mother from her child, or a cow from her calf (vātsalya).[52] Nāmdev is forever like a dependent infant who requires constant care from Viṭṭhaḻ. The crisis of the *Tīrthāvaḻī*—Nāmdev's anxiety away from Paṇḍharpūr—is brought on by Viṭṭhaḻ's decision to allow Jñāndev guardianship of Nāmdev on the pilgrimage trail. The resolution of this crisis of separation comes when Viṭṭhaḻ reunites with Nāmdev and promises never to give him leave again.

The dialectic of separation bears a close relation to the dialectic of different technologies of religious practice (yoga) that emphasize a realization of nondualism (*advaita*) as opposed to simple, interpersonal engagement with god (bhakti) that presumes a dualistic (*dvaita*) relationship between god and devotee. The apparent conflict of these two positions, plentifully debated in the *Tīrthāvaḻī*, is also common in other Krishna traditions. Sūr Dās and Nandadas, for example, take up the dialectic with the *bhramargītā* songs. While Krishna is in Mathurā, Ūdho serves as his messenger to the forlorn gopīs.[53] In Sūr's treatment, Ūdho, similar to Jñāndev, is a scholar and yogi who attempts to reason with the afflicted gopīs as Jñāndev does with Nāmdev: the world is illusory and through inner contemplation, one realizes the indivisibility and immanence of Krishna.[54] The gopīs retort with their incorrigible devotion, as Nāmdev does, and ultimately persuade Ūdho that his ways and means are inferior to their all-consuming devotion to the visible and tangible Krishna.[55] For Sūr Dās, the victory of "simple" religion over the complexities of yoga invokes yet another dichotomy, that of *saguṇa* (with qualities) and *nirguṇa* (without qualities) modes of devotion.[56] However, the *Tīrthāvaḻī* is not concerned with this particular theological distinction.[57] Nāmdev is not necessarily a proponent of saguṇa bhakti. Many scholars have commented on the difficulty of situating Nāmdev within either camp of this theological divide.[58] Instead, the *Tīrthāvaḻī* advocates devotion to a specific deity, to Viṭṭhaḻ in Paṇḍharpūr who stands on his brick. Viṭṭhal̲ dutifully plays his part by taking human form (910:2 above). The complexities of dualism versus nondualism and saguṇa versus nirguṇa are overrun by Nāmdev's singleminded devotion to the image of his god in Paṇḍharpūr, to a deity with definitive anthropomorphic presence, an exact geographical location, and a particular history; who nevertheless remains equated with an ineffable, nonduality preserved in the work of Jñāndev and others. In the *Tīrthāval̲ī*, religious categories are broached only to be disregarded as meaningful in the context of Nāmdev's all-consuming worship. The yogi, and in particular, the unmarried, ascetic Jñāndev, is antithetical to the family values espoused by the relationship between Krishna and Nāmdev. Ironically, these same values are again disrupted by a sant's rejection of his filial obligations, especially to a wife or child, as Eleanor Zelliot has pointed out.

There is evidence within the textual tradition surrounding the *Tīrthāval̲ī* and its several redactions that a transition from a pan-Indian representation of Krishna to a specific Marāṭhī one took place. In the biographical version of the *Tīrthāval̲ī* I have outlined above, and first attested in 1631 CE, the name "Krishna" does not appear. Instead, one finds other proper names like Govinda, Hari, and Keśav, as well as Paṇḍharī Nāth and Yādav Rao. However, in the earliest version of the *Tīrthāval̲ī*, the autobiographical version, first attested in 1581 CE, the name Krishna appears almost fifteen times.[59] From the 1581 CE version to the 1631 CE version the name Krishna is completely eliminated from the story of the *Tīrthāval̲ī*.

In the older version of the *Tīrthāval̲ī* when Nāmdev speaks of the difference he observed during his travels through the North, he mentions that even among fellow Vaishnavas he did not feel at home. The narrative of the *Tīrthāval̲ī* was probably formulated in the sixteenth century, but it certainly reflects an older, burgeoning movement among rural, agrarian, low-caste Marāṭhī speakers. As such, it is one of the first articulations of a unique Marāṭhī identity—one among many others—constructed around geography, religious practice, and language. Vārkarī kīrtankārs were spreading Viṭṭhal̲ bhakti throughout the Deccan and further northward in an environment of diverse political alliances between local and invading Hindu and Muslim rulers, amid a variety of folk religions and literatures, and situated between a vastly expanding literary tradition in the North and an already deep-rooted one in the South. Eknāth, for example, exemplifies the diversity of the sixteenth century: a Brahmin with a guru from a Sufi lineage, he became a famous Vārkarī kīrtankār who utilized the language and images of low-caste Marāṭha life to spread Bhāgavata *dharma* while he remained a scholar of Sanskrit. In Eknāth's era, the period when the *Tīrthāval̲ī* was first committed to writing, the Vārkarī tradition was undergoing a renaissance that included the refurbishment of holy sites (like Jñāndev's samādhi in Aḻandi) and sacred Marāṭhī texts (like the *Jñāneśvarī*), while Sanskrit works like the *Bhāgavata Purāṇa* and the epics were being retold in Marāṭhī literature.

The *Tīrthāvaḻī* is positioned within a discourse of Krishna worship formed by Sanskrit and vernacular devotional literatures, pan-Indian performative traditions like kīrtan and *harikathā*, and a sacred geography of Vaishnava pilgrimage sites. Situated amid this terrain, the *Tīrthāvaḻī* engages these locations of devotionalism and transforms them into Marāṭhī, on the one hand, and onto the religious and physical geography of Mahārāṣṭra, on the other. Krishna is familiarized as Viṭṭhaḻ, a process paralleled in the *Jñāneśvarī*. In the eleventh chapter, when, at Arjuna's insistence, Krishna reveals his cosmic form, Arjuna pleads with his friend and charioteer to assume his familiar appearance. Jñāndev offers this explanation of verse 45, "Your cosmic form fills me with fear, O Lord. Let me see you just as you were before. Like a pilgrim goes in search of wonder and adventure, then returns to the comfort of his home, so your four-armed form is a home to me" (11:493–4). Nāmdev's *Tīrthāvaḻī* and his other songs describe a home life in Paṇḍharpūr surrounded by a family of fellow bhaktas, with Viṭṭhaḻ as their patriarch and matriarch. The *Tīrthāvaḻī* provides a conscious recognition of the Krishna tradition outside Mahārāṣṭra by engaging classical representations, but reinforces a Marāṭhī Krishna, rooted and fixed in Paṇḍharpūr amid a variety of religious and social influences. Nāmdev became anxious when he could not recognize the Krishna images, stories, and songs he encountered on his travels, though he was among fellow Vaishnavas. These strangers, Nāmdev tells us, worshiped Krishna but did not worship Viṭṭhaḻ; they sang songs, but not Marāṭhī songs. Nāmdev may have been among friends, but he was not at home. Only in Paṇḍharpūr is the family portrait complete: Viṭṭhaḻ and Rukmiṇī benevolently gazing upon Nāmdev and other sants, all children and siblings through the Krishna bhakti of the Vārkarī tradition.

Notes

Acknowledgements: I would like to thank Dr. Ashok Kamat, for guidance, encouragement, hospitality, and long discussions about Nāmdev's importance; Dr. Sadanand More, for sharing his insights on Nāmdev and the Vārkarīs with me; Principal Relekar, for his assistance and enthusiasm for my work; Mr. Suresh Subandha, for graciously opening the doors of the Nāmdev Shimpi Mandir to me; Mr. V. Manjul, who has helped me and other scholars in countless ways for many years; Dr. Kalyan Kale, who has patiently reviewed with me my very imperfect translations, thus saving me from certain embarrassment, and has selflessly shared with me his wealth of information; Dr. Tandale, for offering his musical and philosophical talents; Jack Hawley, Anne Feldhaus, Eleanor Zelliot, Mark Nye, Shana Sippy, Anna Schultz, and others who took their time to read and comment on this chapter; and Sunila Kale, my editor.

1. For Sanskrit and Marāṭhī sources for the Puṇḍalīk story see R. C. Dhere (1984), G. A. Deleury (1960), and E. R. Sand (1992, 1994). For oral traditions, see G. D. Sontheimer (1989). E. R. Sand (1994), 132n6, believes that Rukmiṇī is a later addition to the story.

2. This is true of both the Vārkarī tradition, to which this folk story belongs, and of the Mahānubhāv tradition, a bhakti religion as old, if not older, than the Vārkarīs. See Anne Feldhaus (1983b), I. Raeside (1976, 1989) for more on the Mahānubhāv religion and the role of Krishna.

3. In Marāṭhī the first record of devotional-erotic songs (*madhura bhakti*) like those of the *Gītagovinda* appear in the work of Vamana Pandita (1618–95 CE) and are carried on most artfully by *lāvaṇī* poets (*śāhīr*) from the eighteenth century onward, such as Ram Joshi, Honaji, and Saganbhau, who was a Muslim.

4. In Viṭṭhaḻ's temple, he and Rukmiṇī are separated. Rukmiṇī's idol stands in the extreme northwestern corner facing east, with Satyabhāmā and Rādhikā in an adjacent room to her right. However, this does not diminish Rukmiṇī's importance. Aside from the stories of Krishna's life, Rukmiṇī's Svāyamvara ceremony is one of the episodes of Krishna mythology most often retold in Marāṭhī among both Vārkarīs and Mahānubhāvs. See S. G. Tulpule (1979) for literary accounts by at least seven different authors. Rukmiṇī's Svāyamvara is also a fixture of Vārkarī kīrtan.

5. Viṭhobā is arrived at through the diminutive of Viṭṭhaḻ, Viṭṭhu, with the addition of the suffix "ba" as in the ubiquitous "baba" or "father". Viṭṭhāī is again a diminutive, but with a feminine ending. Viṭṭhaḻ is also called simply *māulī* or mother. Indeed, the "feminizing" of Viṭṭhaḻ is so complete at times that Viṭṭhaḻ is said to "feed Nāmdev the milk of love from his own breasts" (*ṇamateṁ pājilā premapānhā*) (*Tīrthāvaḻī* 933:15). The term *māulī* is used by Nāmdev to refer to both Viṭṭhaḻ and to Jñāndev, and later Vārkarīs also use it to refer to Jñāndev and to each other. It is common to hear two or more Vārkarīs greet one another on the biannual pilgrimage to Paṇḍharpūr by calling out "māulī!," reinforcing their metaphor of sharing a common "family" through their devotion to Viṭṭhaḻ and to his sants. The old Marāṭhī word "*kuṭumbā*," or "family," is frequently found in Nāmdev's compositions, those of his fellow sants, and in writing about Nāmdev and his companions, where it refers to all sants and their admirers, past and present.

6. See Eleanor Zelliot (1999a), and Eleanor Zelliot (1999b). I use the word "sant" rather than "saint" to avoid homologies with Christian saints here. For more on the use and history of the term "sant" see Karine Schomer and W. H. McLeod, eds. (1987).

7. See S. More (1994) for a concise and insightful discussion of the *Tīrthāvaḻī*. Charlotte Vaudeville (1996), 250–51, suggests that the *Tīrthāvaḻī*

was "designed to propagate Vaishnava *bhakti* centred on the cult of Viṭṭhaḻa." I am indebted to Dr. More for conversations about this topic in Pune, August 2000.

8. It is interesting to note that like so many of the male sants of the Vārkarī tradition (and figures like Kabir in the North), Nāmdev experiences tremendous problems with the women in his life. Gonāī, Nāmdev's mother, and Rājāī, Nāmdev's wife, both wrote songs condemning Nāmdev's disinterest in the world and his neglect of common daily tasks. On the other hand, Jāṇī, a disciple of Nāmdev's, praised him. Eleanor Zelliot has nicely discussed these problems in the works cited above.

9. In the classical context of Krishna devotion the term "viraha" is often used almost as a technical term to denote separation and the anxiety experienced by the abandoned lover, usually a gopī, and most famously, by Rādhā. However, in the *Tīrthāvaḻī* and in Marāṭhī scholarship about the text, the word "viraha" does not appear. Instead, the words "*viyoga*" and "*udvega*" are used. The term "*vātsalya*," on the other hand, is used both in the text and in Marāṭhī scholarship about the text.

10. See D. B. Mokashi (1987) and G. D. Sontheimer (1989). For Tukarām, see D. Chitre (1991).

11. See S. G. Tulpule (1960, 1979). For some sants, like Jñāndev, Eknāth, and Tukarām, the image of a manuscript is very important, in legend and in iconography: they are often depicted sitting before a manuscript. However, the fixing of a text or the adherence to written statement of belief is not so important among sants before the sixteenth century.

12. The first reference I have found in any British Indological study comes from W. Crooke, who was a district officer in the Bengal civil service in the late nineteenth century. He writes about "Nāmdeo" as a "cotton carder" (1893), vol. I. 84, a "Chhimpi or cotton-printer" (vol. I, 204), who was a follower of Ramanand and a "tribal sant" (ibid.). W. Crooke assigns a particular geographical and tribal identity to those who follow Nāmdev, "Nāmdeo Shimpis of Ahmadnagar," and observed a funeral ceremony involving Nim leaves in a section devoted to such rites across communities (vol. II, 105). In 1896, a second study by Crooke mentions a "Nāmādeo Bhagata" as a tribal sant among the Dhuniyas (299). The Nāmdev of the Dhuniyas is said to have been born in Marwar in 1443, in the time of Sikandar Lodi's reign. Crooke also mentions an account that Nāmdev came from Paṇḍharpūr in the "Dakkin" (ibid.). Crooke's second account probably confuses two figures with the same name, an seemingly intractable problem with regard to Nāmdev, though he does refer to Nāmdev as a traveler who eventually settled in Ghuman, thus in accord with Sikh hagiography about Nāmdev (144).

13. For a more thorough genealogy of Viṭṭhaḻ's names, see G. A. Deulery (1960) and R. C. Dhere (1984).

14. Charlotte Vaudeville (1996), 201.

15. It is possible that Pundarika became the Puṇḍalīk of the story above, transformed from a Śaiva deity into the first devotee of Viṭṭhaḻ. However, this is not the belief of Vārkarīs.

16. Charlotte Vaudeville (1996), 251, agrees that Viṭṭhaḻ's headgear is a Śiva liṅga, whereas G. A. Deleury (1960), 53, disagrees.

17. See R. C. Dhere (1984).

18. Charlotte Vaudeville's assessment was partially based on an analysis of Jñāndev's work. Jñāndev is remembered as both a Śaiva Nātha yogi and a Vārkarī sant, and his songs reflect both elements. For an excellent analysis of Jñāndev's verses and his sectarian affiliations, see C. Kiehnle (1997).

19. I use the term "Mahārāṣṭra" to refer to the Marāṭhī-speaking region, though the region became a state of modern India only in 1960.

20. G. A. Deleury (1960), 193.

21. Cakradar is considered an incarnation of Parameśvar, but he, and the four gurus of the Mahānubhāv sect before him, are collectively called the Five Krishnas. See Anne Feldhaus (1983b).

22. See I. Raeside (1989), xvii–xix. Raeside identifies three significant aspects of the character of the Mahānubhāv Krishna: (1) a lack of erotic elements in his hagiography; (2) the prominence given to his legal wives, especially Rukmiṇī; and (3) the characterization of Krishna as a great warrior.

23. See G. A. Deleury (1960) on two characters named Viththal and Nemdev, described as cattle thieves in the early Mahānubhāv hagiography, the *Līlācaritra*.

24. See G. D. Sontheimer (1989).

25. See Charlotte Vaudeville (1969).

26. The earliest and most complete biography of Jñāndev is attributed to Nāmdev. The *Ādi* tells the story of Jñāndev's parents and Jñāndev's childhood; the *Tīrthāvaḻī* narrates the travels of Jñāndev and Nāmdev and subsequent events; and the *Samādhi* contains Nāmdev's account of Jñāndev taking *sañjīvan samādhi* in Aḻandi. The three texts form the core of Mahipati's eighteenth-century retelling of Jñāndev's life, and are widely adapted elsewhere, as in the famous Prabhat Studios film "Sant Jñāneśvar." See S. Irlekar (1995) for a study of Nāmdev's biography of Jñāndev.

27. Another of Jñāndev's works, the *Anubhāvāmṛta*, is a highly poetic exegesis of Śaiva Siddhānta philosophy. For more on Jñāndev's Śaiva work, see D. Chitre (1996) and C. Kiehnle (1997).

28. The term "samādhi" here refers both to the mental state and to the actual tomb, rediscovered by Eknāth in the sixteenth century, located in Aḻandi, near Pune.

29. Like many figures of the thirteenth and fourteenth centuries in India, little is known for certain about Nāmdev's life or which of the thousands of compositions attributed to him are his. It is very likely that the recorded literary corpus of both Nāmdev and Jñāndev is filled with the compositions of others, amended over the years. Some scholars, like S. B. Kulkarni (1992) of Nagpur, believe that there were as many as four different poets using more or less the same name and the same stock of themes as the first Nāmdev. This is almost certainly true of the work of a late-sixteenth-century poet and translator of the *Mahābhārata*, Vishnudāsa Nāmā, who often referred to himself in his songs as a "slave of Vishnu" (*vishnudās*). Nāmdev is also revered by Kabīr Panthīs, Dādū

Panthīs, and Sikhs. This northern tradition remembers Nāmdev differently than does the Marāṭhī tradition, and it should be recalled that I am engaging the Marāṭhī remembrance of Nāmdev specifically through the *Tīrthāvaḷī*, and not the much broader tradition, which represents Nāmdev as a willing and frequent pilgrim to the North.

30. For more on this subject, see Christian Novetzke (2003).

31. For more on the abhaṅg as a form and the *ovī* as a meter, see C. Kiehnle (1997), 36–51.

32. See W. Callewaert and M. Lath (1989), Charlotte Vaudeville (1993), and N. Singh (1981).

33. The miracle of Viṭṭhaḷ drinking milk from Nāmdev's hand is famous in both Marāṭhī hagiography and in northern hagiographies. See the hagiographies of Anantadās (c. 1588), Nābhādās (c. 1600), and Vyās (c. 1580), as well as pads in the *Guru Granth Sahib* (1604). Also see Mahipati (1762) and Nāmdev's abhaṅg in *Sakaḷa Santa Gāthā* (1999[1908]), no. 7.

34. See *Sakaḷa Santa Gāthā* (1999[1908]), abhaṅg 118–69.

35. The autobiographical version has appeared in P. S. Subandha's anthology (1960), and the government of Mahārāṣṭra's *Śrī Nāmdev Gāthā* (1970).

36. Janābāī (d. c. 1350), a contemporary of Nāmdev, who called herself "Nāmā's disciple" (*nāmyācī dāsī jānī*) in many of her songs, composed a synopsis of the *Tīrthāvaḷī*, attested to as early as 1631 CE. Her synopsis conforms to the biographical *Tīrthāvaḷī* and highlights the pain of separation (*viyoga*) shared by Viṭṭhaḷ and Nāmdev.

37. The number of verses varies among editions. I have used the numbering system of the *Śrī Nāmdev Gāthā*, a semicritical edition published by the government of Mahārāṣṭra in 1970. Though the numbers are different, the text of the *Tīrthāvaḷī* is exactly the same as the one contained in the *Sakaḷa Santa Gāthā* (1999[1908]) edited by Sakhare. This latter collection of Vārkarī sant literature is generally accepted by Vārkarīs as authoritative and used by kīrtankārs in their performances. The text runs from abhaṅg number 612–70 in the 1999 reprint of the *Sakaḷa Santa Gāthā*. For this project, I chose to use the numbering system of the *Śrī Nāmdev Gāthā* because it is a more standard text for academic citation in Marāṭhī scholarship.

38. It is important to note that Brahmins have "owned" and managed the Viṭṭhaḷ temple for hundreds of years, and vital sants, like Eknāth, were Brahmins. The Vārkarī tradition is not an antibrahmanical movement, though it is certainly critical of caste-based discrimination and persecution.

39. This is the autobiographical version and mentions only Nāmdev, who gives a first-person narration of his travels. Jñāndev and Viṭṭhaḷ, as characters, do not appear in this version.

40. The *vārī*, as the pilgrimage is called in Marāṭhī, involves carrying wooden or silver *pādukās*, or sandals, that represent a particular sant, twice a year from the sant's home village to Paṇḍharpūr. The oldest of the sants that are symbolically carried to Paṇḍharpūr is Jñāndev, and a special welcome awaits him outside the city every year. A set of pādukā representing Nāmdev are carried a short distance outside the city, where they meet Jñāndev's contingent who have carried his pādukās from Aḷandi. The two ritually greet and

Nāmdev's contingent escort Jñāndev's into Paṇḍharpūr. Though the vārī takes place twice a year, the particular greeting of Nāmdev and Jñāndev occurs only once a year, in early July, or the *ekādaśī* of the month of *āṣāḍh*. During the other vārī, in November or the ekādaśī of *kārttik*, Nāmdev visits Jñāndev in Aḻandi, in commemoration of the latter's *mahāsamādhi*, the theme of Nāmdev's final biographical work on Jñāndev's life, the *Samādhi*, a lamentation at his friend's passing.

41. All translations are mine from the Marāṭhī, unless otherwise noted.

42. Paṇḍharī is another name for Paṇḍharpūr.

43. See C. Kiehnle's (1997) study of Jñāndev, *The Conservative Vaiṣṇava*, for a discussion of a text the presents some of these ideas through the persona of Jñāndev.

44. See A. G. Gold (1988).

45. See J. T. Molesworth (1996), 629.

46. See S. Pollock (1998), 25, for a discussion of "mutually constitutive interaction of the local and the global" with regard to Kannada and Sanskrit literatures.

47. On the subject of bhakti and the origin of vernacular literatures, S. Pollock (1998), 29, writes that, "many vernacular inaugurations show no concern with religious devotionalism whatever" and makes the case well with Kannada. However, the argument is unsupported within the Marāṭhī milieu where the earliest written literary use of the vernacular occurs in Mahānubhāv hagiographies. See S. G. Tulpule (1979), 314.

48. See Friedhelm Hardy (1983b).

49. I am grateful to W. Callewaert for a complete word index of the *Śrī Nāmdev Gāthā*, provided through personal communication.

50. Though the *Tīrthāvaḻī* has rarely appeared in scholarship in English, Friedhelm Hardy (1983b), 149–50, mentions the text at the end of an essay on viraha in relation to concrete time and space. However, he does not note that the word never appears in the text itself. He does not mention the *Tīrthāvaḻī* in his excellent book-length study of viraha (1983a).

51. See J. S. Hawley (1984), 100–13, where he dicusses viyoga in the context of Sūr Dās, and argues that the term serves as an antithesis to Ūdho's yoga.

52. The word "*vatsa*" in reference to Viṭṭhaḻ's feeling for Nāmdev does appear in the *Tīrthāvaḻī* and in Marāṭhī scholarship on the subject. It is interesting to note that in the oldest collection of songs, from 1631 CE, attributed to Janābāī, a large number of the verses are specifically addressed to *bhaktavatsalatā*. See Dandekar et al., *Śrī Nāmdev Gāthā* (1970), 936–55. Furthermore, in that same manuscript is Janābāī's synopsis of the *Tīrthāvaḻī* (see note 33), thus reinforcing the connection between vātsalya devotion and this text.

53. J. S. Hawley (1984), 98–102.

54. It is interesting to note that Mahipati considered Nāmdev, and not Jñāndev, an avatāra of Ūdho, or Uddhav. Mahipati 1915 (1762) (chapter 9, verses 7–12).

55. The oldest manuscripts used by J. S. Hawley in his work on Sūr Dās are from the same period as those that contain the *Tīrthāvaḻī*, from the late 1580s to the middle of the eighteenth century CE. The direction of influence is uncertain, but it is interesting to note that Sūr Dās, along with Kabīr, Rohidās, and Mīrābāī, are fixtures of Marāṭhī hagiography.

56. See J. S. Hawley (1984), 121, and R. S. McGregor (1973), 47.

57. The word "nirguṇa" appears once in the entire *Śrī Nāmdev Gāthā* and the term "saguṇa" appears forty-one times. Neither term appears in the biographical version of the *Tīrthāvaḷī*.

58. See Friedhelm Hardy (1983a), 150; J. S. Hawley (1984), 194; David Lorenzen (1996), 286; W. Callewaert and M. Lath (1989), 13; Charlotte Vaudeville (1996), 217n16.

59. Manuscript no. 1532 of 1891–95 in the collection of the Bhandarkar Oriental Research Institute, Pune.

60. G. D. Khanolkar (1977).

References

Callewaert, W. M., and M. Lath. *The Hindī Songs of Nāmdev*. Leuven: Departement Orientalistiek, 1989.

Chitre, D. *Says Tuka*. New Delhi: Penguin, 1991.

———. *Shri Jnandev's Anubhavamrut: The Immortal Experience of Being*. Delhi: Sahitya Akademi, 1996.

Crooke, W. *An Introduction to the Popular Religion and Folklore of Northern India*. (1894). New Delhi: Asian Educational Service, 1994.

———. *The Tribes and Castes of the North-Western Provinces and Oudh*. (1890). 4 Vols. New Delhi: Asian Educational Service, 1999.

Dandekar, S.V., et al. *Śrī Nāmdev Gāthā*. Bombay: Śāskiya Madhyavartī Mudranalaya, 1970.

Deleury, G. A. *The Cult of Vitthobā*. Pune: Deccan College, 1960.

Dhere, R. C. *Śrī Viṭhṭhaḷa Eka Mahāsamanvaya*. Pune: Shrividya Prakashan, 1984.

Feldhaus, Anne. *The Religious System of the Mahānubhāva Sect: The Mahānubhāva Sūtrapaṭha*. New Delhi: Manohar, 1983a.

———. "Kṛṣṇa and Kṛṣṇas: Kṛṣṇa in the Mahānubhāva Pantheon." In *Bhakti in Current Research, 1979–1982*. Monika Thiel-Horstmann, ed. Berlin: Deitrich Reimer Verlag, 1983b.

Gold, A. G. *Fruitful Journeys: The Ways of Rajasthani Pilgrims*. Berkeley: University of Califrornia Press, 1988.

Hardy, Friedhelm. "*Viraha* in Relation to Concrete Space and Time." In *Bhakti in Current Research, 1979–1982*. Monika Thiel-Horstmann, ed. Berlin: Deitrich Reimer Verlag, 1983a.

———. *Viraha-Bhakti: The Early History of Krishna Devotion in South India*. Delhi: Oxford University Press, 1983b.

Hawley, J. S. *Sur Das: Poet, Singer, Saint*. Seattle: University of Washington Press, 1984.

Irlekar, S. *Nāmdevakṛta Jñāneśvara Caritra*. Pune: Nihārī Prakāśan, 1995.

Jñānadeva. *Jñāneśvari*. B. A. Bhide, ed. Mumbai: Keshav Bhikaji Dhavale, 1996.

Khanolkar, G. D. *Marāṭhī Vāṅmaya Kośa*. Mumbai: Mahārāṣṭra Rājya Sāhitya Saṁskṛti Maṇḍala, 1977.

Kiehnle, C. *Songs on Yoga: Texts and Teachings of the Maharashtrian Nāthas*. Stuttgart: Franz Steiner Verlag, 1997.

Kulkarni, S. B. Nāmadevagāthyātīla Cār Nāmdev. *Yugavāṇī*. Bombay (July–August, 1992): 6–10.

Lorenzen, David. *Praises to a Formless God: Nirguṇī Texts from North India*. Albany: State University of New York Press, 1996.

McGregor, R. S. *The Round Dance of Krishna, and Uddhav's Message*. London: Luzac, 1973.

Mahipati. *Bhaktavijaya*. Bombay: Nirnaya Sagar, 1915 [1762].

Mokashi, D. B. *Palkhi: An Indian Pilgrimage*. Philip C. Engblom, trans. Albany: State University of New York Press, 1987.

Molesworth, J. T. *Marathi-English Dictionary*. Pune: Shubhada-Saraswat Prakashan, 1996 [1831].

More, S. "Nāmadeva's *Tīrthāvaḷī* and the Vārkarī Tradition." In *Studies in South Asian Devotional Literature*. A. W. Entwistle and Francoise Mallison, eds. New Delhi: Manohar, 1994, 169–74.

Novetzke, Christian. "Divining an Author: The Idea of Authorship in an Indian Religious Tradition." *History of Religions* 42.3 (February 2003): 213–42.

Pollock, S. "The Cosmopolitan Vernacular." *Journal of Asian Studies* 57, 1 (1998): 6–37.

Raeside, I. "The Mahānubhāvas." *Bulletin of the School of Oriental and African Studies* 39, 3 (1976): 585–600.

———. *Gadyarāja: A Fourteenth-Century Marāṭhī Version of the Kṛṣṇa Legend*. Bombay: Popular Prakashan, 1989.

Sakaḷa Santa Gāthā: *Nāmdev Gāthā*. [1999]. Ed. T. H. Avate [1908], R. C. Dhere [1983], and Sakhare [1999]. Pune: Varda.

Sand, E. R. "*Mātāpitṛbhakti*: Some Aspects of the Development of the *Pundalika* Legend in Marathi Literature." In *Devotional Literature in South Asia: Current Research, 1985–1988*. R. S. McGregor, ed. Cambridge: Cambridge University Press, 1992.

———. "The Gopālakalā as Reflected in the *Pāṇḍuraṅgamāhātmya* of Prahlāda Maharāja and the Abhaṅgas of Tukarāma." In *Studies in South Asian Devotional Literature*. A. W. Entwistle and Francoise Mallison, eds. New Delhi: Manohar, 1994, 121–34.

Schomer, Karine, and W. H. McLeod, eds. *The Sants*. Berkeley: University of California Press, 1987.

Singh, N. *Bhagata Nāmdeva in the Guru Grantha*. Patiala: Panjabi University, 1981.

Sontheimer, G. D. *Pastoral Deities in Western India*. Delhi: Oxford University Press, 1989.

Subhanda, P. S. *Śrī Nāmadevarāyañcī Sārtha Gāthā*. Pune: Namdev Shimpi Samaj, 1960.

Tulpule, S. G. *An Old Marathi Reader*. Pune: Venus Prakashan, 1960.

———. *Classical Marathi Literature: From the Beginning to AD 1818*. Wiesbaden: Otto Harrassowitz, 1979.

Vaudeville, Charlotte. *L'invocation, Le Haripath de Dhyandev*. Paris: Ecole Francaise d'Extreme-Orient, 1969.

———. *A Weaver Named Kabīr*. Delhi: Oxford University Press, 1993.

———. *Myths, Saints and Legends in Medieval India*. Delhi: Oxford University Press, 1996.

Zelliot, Eleanor. *Studies in Early Modern Indo-Aryan Languages, Literature, and Culture*. A. W. Entwistle, ed. New Delhi: Manohar, 1999a.

———. *Home, Family and Kinship in Maharashtra*. I. Glushkova and R. Vora, eds. New Delhi: Oxford University Press, 1999b.

Chapter 8

Dance before Doom
Krishna in the Non-Hindu Literature of Early Medieval South India

Anne E. Monius

Krishna shows up in the strangest of places in the early medieval narrative poetry of Tamil-speaking South India. Perhaps most striking is the fact that none of this literature is explicitly Hindu, much less devoted to Krishna. In the *Cilappatikāram*, a long and beautiful poetic narrative composed perhaps in the fourth or fifth century, a text often assumed to be Jain but of uncertain sectarian affiliation,[1] a compassionate herdswoman known as Mātari, in whose care the heroine Kaṇṇaki has been left by her husband, calls to her daughter and the local girls:

> Let us dance the *kuravai* [dance] which Māyavaṉ [Krishna] and his elder brother danced along with Piññai [Krishna's consort] of long spear-like eyes . . . [so that] Kaṇṇaki, a jewel among women on earth, may see it.[2]

The *Maṇimēkalai*, another long and beautiful poetic narrative dating from the sixth century and often paired with the *Cilappatikāram* as its "twin," tells the story of a young woman's gradual awakening to the Buddha's *dharma*.[3] The narrative action suddenly shifts, in chapter 19, from Maṇimēkalai herself heroically feeding the hungry masses from her prison cell to the king of the royal capital of Pukār frolicking with his queen in the royal gardens. Seeing three lovely birds dancing about a tank, the king mistakes them for Krishna, his elder brother, and Piññai dancing the dance known as the *kuravai*. A few lines later he worships a dark green bamboo tree as Krishna and a "*katampu* tree thick with white flowers" (*vāl vī ceṟinta maṟā am*) as Krishna's fair-complexioned elder brother.[4] Virtually no other reference is made to Krishna or to Vaishnava traditions in either text. While Krishna is a Hindu deity well known for his dancing, this particular dance of Krishna, his older brother, and his favorite consort—identified by both texts specifically as the kuravai dance—is unknown to any northern Krishna sources. What do these two substantial scenes mean in each of these non-Hindu Tamil texts, and why do they suddenly appear, seemingly interrupting the flow of the main narrative?

This chapter will explore the nature of these two scenes of Krishna's kuravai dance in the *Cilappatikāram* and the *Maṇimēkalai*, examining each in narrative context and in relation to each other. Like the supposedly "twin" texts that share several characters and subplots, these references to Krishna, Balarāma, and Piññai obviously share a common referent. What are these two extended scenes of Krishna's dance doing in these Buddhist (*Maṇimēkalai*) and perhaps Jain (*Cilappatikāram*) narratives? What, if anything, can each suggest about the place of Krishna worship in the early medieval Tamil literary and religious landscape, at least as seen through the eyes of non-Hindu communities?

Before delving into these "alternative" Tamil materials, it would perhaps be useful to say just a few words about Krishna's more "normative" dance, the *rāsa-līlā* or *rāsakrīḍa* described in, among other places, the "Rāsapañcādhyāyi" section of the ninth-century *Bhāgavata Purāṇa*, in book ten, chapters 29 through 33.[5] Here the stunningly handsome and sexually alluring Krishna plays his flute, calling the *gopī*s out of their homes in the midst of their daily round of activities (and here no single gopī is highlighted as Krishna's favorite). Krishna then abandons them, as each girl is filled with pride at the thought that she alone is the true love of the Lord. The gopīs then proceed to search everywhere for their Lord, singing of their love for him and the anguish at their separation all the while. Krishna finally reappears, and the dancing proper begins: multiplying himself so that each girl has a partner and thinks herself the only one so engaged in rapturous dance with the Divine, all dance in a series of small circles as a crowd of celestial beings looks on. Finally exhausted, all plunge into the river Yamunā for a refreshing bath. This story of the circle dance of Krishna with his beloved gopīs, found in various forms in the *Vishnu Purāṇa* and the *Brahma Purāṇa*[6] and retold countless times in Sanskrit and in a variety of regional languages, is also commonly depicted in visual form, as the *rāsamaṇḍala*, the circle of gopīs, each with her own dance partner, with Krishna also positioned in the center of the circle.

Whatever the precise nature of Krishna's kuravai dance in Tamil literature, it is certainly *not* the rāsa-līlā. As mentioned above, the references to Krishna's dance in the Buddhist *Maṇimēkalai* occur in the middle of the text, when the action suddenly shifts away from Maṇimēkalai herself to the beautiful royal gardens of Kāvirippūmpaṭṭiṉam, where the Cōḻa king frolics with his queen, whose beauty is likened to that of the goddess Śrī (xix.55). Surrounded by birds and bees in a grove of flowers, the king looks toward the garden's tank. The text describes the scene as follows (xix.61–66):

> He felt joy within at seeing to one side there
> a peacock and peahen joining with a swan from the tank
> who had left behind its mate.
> [All three birds] extended their wings and danced about.
> [The king] looked at them and thought:
> "This is the *kuravai* dance danced by Māmaṇivaṇṇaṉ
> [Krishna], his elder brother, and Piññai!"[7]

A few lines later, the king spots some lovely trees and imagines them as Krishna and his brother Balarāma (xix.75–78):

> Seeing the *katampu* tree thick with white flowers and the
> bamboo tree with green roots and dense green foliage,
> [the king] worshiped and praised them with his fair hands
> that were adorned with royal ornaments,
> thinking that [the two trees] were Neṭiyōṉ [Krishna] and the
> one [born] before [him] standing [there].[8]

The king and his queen then simply move on to other parts of their royal park, enjoying the flowers and trees and accompanied by a group of courtesans.

This rather brief but central element in the king's visit to his royal gardens—and the nature of the kuravai dance itself—is greatly elaborated upon in the seventeenth chapter of the *Cilappatikāram*, entitled simply "The *Kuravai* Dance of the Herdswomen" (*Āycciyar kuravai*).[9] At this point in the narrative, the virtuous heroine of the story, Kaṇṇaki, has been left in the care of the herdswoman, Mātari, as her husband, Kōvalaṉ, has gone off to nearby Maturai to attempt to sell their sole remaining possession of worth: Kaṇṇaki's golden anklet. Preparing to make butter for the court of the royal Pāṇṭiyaṉ king sitting on the throne in Maturai, the capital city, Mātari calls on her young daughter, Aiyai, to dance the kuravai dance because she witnesses evil omens:

> The milk has not curdled in the pot;
> the bull with the big hump sheds tears from his fine eyes;
> something [evil] will happen.[10]

As above, Mātari then issues the command to dance:

> "Let us dance the kuravai which Māyavaṉ and his elder brother danced along with Piññai of long spear-like eyes. . . ." Indeed it [the dance] was a prayer that the [impending] evil might depart from the cows and calves.[11]

Seven young girls, in what Hardy assumes to be a holdover from some sort of Tamil folk religion,[12] each then choose a bull to raise as their own. Each girl is then assigned by Mātari a musical note to represent and a role to play in the dance. Each takes her position in the circle, and the dance begins: while dancing in the circle, the girls sing of the deeds of Māyavaṉ or Krishna and the beauty of his favorite young girl, Piññai. They praise and worship the Lord in song throughout the course of the dance, and end with an invocation that Krishna not only protect their cattle, but also their Pāṇṭiyaṉ king:

> May the god who has been extolled in the *kuravai* which we have thus danced remove the afflictions suffered by the cows! May the drum of the Pāṇṭiyaṉ king . . . who wears on his own head the crown of the king of gods armed with with the victorious thunderbolt—may this drum, beaten with the stick, bring about day by day the victory over his enemies, so that all other kings take fright.[13]

The kuravai dance is one that appears many times in various contexts throughout the classical Tamil Caṅkam poetic corpus.[14] Hardy, as noted above, assumes it to be a bit of Tamil folk culture working its way into the highly sophisticated literary narrative that is the *Cilappatikāram*. At several places in the classical poetic anthology known as *Kalittokai*, mention is made of a bullfight, followed by a dance called the *kuravai*.[15] In the Caṅkam literary corpus governed by a sophisticated aesthetic of landscape, kuravai dances are performed particularly by people of the hills and the seaside, and are also mentioned in association with war. Given the close connection of the Tamil deity, Murukaṉ, with hills, seaside, and war, the kuravai dance is most often associated with him.[16] This association of the kuravai dance with Krishna or Māyōṉ (as he is often known in Tamil), in other words, is quite unique to the *Cilappatikāram* and the *Maṇimēkalai*, with the exception of a few references in the poetic anthology mentioned above, the *Kalittokai*.[17]

What no scholar has considered, however, Hardy's impressive study of the connections between bullfights and dancing as indicative of an early "southern Krishnaism" included, is the narrative context in which the *Maṇimēkalai* and the *Cilappatikāram* present Krishna, his brother, and favorite female companion in dance and song. As stated above, the *Maṇimēkalai* is clearly Buddhist in its orientation; the *Cilappatikāram*, of unclear sectarian affiliation and often thought to be Jain, is clearly *not* a Bhāgavata or specifically Vaishnava text, and ultimately ends with expressions of profound devotion to its virtuous heroine, Kaṇṇaki, made goddess. Where Hardy and others have read each text's description of the kuravai as straightforward evidence of the early state of devotion to Krishna in the Tamil-speaking region, the literary sophistication of each text belies such a simple reading. Where each depiction of the kuravai dance is placed in the text reveals less about actual practices of Krishna devotionalism in early medieval South India than it does about non-Hindu attitudes toward the cult and worship of the dark-skinned dancer divine.

Despite the fact that the cowherdess, Mātari, tells her daughter to draw together her friends and enact Krishna's dance in order to dispel the evil omens she has just witnessed, the kuravai dance in both the *Cilappatikāram* and the *Maṇimēkalai* clearly functions in each narrative as a portent of impending doom, doom on a far grander scale than uncurdled milk and cows in pain. In the *Cilappatikāram*, for example, immediately after the conclusion of the dance, Kaṇṇaki learns of her husband's unjust and untimely execution at the hands of the Pāṇṭiyaṉ king of Maturai, and hears the dire prediction from a heavenly, disembodied voice: "A raging fire will consume this city" (an allusion to Kaṇṇaki's growing rage, which will culminate in her tearing off one of her own breasts and flinging it at the city, sending Maturai up in flames).[18] In the *Maṇimēkalai* disaster is forestalled only a bit longer; after the king's dalliance in the garden, Maṇimēkalai persuades him to convert his royal prison into a hospice for wandering ascetics. Immediately after the king orders the razing of the prison, he learns of the violent death of his son, the prince Utayakumaraṉ. In each case, the kuravai dance of Krishna occurs immediately prior to the climactic event of the main narrative: the burning of Maturai in the *Cilappatikāram* and the brutal slaughter of Utayakumaraṉ in the *Maṇimēkalai*. Within only a few hundred lines of his reveries in the garden, the king of Kāvirippūmpaṭṭiṉam will be forced to contemplate the cruel murder of his only son; the dance of Mātari's cowherding neighbor girls ultimately fails to forestall the inevitable news that Kaṇṇaki's husband has been killed by a thieving royal goldsmith and an injudicious king, and the subsequent fury of Kaṇṇaki that will result in the destruction of a great royal city. Far from staving off tragedy, as Mātari insists the kuravai dance will do in the *Cilappatikāram*, the dance of Krishna in these two texts actually *signals* impending doom.

What is one to make of this? Why might Krishna and his kuravai dance be perceived and presented in this way through non-Hindu, non-Vaishnava eyes? On the one hand, one might be tempted to contemplate larger mythological issues in Hindu literature, to consider what Wendy Doniger has called the theme of "death as dancer in Hindu mythology."[19] Considering the two types of dances performed by Śiva—the terrifying *tāṇḍava* dance of destruction and the gentle and generative *lāsya* dance with his consort—Doniger notes that "the two dances, erotic and deadly, are often interchangeable from a cosmic point of view."[20] Given the fact, noted by many scholars, that the deities of Tamil literature tend to share or transfer qualities from one to another with an ease not found in Sanskrit mythology—as Vidya Dehejia has noted, to cite but one example, images of the dancing Śaiva saint, Campantar, have been mistaken in museums and catalogs the world over for dancing Krishna (only the gesture of the right hand is different)[21]—perhaps the presentation of the kuravai dance in the *Maṇimēkalai* and the *Cilappatikāram* amounts to a transference of the "dance of death" more commonly associated with Śiva to Krishna. Krishna here, for historically obscure reasons, has perhaps acquired the deathly aspects of Śiva's tāṇḍava dance, ushering in scenes of tragedy and violent destruction of life with his ironically gentle dance with his elder brother and favorite cowherding girl.

Yet, given the very specific details attached to each presentation of the kuravai dance, such a mythological explanation seems, perhaps, unlikely. Both texts, for example, are insistent that worship of the deity Krishna is an explicitly royal activity. The Cōḻa king in the *Maṇimēkalai* sees Krishna everywhere in his beautiful park, in the animals, the birds, the flowering trees. The *Cilappatikāram* likewise draws unmistakable connections between worship of Krishna and the Pāṇṭiyaṉ king of Maturai; it is the kuravai dance that should make his drumbeat strong, striking fear into the hearts of his enemies.[22] If one considers Krishna's dance in narrative context, this royal attachment to the god, and the dance's protective powers, prove ironic. The dance does nothing to halt impending disaster, specifically disaster striking at the heart of the king and his royal family. The king's son is murdered in the *Maṇimēkalai*, and, in the *Cilappatikāram*, once the king realizes that he has been unjust in killing Kaṇṇaki's husband, he and all his family die of shame right there on the spot. Not only is the kuravai dance of Krishna impotent when it comes to averting disaster, but the dance cannot even save Krishna's most powerful earthly patrons: the king and his royal family.

What is the point of inserting these scenes of the kuravai dance of Krishna, only to show immediately the inability of such a dance to work efficaciously in the world, in these two early medieval—and non-Hindu—texts? Interestingly, the point seems *not* to be to prove devotion to the Hindu god Krishna to be entirely wrong, or weak, or objectionable. In neither text does the king overtly "convert" to the religious orientation championed by the narrative as a whole. Even in the *Maṇimēkalai,* where the king survives his son and lives to see another day, there is no indication that he "becomes" a Buddhist. Rather—and this is quite telling—he engages in the sorts of ethical activity that the young heroine, Maṇimēkalai, prescribes (such as converting the royal prison into a resthouse for ascetics). In both texts—especially in the extended treatment of the kuravai dance found in the *Cilappatikāram*—the dance is presented quite positively, as aesthetically pleasing, full of worship and love for the Lord, in short, as a beautiful expression of devotion to Krishna and a celebration of the love between him and the girl Piññai. Yet something is clearly missing: the Pāṇṭiyaṉ king who worships Krishna fails to realize his error in mistakenly killing Kaṇṇaki's husband, and he and all his subjects suffer dire consequences; the king and his wife-beautiful-as-Śrī in the *Maṇimēkalai* suffer the tragic loss of their son, a prince who ruthlessly and inappropriately pursued the story's young heroine and who was largely governed by his hormones rather than by his head. In short, both royals, absorbed as they are in the worship of Krishna, seem to be lacking a certain moral or *dharmic* sensibility.

It is clearly this element of ethical reflection, of concerning oneself with right ways of living in the world, that both the *Maṇimēkalai* and the *Cilappatikāram* present as missing in the devotion of the kuravai dance of Krishna. Both texts, in different ways, are very concerned with the presentation of *karma* (Tamil *viṉai*). In the religious and cultural milieu of early medieval South India where it has been suggested that the Ājīvika notion of *niyati* or "fate" presented a potent challenge to brahminic notions of karmic cause and effect,[23] both the *Maṇimēkalai* and the *Cilappatikāram* emphasize repeatedly their different visions of karmic activity in the world.[24] In the *Cilappatikāram,* arguably the earlier of the two texts, karma is very much a force in the world, "trapping" characters in its "net." At *Cilappatikāram* xiii.94–95, for example, Kōvalaṉ, waiting with his faithful wife on the outskirts of Maturai, receives a note from Mātavi asking what she has done to deserve such suffering; realizing that Mātavi is without fault, Kōvalaṉ exclaims, "It is *my* bad karma (*tītu*)!" and his burden of guilt or depression over abandoning his lover is thus lifted (*taḻarcci nīṅki*).[25] At xxvi.156, the unscrupulous goldsmith of the Pāṇṭiyaṉ king approaches Kōvalaṉ, who is "trapped in the net of [his] bad karma" (*tīviṉai mutirvalaic ceṉṟupaṭṭiruṇṭa*).[26] Before the queen of Maturai and immediately following her confrontation with the unjust Pāṇṭiyaṉ king (xxi.1), Kaṇṇaki declares, "I am a slave to bad karma!" (*koṭuviṉai āṭṭiyēṉ*).[27] While karma leaves the principal characters of the *Cilappatikāram* seemingly without choice and without much directly articulated sense of personal responsibility, in the *Maṇimēkalai* there is a greater suggestion of moral activity in the world as able to shape karma, as able to transform one's future lives through attention to proper conduct in this life. The *Maṇimēkalai* reworks the *Cilappatikāram*'s presentation of karma in particular in order to articulate a specifically Buddhist vision of karma at work in the world, karma that is redefined in terms of the complex causal processes that underlie the Buddhist doctrine of interdependent origination. The rustic dance of Krishna, his brother, and Piññai, aesthetically pleasing as it may be, especially to the king, cannot intervene in the working out of karma, in the karmic processes that are ultimately said in each text to drive the narrative to its bloody and violent climax. Only ethical action in the world—and the *Maṇimēkalai* makes that clear through its commands to the king to change his manner of rule—can change the contours of karma; even the king, devoted to Krishna and his kuravai dance, is powerless to change what he does not understand. This the *Maṇimēkalai* in particular makes explicit later in the narrative; in cataloguing the shortcomings of various non-Buddhist schools of thought, the text reserves its shortest condemnation, interestingly enough, for the Vaishnavas. What is wrong, in a world ruled by karma, with Vaishnava theology? Only one thing, says the Buddhist *Maṇimēkalai*: the doctrine that "Nāraṇaṉ [Nārāyaṇa] is [our] protection" (xxvii.99).[28]

Considered in these narrative contexts, the *Cilappatikāram* and the *Maṇimēkalai* present very sophisticated and very subtle condemnations of Krishna devotion, particularly as a royal practice, in its lack of attention to the importance of ethical awareness in the context of a world ruled by karmic processes. Through the image of the kuravai dance, Krishna is presented in an aesthetically pleasing way, yet his dance is somehow limited, impotent against larger forces at work in the narrative—and, by extension, the world—that shape the human condition. Singing, dancing, and lovemaking all yield their aesthetic delights, but Krishna's dance is powerless to help the king who does not understand the proper way to rule, to live.

The question remains, of course, to what extent the kuravai dance of Krishna represents a truly "alternative" vision of Krishna as assumed throughout this volume. Certainly the early Tamil dance of Krishna is not the rāsa-līlā of Sanskritic tradition; yet, at the same time, the Tamil association of Māyōṉ and Māyavaṉ with an elder brother, a female milkmaid, and the rustic landscape of the forest echoes the Sanskritic traditions of Krishna and his gopī friends so ubiquitious in later North Indian text and imagery. What is perhaps most compellingly "alternative" about this kuravai dance of the Tamil Krishna is, in fact, its incorporation into narratively crucial sequences in non-Hindu texts. As presented in both the *Cilappatikāram* and the *Maṇimēkalai*, the power and beauty of Krishna's bucolic dance are seemingly recognized, even celebrated in the case of the *Cilappatikāram*'s extended treatment of the dance. Yet for the literary connoisseur familiar with the Vaishnava imagining of the dancing deity, each narrative subtly undermines the efficaciousness of such a dance. The beauty of Krishna, without an accompanying understanding of the power of karmic forces at work in human lives, is a portent of doom in these early medieval non-Hindu texts. The dance to ward off evil becomes instead a prelude to the suffering of karmically unaware royal patrons and devotees.

Notes

1. The *Cilappatikāram* tells the story of a young couple, Kaṇṇaki and Kōvalaṉ, whose conjugal devotion is tested by Kōvalaṉ's dalliance with a young courtesan, Mātavi. Eventually returning penniless to his ever-faithful wife, Kōvalaṉ takes Kaṇṇaki with him to Maturai in search of a fresh start on life. When Kōvalaṉ attempts to sell the couple's sole remaining possession of value—Kaṇṇaki's anklet—in the city, he is accused by an unscrupulous goldsmith of having stolen the anklet of the queen, and he is put to death by the king's henchmen. Kaṇṇaki, in a rage at the unjust murder of her beloved husband, tears off her breast and hurls it at the city, sending Maturai up in flames. The final section of the text narrates Kaṇṇaki's deification and the erection of a shrine in her honor by a powerful South Indian king. For a brief overview of the text and a detailed bibliography of the secondary scholarship, see Kamil V. Zvelebil (1995), 144–48.

2. Iḷaṅkovaṭikaḷ, *Cilappatikāram mūlamum Arumpatavuraiyum Aṭiyārkkunallāruraiyum*. U. Vē. Cāminātaiyar, ed. (1892; reprint ed., 1978), 438:

> *maṇṇiṉ mātark kaṇi ākiya kaṇṇakiyum tāṉ kāṇa . . . māyavaṉuṭaṉ tam muṉāṭiya . . . vēl neṭuṅkan piññaiyōṭu āṭiya kuravai āṭutum yām*

All references to the text of the *Cilappatikāram* below are taken from Cāminātaiyar's edition. Translation by Friedhelm Hardy (1983), 173.

3. The *Maṇimēkalai* obviously builds on the story told in the earlier *Cilappatikāram*. Its central character, Maṇimēkalai, is the illegitimate daughter of the wayward Kōvalaṉ and his mistress, Mātavi. For an overview of the text and a list of references to both translations and secondary scholarship, see Kamil V. Zvelebil (1995), 408–13.

4. Cāttaṉār, *Maṇimēkalai.* U. Vē. Cāminātaiyar, ed. (1898; reprint ed., 1981), xix.76, 209. All references to the text of the *Maṇimēkalai* below are taken from Cāminātaiyar's edition.

5. For both the Sanskrit text and an accessible English translation, see *Rāsapañchādhyāyī, in Śrīmad Bhāgavatam,* Swami Gambhirananda, ed. and trans. (1997).

6. See Friedhelm Hardy (1983) for the relevant Sanskrit passages, 592–99, and an English translation, 91–97.

7. *Maṇimēkalai,* 208:

puṇar tuṇai nīṅkiya poykai aṉṉamoṭu
maṭamayil pēṭaiyum tōkaiyum kūṭi
iru ciṟai viritta āṅku eḻuntu uṭaṉ koṭpaṉa
oru ciṟaik kaṇṭu āṅku uḷ makiḻvu eyti
māmaṇivaṇṇaṉum tam muṉum piññaiyum
āṭiya kuravai iḵtu ām eṉa nōkkiyum

8. *Maṇimēkalai,* 209:

pācilai ceṟinta pacuṅkāl kaḻaiyoṭu
vāl vī ceṟinta marā am kaṇṭu
neṭiyōṉ muṉṉoṭu niṉṟaṉaṉ ām eṉat
toṭi cēr ceṅkaiyil toḻutu niṉṟu ēttiyum

9. *Cilappatikāram,* 437–57.

10. *Cilappatikāram,* 437:

kuṭappāl uṟaiyā kuviya imil ēṟṟiṉ
maṭam kaṇ nīr cōrum varuvatu oṉṟu uṇṭu

Translated by Friedhelm Hardy (1983), 172.

11. See note 2 above.

12. Friedhelm Hardy (1983), 182: ". . . it may be suggested here that the *Āycciyarkuravai* documents areas of popular folk culture in literature for the first time."

13. *Cilappatikāram,* 446:

eṉṟi ām
kōtta kuravai uḷ ēttiya teyvam nam
āt talaip paṭṭa tuyar tīrkka vēttar
maruḷ vaikal vaikal . . .
veṟṟi viḷaippatu . . . koṟṟattu
iṭip paṭai vāṉavaṉ muṭit talai uṭaitta
. . . teṉṉavaṉ kaṭippu ikum muracē

Translation by Friedhelm Hardy (1983), 178.

14. Caṅkam literature, literally literature of the "community" or "assembly" (Sanskrit *saṅgha*), refers to a collection of six anthologies (*tokai*) and nine long poems (*pāṭṭu*) composed in Tamil during the early centuries of the common era. Addressing themes of love and war, these poems are noted for their unique style and aesthetic, and deal largely with nonreligious or "secular" topics. For a brief overview of the tradition, see Kamil V. Zvelebil (1995), 108–10.

15. Friedhelm Hardy (1983), 618.
16. Friedhelm Hardy (1983), 618–20.
17. Friedhelm Hardy (1983), 185–89.
18. *Cilappatikāram*, xviii.53, 460: *oḷḷeri uṇṇum ivv ūr*
19. Wendy Doniger O'Flaherty (1980), 201.
20. Wendy Doniger O'Flaherty (1980), 204.
21. Vidya Dehejia (1988), 50–51.
22. Friedhelm Hardy (1983), 610–12, assembles the classical Tamil literary evidence for a connection between Krishna as Neṭiyōn̲ and the Pāṇṭiyas.
23. R. Vijayalakshmy (1988).
24. For a detailed discussion of the *Maṇimēkalai* and the *Cilappatikāram* on the question of karma, see Anne E. Monius (2001), 71–74.
25. *Cilappatikāram*, 333–34.
26. *Cilappatikāram*, 421.
27. *Cilappatikāram*, 483.
28. *Maṇimēkalai*, 310: *nāraṇan̲ kāppu en̲r̲u*.

References

Cāttan̲ār. *Maṇimēkalai*. U. Vē. Cāminātaiyar, ed. Cen̲n̲ai: Ṭākṭar U. Vē. Cāminātaiyar Nūlnilaiyam, 1898; reprint ed., 1981.

Dehejia, Vidya. *Slaves of the Lord: The Path of the Tamil Saints*. New Delhi: Munshiram Manoharlal, 1988.

Hardy, Friedhelm. *Viraha-bhakti: The Early History of Kṛṣṇa Devotion in South India*. Delhi: Oxford University Press, 1983.

Iḷaṅkōvaṭikaḷ. *Cilappatikāram mūlamum Arumpatavuraiyum Aṭiyārkkunallāruraiyum*, U. Vē. Cāminātaiyar, ed. Cen̲n̲ai: Ṭākṭar U. Vē. Cāminātaiyar Nūlnilaiyam, 1892; reprint ed., 1978.

Monius, Anne E. *Imagining a Place for Buddhism: Literary Culture and Religious Community in Tamil-speaking South India*. New York: Oxford University Press, 2001.

O'Flaherty, Wendy Doniger. "Death as a Dancer in Hindu Mythology." In *Sanskrit and Indian Studies: Essays in Honour of Daniel H. H. Ingalls*. M. Nagatomi, et al., eds. Boston: Reidel, 1980, 201–16.

Śrīmad Bhāgavatam. Swami Gambhirananda, ed. and trans. Mumbai: Bharatiya Vidya Bhavan, 1997.

Vijayalakshmy, R. *Tamiḻakattil ācīvakarkaḷ*. Cen̲n̲ai: International Institute of Tamil Studies, 1988.

Zvelebil, Kamil V. *Lexicon of Tamil Literature*, Handbuch der Orientalistik, Zweite Abteilung: Indien. J. Bronkhorst, ed. New York: E. J. Brill, 1995.

Chapter 9

Hero of Wonders, Hero in Deeds
Vāsudeva Krishna in Jaina Cosmohistory

Jerome H. Bauer

Jaina teachers have masterfully adapted the Hindu Krishna stories popular among their laity, retelling them to conform to Jaina orthodoxy and to promote orthopraxis. As such, Jaina Krishna mythology presents an "alternative" Krishna, which stands alongside the well-known Hindu stories that are simultaneously popular among the Jaina laity. Krishna in the Jaina tradition is no more a god than any other human being capable of liberation from karma and rebirth, but neither is he an ordinary human being. Krishna Vāsudeva is on the one hand an archetypal Jaina layman and king, and, on the other hand, a *Śalākāpuruṣa*, an Illustrious Person, with an illustrious destiny. As such, he has the role of *karmavīr*, or "action hero," rather than *dharmavīr*, the role played by the Tīrthaṁkaras (exemplary saviors) and other renunciants. As karmavīr, he is also *āścaryavīr*, "wonder hero," an apparent worker of miracles. The Śvetāmbara Canon tells a unique story of an *Āścarya* or singular wonder worked by Krishna: his marvelous journey across spatiotemporal boundaries to rescue the heroine Draupadī.

While Hindu theologians and devotees are divided on the issue of whether Krishna, as an *avatāra* of Vishnu, is subject to the "law of karma," Jaina teachers have no doubt. Krishna must go to hell, for his (necessary) deeds of violence, committed to uphold the order of society and divine custom, and for his well-known sexual misconduct, as troubling for Jaina teachers as it is for their Christian and Muslim counterparts. Sin is real, and must be worked off, even by such an exalted personage as Krishna, whose penultimate destiny is to become an exalted Jaina teacher, the twelfth (or thirteenth) Tīrthaṁkara of the coming age, and whose ultimate destiny is liberation. Both Jaina sects, Śvetāmbara and Digambara, agree on most details of this story.

It is commonplace, especially among Jaina scholars with an ecumenical bent, to downplay the differences between the two major sects of Jainism. Often this can be justified, since the doctrinal differences do sometimes seem trivial. Furthermore, although the Digambaras reject the entire *Āgama*, or Canon, upon which Śvetāmbara mythology is based, Digambara mythology is actually very similar to that of the Śvetāmbaras. Both Digambara and Śvetāmbaras accept the same "Universal History"[1] or "cosmohistory,"[2] with some differences of detail reflecting differences of doctrine. This basic scheme incorporates much Hindu mythology, for example the stories of the *Rāmāyaṇa* and the *Mahābhārata*, with suitable changes according to Jaina doctrine and tradition. For the most part, the two sects tell the same stories.

Even so, Digambaras make a point of rejecting some stories from the Śvetāmbara Canon, notably those concerning the ten Aścaryas, singular wonders or authorized rule violations accepted only by the Śvetāmbaras. Since one of these Āścarya stories involves Krishna[3] (the distinctively Jaina tale of Krishna's wondrous journey across the mythical Salt Sea to rescue the heroine Draupadī), it is not possible to write a comprehensive article about "the Jaina Krishna" without pointing up the difference between Śvetāmbara and Digambara. The Draupadī story is omitted without comment from Digambara texts, making it difficult to determine the issues behind its rejection. Just because there is so little discussion, we cannot assume that there is no significance to this omission. Indeed, this is the main point of distinction between these two alternative Krishna mythologies, and also a point of distinction between the Jaina and Hindu story cycles.[4] I will argue that this story is significant for its *Āścaryatva*, its "Āścarya-ness," an untranslatable word, denoting a concept unique to Śvetāmbara Jaina mytho-doctrine.[5]

Stories of Krishna in his role as karmavīr address the Jaina problems of suffering and ethical paradox, while stories of Krishna regarded as āścaryavīr address the problem of bafflement, the sense of anomaly in the world.[6] The Jaina Krishna stories, like the Hindu myths, may be treated as part of the "miracle system" of the Jaina faith, the cultural system of anomaly containment and boundary maintenance. I argue that the "Jinalogians," Jaina teachers such as Hemacandra, knew what they were doing in this regard. Like mainstream Protestant cessationists who tried to debunk Catholic shrine miracles,[7] some Jaina teachers tried to debunk exaggerated miracle claims made for Krishna by Hindus. Like the Deists and Protestant cessationists, some authors of the Jaina Krishna stories seem to have adopted a rather "antimiracle" perspective. Many doctrinally astute Jaina layfolk today are similarly hostile to the miraculous, yet for all that, they know how to tell stories of wonder, for homiletic purposes.

Karmavīr Krishna (Krishna the Layman)

In his classic article, "Dharmavīr Mahāvīr ane Karmavīr Krishna,"[8] the Śvetāmbara Jaina pandit Sukhlal Sanghvī contrasts the "action hero" Krishna with the "soteriological hero" Mahāvīra, comparing their mythological life stories, which run parallel to one another, at some points and in some respects. Whatever the similarities, their respective roles are quite different: Mahāvīra is a Tīrthaṁkara, literally a "Ford Maker" or "Maker of the River Crossing," founder of a *Tīrtha*, a soteriological dispensation;[9] this role is equivalent to a Buddha, or a god. A Tīrthaṁkara is an exalted teacher in his (or her) last birth, before liberation. Krishna, on the other hand, is a mere Vāsudeva, a kind of Illustrious Person (*Śalākā-puruṣa*) ranking below a Cakravartin (a Universal Emperor),[10] and well below a Tīrthaṁkara. His role is to wield temporal power, to be a warrior in the literal sense, rather than to pursue the higher calling of renunciation and spiritual conquest. Krishna the Vāsudeva is still active in the ordinary world of *saṁsāra* (transmigration), and he must work off his karma in subsequent lifetimes, including time spent in the Jaina hells (which are really temporary purgatories). He is karmavīr not only in the sense of karma as "action," but also in the sense of karma as "sin": that is, the results of actions that obscure the soul's innate properties of infinite bliss, knowledge, and potency.

The Jaina Krishna myths portray Krishna as an extraordinary Jaina layman, a kind of superhero, but without innate superpowers. He has an illustrious destiny, as a result of the fruition of karma from past lives. However, the apparently miraculous or marvelous events associated with his life (well known to both Jainas and Hindus), are performed by the Jaina gods, who are themselves beings within saṁsāra, or by wizardlike "flying ascetics," who play the role of tricksters (often aided by personified *vidyā-s* or magic arts). These gods and wizards, preternaturally long-lived and able to cross spatial boundaries, keep the narrative moving along, but are clearly inferior to Krishna. Krishna, in turn, is subordinated to the Jaina ascetics, especially those on the direct path to liberation, who are omniscient, in contrast to Krishna, who has rather limited knowledge.[11] Krishna is not, for the Jainas, an incarnation of god, but an illustrious (although hardly exemplary), layman. The Jaina Krishna is the cousin of the twenty-second Tīrthaṁkara, Neminātha, who is Krishna's compatriot in war and peace, before his renunciation of the life of a layman.

We cannot know for certain the intentions of the authors of Jaina texts, since we have very little biographical information about them. The great Jaina theologian and mythographer Hemacandra is said to have answered an indignant Hindu, who objected to the Jaina claim that the Pāṇḍavas became Jainas, by asserting that if you count the Pāṇḍavas' descendents as Pāṇḍavas, then *some* of the Pāṇḍavas must have become Jainas.[12] This story suggests self-conscious irony on Hemacandra's part. Some scholars suggest that the Jaina mythographers deliberately coopted Hindu mythology to serve the spiritual and entertainment needs of their laity.[13]

Padmanabh S. Jaini (Jaini 1993) labels the Jaina *Purāṇas* as a "countertradition," while John E. Cort (Cort 1993) emphasizes the parallel development of traditions that borrowed back and forth from one another. These positions are not mutually exclusive. The term "countertradition" implies intentionality on the part of the author/redactor (perhaps with the negative connotations of artificiality and censorship), while the term "parallel tradition" suggests a natural cultural flow, out of human control, "in the air" like language change. The term "alternative tradition," on the other hand, suggests a middle way between these two views: Jaina stories may be viewed as skillful means to convey Jaina doctrines and cultural values, organically Jaina mytho-doctrine.

Hindu Krishna, Jaina Krishna

Various Jaina Krishna stories are told in many texts, including several Digambara Purāṇas, for example, the *Pāṇḍava Purāṇa* of Śubhacandra (sixteenth century),[14] the *Mahāpurāṇa* of Jinasena (ninth century), the *Harivaṃśa Purāṇa* of Punnāṭa Jinasena (eighth century), and Śvetāmbara Caritras, such as the *Triṣaṣṭiśalākāpuruṣacaritra* of Hemacandra (twelfth century). The Jaina Krishna stories are called "Harivaṃśa Purāṇas," after the oldest version of the Hindu Krishna story cycle.[15] Biographies of Neminātha are more numerous than those of other Tīrthaṁkaras in the Jaina Purāṇas, and these texts presumably all contain references to Krishna.[16] Some stories involving Krishna are also told in the Śvetāmbara Āgama or Canon, and its commentaries, for example, the *Sthānāṅga Sūtra* and the *Jñātādharmakathāṅga Sūtra* (redacted in the fifth century CE). This chapter will follow Hemacandra's elaborate account, with supplementary references from other texts.[17]

Krishna's Marvelous Nativity and Youth

The nativity story of Krishna is somewhat similar to the Hindu account, although the birth story of his elder brother, Balarāma, is quite different.[18] A prophecy that the seventh child of Devakī will kill the evil king Kaṁsa leads the latter to order their destruction. When the seventh child, Krishna, is born, Kaṁsa's watchmen are put to sleep by the child's guardian deities, and the newborn is exchanged with a girl child by Krishna's father, Vasudeva.[19] As in the Hindu tale, Krishna is raised by his foster father, Nanda, in a village of cowherds.

Hemacandra gives the "true story" of the well-known miracles attributed to the young Krishna. For example, the child Krishna is afflicted by two Khecarī witches, Śakuni and Pūtanā, whose enmity for Vasudeva from past lives is directed against his son. Śakuni stands on a cart and calls to Krishna, while Pūtanā thrusts her poisoned breast into the baby Krishna's mouth. Krishna's guardian deities overturn the cart and kill both Khecarīs with it. Nanda asks some herdsmen who witnessed the event what had happened, and they insist that the child Krishna killed the two demonesses without help. Thus is born the legend of Krishna's preternatural[20] strength, arising out of the misunderstanding of ignorant herdsmen.

Krishna becomes the darling of the herdsmen, milkmaids, and other local people. They spoil Krishna, failing to restrain him properly. His mischievousness and unrestrainability are not celebrated as in the Hindu tradition, and the people's affection, or *bhakti*, for Krishna is not liberating but the opposite: an obstacle to good discipline, a bond to be broken before salvation is possible. Even so, the appeal of the naughty boy Krishna is not denied.[21]

Vasudeva hears about Krishna's exploits, and fears that Kaṁsa will learn of them and become suspicious, so he sends Balarāma to be Krishna's protector. The two grow up as brothers, learning archery and earning the admiration of the milkmaids (*gopīs*), who neglect their work to watch the inseparable pair. Krishna delights in seizing bulls by the tail, demonstrating his extraordinary if not preternatural strength with feats unmatched by his older brother.

Hemacandra describes Krishna's youthful exploits with the gopīs: their love for him is "like a disease," which drives them to distraction and the neglect of their duties. They knock over the milk pails and milk the cows on the ground without knowing it. The gopīs pretend terror in order to be comforted by Krishna, and they pretend not to know the words of songs, in order to be taught by him. They touch him whenever they can, their passion unconcealed.[22] This is as explicit as Hemacandra's narrative gets. We are not given much detail about Krishna's sport with the gopīs, but we are told that the two youths pass eleven years happily in this way. During that time Krishna's cousin, the Tīrthaṁkara Neminātha, is born.

Meanwhile, Kaṃsa, learning that his nemesis is alive, arranges a wrestling match to trap Krishna, and is killed. Krishna marries Kaṁsa's sister, Satyabhāmā, and heads west to found the city of Dvārakā, where he and Balarāma rule in great wealth and splendor, protected by their guardian deities.[23] There they are assailed by the father of Kaṃsa's widow, the Prativāsudeva Jarāsandha.

The Jaina Mahābhārata and the Killing of Jarāsandha

Although the *Triṣaṣṭiśalākāpuruṣacaritra* recounts many of the events of the great Hindu epic *Mahābhārata*, there is no discrete chapter that may be labeled "the *Jaina Mahābhārata*," corresponding to "the *Jaina Rāmayaṇa*." Nevertheless, the basic story of the familiar epic is told, with some specifically Jaina stories interspersed. As in the Brahmanical epic, King Pāṇḍu gives the throne to Yudhiṣṭhira, and the Pāṇḍavas gamble away their kingdom to Duryodhana and go into exile in the forest with Draupadī. They make their way to Dvārakā, where they join forces with Krishna, Balarāma, and all the Yādavas, and dwell there happily for some time, unknown to their enemy Jarāsandha. Eventually, Jarāsandha learns their location, and gathers a huge army, including Duryodhana and all the Kauravas, to assail Krishna's forces. Jarāsandha's forces are met by the army of Krishna and Balarāma, along with all the Pāṇḍavas, Krishna's father Vasudeva, and even the Tīrthaṃkara Neminātha. Both sides have the help of minor divinities and wizards.

Conspicuously absent from Hemacandra's account is any sort of "Jaina Bhagavad Gītā." Krishna does not have to urge a reluctant Arjuna to do his duty as a warrior, as in the Hindu *Mahābhārata*. Instead, Hemacandra provides a sort of "anti-Gītā." On the eve of battle, the Prativāsudeva is given the opposite advice: Jarāsandha's minister Haṁsaka advises him not to fight, but this good advice is rejected.[24] Other Jaina Purāṇas do have Krishna urging bravery in battle, but he is not Arjuna's charioteer, as in the Hindu story.[25]

The Tīrthaṁkara Neminātha, out of loyalty to his relatives, wishes to participate in the battle. Neminātha at first takes a mainly defensive role in the battle, deflecting the weapons of the enemy and destroying their bows, apparently without taking life. However, when the battle seems to be turning to the enemy's advantage, he is urged to intervene. The Tīrthaṁkara, "without anger," blows his conch shell, terrifying the enemy and encouraging the Yādava army. With a rain of arrows, he destroys the banners, bows, chariots, and crowns of the opposing warriors. Up to this point he has killed no one; now, ". . . the Master alone killed a lac of crowned kings. What are mountains compared with the ocean enraged?"[26] The Tīrthaṁkara acts without anger, yet he is compared to a force of nature, an ocean acting as if enraged. Neminātha has the opportunity to slay Jarāsandha, but he reflects that it is the role of "Vishnu" (the Vāsudeva) to slay the "Prativishnu" (the Prativāsudeva), and so spares his life. Krishna intercepts Jarāsandha's own *cakra* (discus), which has glanced off his breast, and offers to let him live and rule his kingdom as his vassal. When this offer is rejected, Krishna kills Jarāsandha with his own weapon,[27] fulfilling his cosmic role.

Krishna is not wounded by the enemy's discus: "The cakra, as if weaned apart by the policy of dissension, stayed at his side and Krishna took it in his hand like his own majesty that had been offered. 'The ninth Vāsudeva has arisen,' the gods, proclaiming this, rained a shower of perfume and flowers on Krishna from the air."[28] Previously, Krishna's legendary exploits have been explained away as exaggerations of his extraordinary strength, or as accomplished by his guardian deities. The fulfillment of his destiny, however, is accompanied by a genuine miracle: Krishna's invulnerability to a discus that no other warrior could withstand, and Krishna's veneration by the gods, who perform the usual *atiśayas* (signs and wonders) that accompany an auspicious event.[29] The auspicious event of Krishna's fulfillment of his destiny as a Vāsudeva is preceded by a most unusual and seemingly inauspicious event: a future Tīrthaṁkara's slaying of enemies, performed dispassionately, as if by a force of nature.

Krishna's Līlā, Neminātha's Līlā

Just as Neminātha performs the actions of war dispassionately, in a Jaina counterpart to the *karma yoga* prescribed by the Hindu Krishna in the Hindu Bhagavad Gītā, so he performs the actions of love. Krishna, in the Jaina stories, is an "action hero" par excellence, passionate and violent, in pointed contrast to Neminātha, who is "in this world but not of it," even in his early life as a layman.

Some time after the great battle, the young Neminātha, in a competitive mood, challenges Krishna to arm wrestle, and wins.[30] Krishna, now submissive to Neminātha, offers him the freedom of his harem, and embarks on a determined campaign, in collusion with his wives, to turn Neminātha toward a life of pleasure. He is perhaps motivated by good-natured sibling rivalry, if not jealousy. Having suspected that his cousin will be not an ordinary mendicant but a Tīrthaṁkara, he attempts to bring Neminātha "down to earth," to share with him the life of a layman, before his destined elevation. The scenes of Krishna and Neminātha sporting together in Krishna's garden and pool, along with Krishna's wives, decorate many Jaina temples, and these stories are well known to contemporary Jainas. Despite all of this, Neminātha is unmoved. He finally agrees to be married, but only out of politeness. On the advice of the Jaina layman, Krishna, he does what is expected of him (*dharma*) in the matter of marriage, just as Arjuna in the Hindu Bhagavad Gītā does what is expected of him (dharma) in battle, on the advice of the Hindu God, Krishna. He does so dispassionately, and with some intimation of the events to follow: "At the right time I must necessarily do what is suitable for myself."[31]

Neminātha, having agreed, reluctantly, to marry, is on his way to the wedding ceremony when he hears the cries of all the animals about to be killed for the feast,[32] who beseech his protection, each in its own language. He orders all the animals set free and renounces marriage and the lay life at that moment. Krishna and the other Yādavas cannot dissuade him from taking the mendicant path without delay. This story is often told by contemporary Jaina layfolk as an example of *ahiṃsā*, and the scene is frequently depicted in temple illustrations and even occasionally in metal images.

The Death and Destiny of Krishna

After the destruction of Dvārakā, Krishna wanders in the forest and is accidentally shot in the foot by a hunter. After a thousand-year lifespan, Krishna dies "in cruel meditation," making a *nidāna* (sinful resolution)[33] of revenge. Since the last moment of his life is spent in cruel thoughts, he must go to hell.[34] He is destined to become the twelfth, or according to the *Samavāyāṅga Sūtra*, the thirteenth[35] Tīrthaṁkara of the coming *utsarpiṇī* (ascending world-period).[36]

Although the Jainas make a point of sending Krishna to hell for his various sins, they also make a point of giving him the most exalted status in the far future: the status of Tīrthaṁkara, exemplary teacher. Krishna is an example to all layfolk, who live ordinary lives, which necessarily involve the commission of sins and the accumulation of karma.

Jaina Krishna, Jaina Vishnu

In the Hindu Purāṇas, the preserver god Vishnu descends to earth as an *avatāra*, or incarnation, in order to protect the earth and its denizens from the oppressive weight of the demons, led by their king, Kaṁsa. It is Krishna's mission, his dharma, to kill his nemesis Kaṁsa and thereby uphold ($\sqrt{}$*dhṛ*) the balance of the cosmos. In the Jaina stories, the nemesis of Vāsudeva Krishna is not Kaṁsa but Jarāsandha (although both are killed by Krishna). In the Hindu stories, Vishnu becomes Krishna in order to kill a demon king. In Hemacandra's *Triṣaṣṭiśalākāpuruṣacaritra*, Krishna becomes "Vishnu" (a mere title) when he fulfills his destiny by killing his worthy opponent. The gods proclaim, "Jarāsandha has been killed and Krishna has become Vishnu."[37]

Even so, Krishna must perform a ritual feat of strength before the assembly of the gods, in order to convince them that he has indeed earned the status of Vishnu. Krishna must lift a special stone. As the ninth and final Vishnu of this descending period, he can barely get it off the ground, due to the general waning of powers.[38] In the Hindu Krishna mythology, the avatāras of Vishnu seem to follow an evolutionary progression from sea, to land, to partially human, to deformed human, to fully human. No such progression is evident in the Jaina mythology: the powers of the Vishnus decline along with those of all other transmigrating beings.

The Wondrous Journey

Krishna's Trip to Avarakaṅkā

The Digambara and Śvetāmbara mythologies of Krishna are substantially the same, with the exception of one incident: Krishna's trip across the Salt Sea to rescue Draupadī. This unusual event is classified as the fifth Āścarya, or Wonder, according to the Śvetāmbara Āgama, or Canon.

The ten Āścaryas are listed in the *Sthānāṅga Sūtra* (redacted in the fifth century CE), and the stories are told in various Śvetāmbara canonical and noncanonical texts, and in the commentaries upon these texts, especially the *Kalpa Sūtra* embryo-transfer sequence. The story of Draupadī's abduction[39] and rescue by Krishna is told in the *Jñātādharmakathāṅga Sūtra* and by the eleventh-century commentator, Abhayadeva. In his commentary on *Sthānāṅga Sūtra* (777),[40] Abhayadeva tells this story in full, in contrast to his truncated versions of most of the other Āścarya stories, perhaps attesting to the story's popularity at that time.

The basic story, as told by Abhayadeva, is as follows: Draupadī, wife of the Pāṇḍavas, was abducted by King Padma, who dwelt in the city of Avarakaṅkā, capital of the Bharatakṣetra (that is, the India region) of the continent of Dhātakīkhaṇḍa. This abduction was carried out by a demigod. Having received information about this event from the "flying ascetic" Nārada, Krishna Vāsudeva, after having propitiated the god named Susthita, lord of the Lāvaṇa Samudra, or Salt Sea. Krishna then crossed over the deep ocean along with the five Pāṇḍavas. They conquered King Padma in a decisive battle and rescued Draupadī. Kapila Vāsudeva heard the news of the arrival of Krishna Vāsudeva from the Jina Munisuvrata (the Tīrthaṁkara of that continent), and came respectfully for the sight (*darśana*) of Krishna. At that moment Krishna was already crossing back over the ocean. When Vāsudeva Kapila blew his conch, and Krishna did the same thing, they simultaneously heard the sound of each others' conches.[41]

This "continent," Dhātakīkhaṇḍa, is really a "heterocosm," another world within the realm of saṃsāra (transmigration), with different physical and temporal laws. For example, liberation is possible in some of the other continents that are not in Avasarpiṇī. Just as, in the past, human beings had greater physical stature and powers, the same may be true in these other worlds. Even so, these heterocosms or continents, although they may be subject to different rules in many respects, are all part of the Jaina multiverse, and must conform to the overarching rules of Jaina cosmohistory, including the laws governing Āścaryas. The general rule is that the other continents have the same ten Āścaryas as our own, with some qualifications. Krishna's crossing of the Salt Sea is thus no ordinary ocean voyage, but has the character of a wondrous journey, across the boundary between worlds. Since this is a "one time only" event (as far as we in this age and place are concerned), the effect of the story is to reinforce our idea of secure and impermeable boundaries between worlds, a comforting thought indeed.[42]

The account of the rescue of Draupadī given by Hemacandra is not substantially different, but he supplies a few more details. Krishna refuses an offer from Susthita to rescue Draupadī, and to drown King Padma and his army as well. He asks instead for an unobstructed path over the water for the six chariots of the Pāṇḍavas and himself, so that Draupadī may be won back in honorable battle.[43]

The Pāṇḍavas are first defeated and forced to retreat. Krishna assumes the form of a "man-lion." He stamps his feet, and the walls of King Padma's city tumble down. Padma, terrified, flees for protection to Draupadī. She advises him to put on women's clothing and stand behind her, asking for protection. This he does, and his life is spared.[44]

Note the assumption, by the Jaina Krishna, of the form of another Hindu avatāra of Vishnu: the man-lion. Ordinarily, changes of bodily form are not permissible according to the Jaina rules of karma, but here is an exception.[45] Hemacandra is apparently troubled by the implications of this unnatural, magical transformation into a man-lion, and so attempts to account for it in terms of orthodox Jaina karma doctrine, using the technical term *vaikriya-samudghāta*,[46] which involves the expansion of one's space-points and reconfiguration around a new center. This power, possessed by gods, hell dwellers, and some humans, enables one to move great distances and walk through solid objects.

Here it is also used to explain Krishna's anomalous transformation into a giant man-lion with truly superhuman strength. Generally this preternatural power is available to humans only for a special purpose; Krishna does not have it in his home world.

Hemacandra's account of the near meeting of the two Vāsudevas is substantially the same as Abhayadeva's, except that Hemacandra has Krishna blow his conch with the sound of distinct words, "We have come far. We must not talk with you."[47] Hemacandra has the Vāsudeva Kapila depose the humiliated and contrite King Padma and put his own son on the throne.

Hemacandra adds a postscript to the story of Krishna's wondrous journey. Krishna, having returned to his home continent, seems to have lost his supernormal powers. He is tired crossing the river Ganges, and accomplishes this feat only with help of the river goddess. Presumably his guardian deities are involved as well, although they are not mentioned. In Dhātakīkhaṇḍa he had the powers of a god, including the divine power of vaikriya-samudghāta. In the other world, he did not need the help of any other being. Here, in his own world, he is a mere mortal once again. Hemacandra is clear: Krishna's odyssey has not transformed him into a superhuman or a god.

All the commentators agree that this story's Āścaryatva, the reason for its classification as a Singularity, a Wonder of the Age, is the temporary presence of two Vāsudevas in the same *sthāna*, the same cosmohistorical "slot," at the same time, along with their exchange of conversation through their magic conches. The story is thus an Āścarya because of a boundary violation, not because of any particular violation of a karmic rule of rebirth, even though some versions of the story seem to involve anomalous transformations outside the natural law. The "Fifth Wonder" is not really a violation of the Jaina law of karma, but a violation of an order of custom, the rules of the Jaina cosmohistory.

The commentaries on the *Kalpa Sūtra* maintain that each "continent" or "subcosm" has ten identical Āścaryas, but this is qualified by excluding two Āścaryas that involve boundary violations, including Krishna's trip to Avarakaṅkā. The sixteenth-century polemicist Dharmasāgara, although following tradition in most respects, makes one interesting departure. He clarifies the comment about the impossibility of the repetition of Krishna's trip from one continent to another by stating a reason: Vāsudevas of other worlds may not come here for a visit, as Krishna did to them. There is no logical reason why this should be so in terms of Jaina cosmology, but it is explicable in terms of religious authority. What if people could reasonably expect a visit from an extracontinental Vāsudeva at any time? That belief could be dangerous, spawning millenarian movements.

Therefore, a containment strategy becomes necessary: the Vāsudevas of other subcosms are declared unavailable to us. The violation of cosmic boundaries is relegated to the distant past, *anantakālāt*, "an endless time ago."

Digambara Krishna's Wondrous Journey

Digambara mythology includes a story, not found in the Śvetāmbara accounts, that preserves some features of Krishna's wondrous journey across the waters. According to the *Mahāpurāṇa* of Puṣpadanta, this incident occurs after the death of Kaṁsa and the pursuit of the Yādavas by Jarāsandha.[48] After the rumor is spread that the Yādavas have perished in a fire, Jarāsandha's army withdraws, and the Yādavas set up camp on the seashore. At this point, the god Naigama (called by the Śvetāmbaras Hariṇegamesī), "dressed as a horse," appears to Krishna and asks him to ride on his back, and to have the Yādava army follow. Krishna does so, and the horse enters the sea, the waters are parted, and Krishna and the Yādavas follow the narrow strip of land to the site of Dvārakā, where they found their city.

This story is remarkable in a number of ways. First, the parting of the waters is unambiguous, in contrast to the story of the rescue of Draupadī, which seems to refer to "walking on water."[49] Second, this is a Digambara reference to Hariṇegamesī, a sinister child-seizing and embryo-seizing demon or demigod who doubles as god of procreation. The Śvetāmbaras have domesticated him, turning him into Indra's obedient infantry commander, an angelic being who may grant a child at the request of a devotee, but will take one away only on orders from Indra. The Digambaras reject the major Śvetāmbara stories about him, such as the canonical Āścarya story of Mahāvīra's embryo transfer, and he is less prominent in their mythology. Here he appears as a magical helper of Krishna, without any association with procreation. He leads Krishna and his army to a safer camp across an unspecified body of water. This journey, although wondrous, involves no boundary violation, as does the Śvetāmbara story of Krishna's journey between worlds. The story is "āścarya," a wonder, but not "Āścarya" in the Śvetāmbara sense, a proper noun referring to one of a set of ten "Strange Events," authorized rule violations.

Krishna Stories Told by Contemporary Jaina Laity

Even a casual observer of contemporary Jaina layfolk cannot fail to notice that many Jainas seem more familiar with the Hindu stories of Rāma and Krishna than with those of their own tradition. For example, on a pilgrimage bus tour of Gujarat in 1989, I observed a group of Jaina laymen reading comic books on the life of Krishna published by the International Society for Krishna Consciousness (ISKCON). When I asked them what Jainas believe about Krishna, they seemed embarrassed, apologetic, and noncommittal. This reaction suggests some awareness of the Jaina Krishna stories, but a clear preference for the Hindu versions. Is this typical? I have not conducted a systematic, scientific survey of Jaina attitudes toward Krishna, so we cannot generalize. However, a formal interview with Dr. Shah,[50] a Gujarati-born American Śvetāmbara Jaina, one of the founders and trustees of a major North American Jaina temple, in the summer of 2000, may provide insight into how some educated Śvetāmbara Jainas regard Krishna and Neminātha.

Dr. Shah, before agreeing to the interview, insisted that Jainas have very few Krishna stories, since Krishna is only the helper of Neminātha, about whom many stories are told. We ought to tell stories about the Tīrthaṃkara, not his helper (just as Hindus should worship Ganesh and not his helper, the rat). The first story told by Dr. Shah involves Krishna's interaction with Neminātha, clearly establishing the superiority of the latter. He told this story over the phone, "off the top of his head," and later repeated the same story in the interview. During the interview, I was accompanied by two friends, one of whom is a Hindu.

According to the story, Neminātha has all twelve thousand of his monks line up to receive Krishna's homage. Krishna and his servant bow to each in turn, but at the end of the line, Krishna feels tired, and says so in the presence of Neminātha, who admonishes him. According to Neminātha, Krishna, because of his involvement in the Pāṇḍava wars, has earned a place in the seventh and lowest hell. If he had not said "I am tired," he would have "destroyed seven *narakis* [hells]," but because of his mistake, he was destined to go to the third hell. At this point Dr. Shah asked pardon of my Hindu friend for saying Krishna was in hell, and he clarified the status of Krishna according to Jaina doctrine. He repeated his contention that Jainas tell very few Krishna stories, preferring stories of the Tīrthaṁkaras. He concluded the story by returning to the servant of Krishna, who accrued neither good nor bad karma by bowing to the monks, since he was merely following orders.

Next, Dr. Shah told the story of Krishna's wife Rukmiṇī and the reason for her twelve-year separation from her son Pradyumna. This is the karmic consequence of her having touched a peahen's egg with her hand, which was stained with red powder. The mother peahen rejected the egg for twelve days, after which a rainstorm washed off the powder and she resumed incubating the egg. Hemacandra tells a similar story, in which Krishna plays only a marginal role and his wives, in their maternal roles, are central.[51]

Dr. Shah next told the story of Krishna's brother Gajasukumāla, who became a monk shortly after his marriage. The offended father-in-law tortured the meditating monk with burning coals. Gajasukumāla endured the pain with equanimity, forgave his tormenter, and thereby became omniscient.[52]

According to Dr. Shah, "basically, this is the Krishna story," even though only one of the three stories directly involves Krishna. I then asked about the Draupadī story. which he proceeded to tell, although without much detail. Draupadī is kidnapped by somebody from "another part" of the universe. Krishna, being a Vāsudeva, came to know she was there, and went to rescue her (no mention is made of the wondrous passage of the ocean). Since two Vāsudevas cannot be in the same place, Krishna blows his horn in order to let his counterpart know of his presence, so that he may withdraw. This is done so as not to violate the custom, or rule, according to which two Vāsudevas may never meet or converse. In this account, the two Vāsudevas avoid each other out of courtesy and a sense of protocol, instead of missing each other by chance, as in the Hemacandra and *Kalpa Sūtra* commentarial versions. Dr. Shah notes that the Vāsudeva from our world can travel to another "place," but in our world there can never be two Vāsudevas, Cakravartins, or Prativāsudevas at the same time (apparently following the tradition of Dharmasāgara's commentary, according to which Vāsudevas from another continent may not come here).

I asked about the many miracles and marvels attributed to Krishna. Dr. Shah responded: "We do not believe in miracles, none whatsoever. Everything happens because of our own karma; God does not give us anything, nor does he create." This was followed by a long discourse on karma, merit, heavens and hells. By "miracles" Dr. Shah apparently thought I meant special answers to prayers (in the Christian and Hindu traditions), and the miracle of creation ex nihilo, according to the Christian tradition. He did not discuss any superhuman feats performed by Krishna or associated with his life story.[53]

I next asked why Krishna had to go to hell: was it because of his deeds of violence, even though he was just performing his role as a king or a Vāsudeva? Dr. Shah responded that Vāsudevas always go to hell, but he went on to emphasize that Tīrthaṁkaras such as Mahāvīra, Śāntinātha, and Neminātha were kings too, but they gave it up. Dr. Shah was emphatic that Krishna had free will: he could, and should, have given up his worldly life at any time. As to the specific act that led him to hell, Dr. Shah said it was no specific act, but the fruition of karma, which is constantly accumulated and constantly coming into fruition.

I next inquired about Krishna's dalliance with the cowherd women (gopīs), and his many wives. According to Dr. Shah, "We do not have these stories," and "these are just stories for laypeople." He went on to explain that, for erudite Hindus, the various gopīs are symbols for the various cakras (power centers of Haṭha Yoga).

In the absence of a scientifically conducted survey of lay Jaina attitudes toward Krishna, Dr. Shah's remarks perhaps may be taken as representative, if not of Jaina laymen, at least of doctrinally astute Jaina community leaders, on the *moksha-mārga*, the path to liberation.[54] The emphasis on Neminātha as opposed to Krishna, as well as his choice of stories, all underline the cardinal Jaina value of ahiṃsā, or noninjury (for example, the egg story, a tale tangential to the Krishna cycle but illustrative of the "natalist" side of Jaina tradition). I had to prompt him to tell the distinctively Śvetāmbara Draupadī story; this story is tangential as well, yet he could tell it without preparation, suggesting that it is in his repertoire of stories. Finally, it is noteworthy that, although Dr. Shah always seizes every opportunity to discourse on the "orthodox" doctrine of karma, and to emphasize the inefficacy of divine grace, and so on, his view of "the law of karma" is far from fatalistic. He stresses the free will of individuals to choose the path of perfection, asserting that even Krishna had that freedom, but decided not to exercise it. For Dr. Shah, karma is clearly a moral law, a cosmic legal system set up to give us opportunities for self-reform and character building, rather than a juridical law, a mechanical cosmic justice system. The juridical law of karma always dispenses "an eye for an eye," as in many of the Śvetāmbara Canonical texts—for example, the *Vipāka Sūtra*.[55] While not denying the inevitability of karmic retribution, Dr. Shah's view of the future is not pessimistic.

Conclusion: Jaina Krishna as Alternative Krishna

Do the Jaina Krishna stories represent an "alternative tradition" or "countertradition," or are they a "parallel tradition"? Is the Digambara version of the Krishna story a countertradition to the Śvetāmbara story, or vice-versa? It is difficult to establish the priority of these stories, as it is difficult to establish the motives of the authors (even though we know the authors and approximate dates for most of these texts). It is therefore difficult to give definitive answers to these questions. Even so, some striking differences are apparent, between the Krishna of Hindu and Jaina, Śvetāmbara and Digambara.

Jītavīr Krishna

Digambaras and Śvetāmbaras share a common mythology of "Universal History" or "cosmohistory": history of the Jaina "multiverse," composed of different worlds, in which time flows differently and natural laws governing bodily stature, and perhaps magical transformations, seem to function differently. Even so, all of these worlds are governed by the natural law of karma and subject to the same karmic rules of rebirth. For the Śvetāmbaras, all the worlds are also governed by the same "suprakarmic" order of divine custom, rules of precedent, ordained by the previously liberated Tīrthaṁkaras, which the gods are bound to uphold when karmic rules are broken, to restore the cosmic balance. This "order of custom" is seldom referred to or given a name, but in the *Kalpa Sūtra*, in one very significant context, this ancient custom is designated *"jīyaṃ,"* from Sanskrit *"jīta,"* "of old."[56] The Śvetāmbaras thus implicitly introduce into their mythology something which their theology, "Jinalogy," and philosophy will not allow: a quasi-theistic administrator of karma, available to solve problems of the coordination of karma, and to ensure its correct and just administration.

According to Hemacandra, the first Tīrthaṁkara Ṛṣabha is the "stage-director of the play of the order of the world."[57] In the *Kalpa Sūtra*, the gods may sometimes be called upon to intervene in the karmic process, in order to restore the immemorial custom (jīyaṃ), "as directed (or predicted) by the previous Tīrthaṁkaras" (Pkt. *puvvatitthayaraniddiṭṭhe*, Skt. *pūrvatīrthaṃkaranirdiṣṭa*).[58] How can a previously liberated Tīrthaṁkara direct the play of the world? If "all the world's a stage," and we are all actors in a play without an author, do any of us have free will? Could Krishna really have chosen other than he did, or was he, as a character type, fated to play the part written for him? What is the relationship between karma (which we can control), and fate (which is perhaps beyond our control)? Is this a realm of mystery officially beyond human understanding?

Krishna, at least in the Śvetāmbara tradition, acts as *"jītavīr,"*[59] "hero of the divine order," "superhero," or "hero of fate." He is a human preordained to enforce the suprakarmic order of divine justice, to establish "cosmodicy,"[60] preordained by the previously liberated Tīrthaṁkaras.

Karmavīr Krishna

A. L. Herman has coined the term "karmadicy" for what he calls the "karmalogical problem of evil," stated as follows: (1) if karma controls God, God is not omnipotent; (2) if God controls karma, God causes suffering; (3) either karma controls God, or vice-versa; (4) therefore, either God is not omnipotent, or God causes suffering.[61] Herman believes that the problem may be solved, in a Hindu context, by deifying "Karma Law," regarded not as an impersonal, mechanistic natural law, but as a kind of Person. Herman justifies this position on scriptural grounds. For the Jainas, however, there is "officially" no God, and so, the "karmalogical problem of evil" cannot arise. Even so, the collectively liberated Jinas are often called "God," especially by Jaina layfolk, although this usage is controversial. Dr. Shah, in a formal interview and in informal conversation, insists that Jainas do not believe in "a God as such." In place of a God who administers the law of karma to uphold cosmic justice, this cosmic justice is upheld by the will of the previously liberated Tīrthaṁkaras, who use the transmigrating gods to uphold the immemorial divine custom, in quite a paradoxical way. The "Jinalogical problem of evil" is extralogical.[62] Evil exists within saṃsāra, and is a problem only for beings who are not liberated.

Krishna, and Neminātha in the time before his liberation, are both karmavīr, although in different ways, corresponding to their different roles. Neminātha has the role held by the Hindu Krishna in the Bhagavad Gītā: he is Karmavīr, with a capital *K*, performing actions neither purposive nor nonpurposive, like a force of nature.[63] The Jaina Krishna is karmavīr with a small *k*, performing the passionate deeds of a warrior and suffering the consequences. In this sense, the Jaina Krishna can be called an "alternative Krishna."

Dharmavīr Krishna

The Jaina Krishna sets a generally bad example in his life as Krishna, but he has a role to play in the drama of the world, which is necessary to "uphold" (√*dhṛ*) the Jaina social order and cosmohistory. In the strict sense of the term, the Jaina Krishna is dharmavīr (dharma is the "right way to uphold the balance of the cosmos"). Also, Krishna, like the other Vāsudevas, will be a Tīrthaṁkara, an exemplary Dharmavīr, in the far future. So, what is taken away with one hand is given back with the other! Krishna's fate is expressed in terms of his karma: in these stories, everything happens because of karma, coordinated by Divine Omniscience (if not functionally Divine Omnipotence).

Āścaryavīr Krishna

Only for the Śvetāmbaras, Krishna is Āścaryavīr, that is, Wonder Hero, the only Vāsudeva of our world associated with an Āścarya, one of ten canonized, and therefore singularized, Wonders. His Wondrous Journey takes him to meet his otherworldly counterpart, the Vāsudeva Kapila, in a sort of folkloric doubling, which serves to amplify the fabulous crossing of boundaries. Not only is Krishna the only Vāsudeva associated with an Āścarya, he is the only non-Tīrthaṃkara Śalākāpuruṣa who is Āścaryavīr (the other being Mahāvīra, the Dharmavīr par excellence, whose embryo transfer and other life events are also Āścaryas). The Āścaryas can be interpreted as authorized rule violations, exceptions that prove the rule. Āścaryavīr Krishna is authorized to uphold the Jaina Dharma through his exceptional actions (karma), performed with passion, as befits a layman. His necessary actions uphold the usual and customary order of things, the Jaina cosmohistory.

Hemacandra tells the Krishna story like a cessationist Protestant, maintaining a limited age of miracles. The cessationists are antimiracle (disbelieving in significant wonders in the modern age), but pro-Miracle (believing in the Great Miracles of the Creation, the Incarnation, and the Resurrection). Similarly, Hemacandra takes pains to debunk the popular Hindu miracles of Krishna as legendary embellishments of extraordinary but not unnatural feats of strength. Hemacandra is anti-*āścarya,* but pro-Āścarya. His Krishna is Āścaryavīr, and atiśayavīr as well: wonders attributed to him are really the acts of his guardian deities, who truly have the power to perform preternatural wonders, within the law of karma and in accord with the order of custom.

Some modern Jainas tell these "alternative Krishna" stories, but, if Dr. Shah is typical (except for the Draupadī story, which is regarded as tangential), these are not told as "miracle stories" in any currently accepted sense of the term. "Miracles" and "Āścaryas" are consigned to a past age, and are soteriologically irrelevant. Two versions of the Krishna story are available to the Jaina laity: their own "karmavīr Krishna," and the "āścaryavīr Krishna" of the Hindus. A separate Jaina identity is maintained, expressible through stories of an "alternative Krishna," available in two alternative versions: Digambara and Śvetāmbara. These stories exemplify both the asceticist and natalist values shared by all Jainas, men and women.

Notes

1. This term "Universal History," *Universalgeschichte* or *Welthistorie,* is used by many Western scholars, including Helmuth von Glasenapp, Walter Schubring, Ludwig Alsdorf, Klaus Bruhn, A. K. Warder, Paul Dundas, and John E. Cort. See John E. Cort (1995), 479; John E. Cort (1993), 193–202. For a bibliography, see John E. Cort (1995). The Jaina Krishna mythology is set within this "Universal History," according to which every world age has a series of sixty-three "illustrious persons" (*Śalākāpuruṣas* for the Śvetāmbaras, *Lakṣaṇapuruṣas* for some Digambaras). Generally, twenty-four of them are Tīrthaṃkaras;

twelve are Cakravartins (Universal Monarchs); nine are Vāsudevas (heroes patterned on the Vāsudeva Krishna, who perform necessary deeds of violence), nine are Prati-Vāsudevas (the enemies of the Vāsudevas), and finally, nine are Baladevas (the elder brothers and helpers of the Vāsudevas, righteous Jaina kings, including the Jaina Rāma). In some early traditions, there are fifty-four or seventy-two Illustrious Persons. See John E. Cort (1993), 196–97.

2. I prefer the term "cosmohistory" to "Universal History" because the Jaina world may be considered a "multiverse," with many regions governed by different laws, in which time flows differently.

3. In this chapter, I use the English spelling "Krishna," rather than the Sanskrit *Kṛṣṇa* or Prakrit *Kaṇha*. Many Jaina reference works use the Prakrit form.

4. One easy way to tell a Digambara from a Śvetāmbara reference work is to look up the Krishna story and note the presence or absence of the word "Draupadī," or other key words relating to the Āścarya stories.

5. Mythology and doctrine are not clearly distinguished in Jaina tradition. Both are often glossed by English-speaking Jainas as "philosophy," in the original sense of "love of wisdom."

6. For a discussion of the problems of bafflement, suffering, and ethical paradox, see Clifford Geertz (1973).

7. For a history of the mainstream Protestant concept of a limited age of miracles, now often called "cessationism," and the recent demise of this idea, see Robert Bruce Mullin (1996).

8. Pandit Sukhlalji Sanghvi (1957).

9. In the Protestant Christian tradition, a dispensation is a discrete age with discrete properties or rules. Jaina cosmohistory may be characterized as dispensational in the general sense of the term.

10. A Vāsudeva is sometimes called an Ardhacakrin, literally "half a Cakravartin."

11. Krishna proclaims "I am not omniscient." Helen Johnson, trans. (1962), 212.

12. George Bühler (1936), 19–20.

13. According to Padmanabh S. Jaini, "Even a cursory glance at the Jaina Purāṇas makes it clear that the Jaina authors who composed them knew the Hindu Epics and Purāṇas well, studying them with the attention worthy of a board of censors examining the offensive portions of a story, and finally decided to rewrite the script in conformity with their own doctrines and sensibilities." Padmanabh S. Jaini (1993), 207.

14. Pravīṇacandra Jain, Darbārolāl Koṭhiyā, and Kastūrchandra Suman, eds. (1993), 96.

15. John E. Cort (1993), 191.

16. There are thirty-four biographies of Nemi, compared to twenty-nine of Śāntinātha, twenty-four of Ṛṣabhanātha, twenty-four of Pārśvanātha, nineteen of Mahāvīra, seventeen of Candraprabha, fourteen of Mallinātha, and twelve of Munisuvrata, according to Velankar, H. D., *Jinaratnakośa*, cited in John E. Cort (1993), 189.

17. Hemacandra's *Triṣaṣṭiśalākāpuruṣacaritra* is still the only Jaina Purāṇa translated in entirety into a European language, English. See John E. Cort (1993), 192–93.

18. In Hemacandra's account, Balarāma is conceived in, and born from, the womb of Rohiṇī. In the *Bhāgavata Purāṇa* and other Hindu texts, Balarāma is conceived in the womb of Devakī, Krishna's mother, and transferred to the womb of Rohiṇī by Yogamāyā, Vishnu's power of illusion personified as a goddess (Swami Tapasyananda, trans. 1981, 37–48), or Jagaddhātrī, the nurse of the universe (H. H. Wilson, trans, 1840, 400).

19. The previous six children of Devakī had been exchanged at birth with the stillborn babies of another woman by the deity of childbirth, "Hari's god" Hariṇegamesi, who synchronizes their reproductive cycles. See Helen Johnson, trans. (1962), 158–59.

20. Hemacandra portrays Krishna as a strong man, rather than a superman. Most of his deeds are neither supernatural (performed by God), nor preternatural (performed not by God but by angelic or demonic beings). Many of Krishna's "miracles" are really preternatural actions by his guardian deities, who follow laws appropriate to the *devagati*, the divine realm. Most of Krishna's own actions, including many that in the Hindu tradition are unambiguously miraculous, are portrayed by Hemacandra as unusual feats of strength, but not out of character for a heroic human. For discussion of the Hindu Krishna as strong man, see Benjamin Preciado-Solis (1984). For a history of the categories of "supernatural," "natural," and the unstable mediating category, "preternatural," see Lorraine Daston (1991). In a Jaina context, these three terms may be used to designate, respectively, the realm of liberated souls and the suprakarmic order of custom ordained by them, the natural law of karma, and the liminal realm of miscellaneous, morally ambiguous beings, such as *vidyādharas* (wizards), *yakṣas* (demigods), and so forth, who are within saṁsāra but sometimes have suprakarmic roles. Some Jainas, especially North American Jainas who are in dialogue with their Christian neighbors, are already beginning to use some of these Christian categories in their instructional materials. For example, Mahāvīra's soul before his birth is called an "angel," and so is the demigod Hariṇegamesi (whose role as messenger makes this term especially appropriate for him). See JAINA (1999), 97.

21. Helen Johnson, trans. (1962), 161–62.

22. Helen Johnson, trans. (1962), 163.

23. Helen Johnson, trans. (1962), 175–79.

24. Helen Johnson, trans. (1962), 224–26.

25. Padmanabh S. Jaini (1993), 221.

26. Helen Johnson, trans. (1962), 238.

27. Helen Johnson, trans. (1962), 240.

28. Helen Johnson, trans. (1962), 240.

29. For a discussion of *atiśayas*, *prātihāryas*, *Āścaryas*, and other terms comprising the Jaina "miracle system," see Jerome H. Bauer (1998).

30. Helen Johnson, trans. (1962), 249–50.

31. Helen Johnson, trans. (1962), 255.

32. Why animals would be killed at a Jaina wedding feast is not made clear.

33. Not all *nidānas* are made in the hour of death.

34. Helen Johnson, trans. (1962), 305. One's thoughts at the time of death are more likely to determine the fixing of life-span determining karma (*āyuḥkarma*), after which all other karmas fall into place. See Padmanabh S. Jaini (1980).

35. Mohan Lal Mehta and K. Rishabh Chandra (1970), vol. 1, 153.

36. Helen Johnson, trans. (1962), 297.

37. Helen Johnson, trans. (1962), 242.

38. Helen Johnson, trans. (1962), 242–43.

39. The Hindu Purāṇic and epic traditions contain stories of Draupadī's abduction and rescue, although these stories do not involve Krishna, nor do they involve a wondrous journey to another realm. According to Maurice Winternitz, "The whole episode of Draupadī's abduction [by the lustful king Jayadratha, told in the *Draupadīharaṇa*] is certainly only a duplicate of Sītā's abduction in the *Rāmāyaṇa*. In the latter this abduction is the nucleus of the whole legend and the poem whereas in the *Mahābhārata* Draupadī's abduction has almost no significance for the course of the story." (Maurice Winternitz, 1981, 481). See the *Draupadīharaṇa Parva* of the *Vana Parva, Mahābhārata*, chaps. 262–71; J. A. B. Van Buitenen, trans. (1975), 705–23; Vettam Mani (1975), 353. Draupadī is also abducted by the demon Jaṭāsura. See Mani (1975), 351. See also Vettam Mani (1975), 246, 548–52. Conspicuously absent from the Jaina Draupadī stories is the well-known account of her disrobing by the Kaurava Duśśāsana, and the miracle of her infinite sari (in some tellings, a boon of Krishna). Apparently, the Jaina "board of censors" found this story unacceptable. Perhaps the Śvetāmbara abduction story is a "counter tradition," a deliberately constructed substitute for the unacceptable story. However, the two tales are so different that this is unlikely. Alternatively, the story of Krishna's protection of Draupadī from molestation may have originated with the Jainas.

40. Sāgarānanda Sūri Jī Mahārāja and Muni Jambuvijayajī, eds. (1985), 349–50.

41. Abhayadeva clearly states that Kapila Vāsudeva blows the conch Pañcajanya, which, in Hemacandra's account, had been given to Krishna earlier by the lord of the Salt Sea, Susthita, before the foundation of Dvārakā. Did Krishna leave this conch behind for Kapila to find? Did both Vāsudevas have identical horns, both named Pañcajanya, both given to them by Susthita? Abhayadeva does not say. The other "continents" are identical yet different, in a mysterious way that does not bear too much scrutiny. Hemacandra does not name the conch of either Vāsudeva.

42. For discussion of singularization as a possible motive for canonization of Āścarya stories, see Jerome H. Bauer (1998).

43. Helen Johnson, trans. (1962), 276.

44. Compare the Hindu *Mahābhārata* story of Draupadī's abduction by King Jayadratha, the latter flees the battlefield, but is caught by the Pāṇḍavas

and humiliated by having his head shaven. Vettam Mani (1975), 353; J. A. B. Van Buitenen, trans. (1975), 722–23.

45. Under certain circumstances, karma bound as one type may come into fruition as another, but this would not apply here.

46. *Vaikriya-samudghāta* is the usual means of locomotion of the gods, and the audience is assumed to know this. It is not unknown in Jaina narrative literature for two accounts to be given of the motion of the gods, one vivid and descriptive, the other technical, as if the storytellers were assuming a dual audience, one with technical knowledge of the workings of the "natural law" of karma and the technical jargon of this literature, and a less sophisticated audience who respond better to pantomime. For example, in the Śvetāmbara *Kalpa Sūtra*, Hariṇegamesi's paces are described as events in real time, but the Prakrit term for *vaikriya-samudghāta* (*veuvviya-samugghāya*) is also employed, translated by Lalwani as "magical powers." (Kastur Chand Lalwani, trans. 1979, 19). For detailed discussion of *vaikriya-samudghāta*, based on Jaina commentaries, see Helen Johnson, trans. (1931), 118–19.

47. Helen Johnson, trans. (1962), 268. According to Muni Ratna Prabha Vijaya, "both the Vāsudevas met each other by the exchange of the sound of their individual conch. Such a thing had never happened; two Vāsudevas never meet each other, and therefore, this meeting is a strange event." Ratna Prabha Vijaya (1989), vol. 2.1, 43–44.

48. P. L. Vaidya, ed., and Devendra Kumar Jain, trans. (1970), xxiii.

49. The stories of Krishna's wondrous trip may be told as miraculous walking on the water (like Jesus) or miraculous parting of the waters (like Moses). This ambiguity is present in the early textual accounts, whose authors were probably not familiar with the Abrahamic stories. The trip itself may be regarded as "āścarya," not "Āścarya": a minor wonder, a mere detail.

50. This is a pseudonym.

51. Compare Helen Johnson, trans. (1962), 188–97. Hemacandra includes in his Krishna story a substantial amount of material concerned with women and motherhood, including the rivalries and reproductive competition of Krishna's cowives, in which Krishna and other men are marginalized. See Helen Johnson, trans. (1962), 212–14.

52. For Hemacandra's version, see Helen Johnson, trans. (1962), 281–93.

53. Dr. Shah seems to have assumed, not a "violation of natural law" definition of a miracle, nor an "evidentialist" definition (that is, miracle as public evidence for a doctrine, or its messenger), but instead, a "sacramentalist" definition. This is what "miracle" means to Hindus (and also, to many Catholics), but not to the Jainas. Dr. Shah rejects this sort of "miracle," along with the charismatic Christian experience of miracles as gifts of the Holy Spirit (Dr. Shah enjoys amicable dialogue with his Christian patients).

54. Perhaps Jaina women tell the stories with different emphasis (or perhaps not; Dr. Shah frequently consults laywomen during storytelling sessions).

55. For a discussion of the "law of karma" as a juridical law and as a moral law, see Bruce Reichenbach (1990). Reichenbach argues in favor of karma as a juridical law, since it apportions punishment, for crimes which we cannot remember, and so cannot repent. The Jaina karma mytho-doctrinal texts on karma, e.g., the *Vipāka Sūtra*, emphasizes the knowability of one's past lives and

sins, and the virtual certainty of liberation for anyone with the desire. Reichenbach characterizes the Hindu *darśanas* as libertarian or indeterminist with respect to moral agency, while Buddhism is characterized as compatibilist, stressing as it does the twelve-fold chain of dependent origination, on the one hand, and the Noble Eightfold Path to liberation, on the other hand. Reichenbach does not seem to know how to characterize Jainism in terms of Western philosophical ethics, but perhaps the label "compatibilism" is not far wrong. Order is compatible with freedom, justice with reform.

56. The *Kalpa Sūtra* uses this term, defined by the *Illustrated Ardhamāgadhī Dictionary* (Ratnachandraji Maharaj, 1988) as "traditional usage or convention," or duty; that which ought to be done," and derived from Sanskrit *jīta* (from Sanskrit 1√*jyā*, "become old" or "hoary with age"). In the *Kalpa Sūtra* (Kastur Chand Lalwani, 1979, 15), the phrase "*Taṃ jīyam eyaṃ tīya-paccuppaṇṇa-maṇāgayāṇam Sakkāṇam* . . ." is used, which may be translated, "In such a situation, it is the custom for the Śakras, in the past, present, and future." (Lalwani translates "*jīyam*" as "eternal practice.") My phrase, "the order of custom" is a construction, not a translation from any text. The concept of jīta implies a deterministic framework, in contrast to dharma, implying ethical indeterminism, two sides of Jaina compatibilism. For more on "Śakrajītatvāt" and "jīyam," see Jerome H. Bauer (1998).

57. Helen Johnson, trans. (1931), 155.

58. Kastur Chand Lalwani (1979), 4–5, 12–13. See Jerome H. Bauer (1998), 199–200.

59. In this section, I have followed Pandit Sukhlalji Sanghvi in using his coined terms, "Karmavīr" and "Dharmavīr," and have coined two new terms: "Jītavir" and "Āścaryavīr."

60. This term, "cosmodicy," has been suggested as a replacement for "theodicy" in nontheistic systems. (Wilhelm Halbfass, personal communication, spring 2000).

61. Arthur L. Herman (1987), 237.

62. For discussion of the Jaina theory of omniscience as paradoxical and "extralogical," see Ramjee Singh (1964), (1974a), (1974b).

63. Both Shankara and Rāmānuja agree that there is a class of actions, performed by God, which are neither purposive nor nonpurposive, and therefore God may act in the world, without accruing karma. See Bruce Reichenbach (1990).

References

Bauer, Jerome H. *Karma and Control: The Prodigious and the Auspicious in Śvetāmbara Jaina Canonical Mythology*, Ph.D. Dissertation, University of Pennsylvania, Department of Asian and Middle Eastern Studies, 1998.

Bühler, George. *The Life of Hemacandrācarya*. Śāntiniketan: Singhi Jaina Jñānapīṭha, 1936.

Candrasāgarasūrivaraḥ, Ācāryadeva. *Śrījñātādharmakathāṅge*. Śrī Ānandacandragrantha Series no. 18. Surat: Śrī Siddhacakra Sāhitya Pracāraka Samiti, 1952.

Cort, John E. "An Overview of the Jaina Purāṇas." In Wendy Doniger (1993), 185–206.

———. "Genres of Jain History." *Journal of Indian Philosophy* 23.4 (1995): 469–506.

Daston, Lorraine. "Marvelous Facts and Miraculous Evidence in Early Modern Europe," *Critical Inquiry* 18.1 (1991): 93–124.

Dharmasāgaragaṇi. *Kiraṇāvalīvṛtti* [*Kalpa Sūtra* commentary]. Śrī Ātmānanda Jaina Text Series (Grantha Ratna Mālā) no. 71. Bombay: Nirṇayasāgara, 1922.

Doniger, Wendy, ed. *Karma and Rebirth in Classical Indian Traditions*. Berkeley: University of California Press, 1980.

———, ed. *Purāṇa Perennis: Reciprocity and Transformation in Hindu and Jaina Texts*. Albany: State University of New York Press, 1993.

Geertz, Clifford. "Religion as a Cultural System." In Clifford Geertz, ed. *The Interpretation of Cultures*. New York: Basic, 1973, 87–125.

Hawley, John Stratton. *Krishna, the Butter Thief*. Princeton, NJ: Princeton University Press, 1983.

Herman, Arthur L. *The Problem of Evil and Indian Thought*. Delhi: Motilal Banarsidass, 1976.

———. "Karmadicy: Karma and Evil in Indian Thought." In S. S. Rama Rao Pappu, ed., *The Dimensions of Karma*. Delhi: Chanakya, 1987.

JAINA (Federation of Jain Associations in North America). *Jain Pathshala, Book for Level 3*. Jain Education Series no. 9. Phoenix: Jain Center of Greater Phoenix, 1999.

Jain, Pravīṇacandra, Dārbarolāl Koṭhiyā, and Kastūrchandra Suman, eds. *Jaina Purāṇa Kośa*. Rājasthān: Jainavidyā Saṃsthān, 1993.

Jaini, Padmanabh S. "Karma and the Problem of Rebirth in Jainism." In Wendy Doniger (1980), 217–40.

———. "Jaina Purāṇas: A Purāṇic Counter Tradition." In Wendy Doniger, ed. (1993), 207–49.

Jayavijayagaṇi. *Kalpadīpikā* [*Kalpa Sūtra* commentary]. Gujarat: Paṇḍit Maphatlāl Jhavercandra, 1934.

Jinendra, Varṇi. *Jainendra Siddhānta Kośa* (Hindi) 4 vols. Delhi: Bhāratīya Jñānapīṭha, 1970–73.

Johnson, Helen, trans. *Triṣaṣṭiśalākāpuruṣacaritra*, vol. 1. Gaekwad Oriental Series. Baroda: Oriental Institute, 1931.

———, trans. *Triṣaṣṭiśalākāpuruṣacaritra*, vol. 5. Gaekwad Oriental Series. Baroda: Oriental Institute, 1962.

Kanhāiyālāljī, Śrī Paṇḍitamuni Maharāj, ed. and trans. (Hindi and Gujarati) *Śrī Jñātādharmakathāṅga Sūtram*. Rajkot (Gujarat): Jainaśāstroddhāra Samiti, 1963.

———. *Śrī Sthānāṅga Sūtram*. Rajkot (Gujarat): Jainaśāstroddhāra Samiti, 1966.

Koṭiyā, Mahāvīr. *Jain Sāhitya Meṃ Kṛṣṇa*. Delhi: Bhāratiyā Jñānpīth Prakāśan, 1984.

Lakṣmīvallabha. *Kalpadrumakalikāvṛtti* [*Kalpa Sūtra* commentary]. Bombay: Nirṇayasāgarmudrālaya, 1918.

Lalwani, Kastur Chand, trans. *Kalpa Sūtra of Bhadrabāhu Svāmī*. Delhi: Motilal Banarsidass, 1979.

'Madhukar' Muni, Yuvācārya Śrī, ed.; Shastri, Pt. Hiralal, trans. *Sthānāṅga Sūtra* (Hindi). Beawar: Sri Agama Prakashan Samiti, 1981.

Mani, Vettam. *Purāṇic Encyclopedia: A Comprehensive Dictionary with Special Reference to the Epic and Purāṇic Literature*. Delhi: Motilal Banarsidass, 1975.

Mehta, Mohan Lal, and K. Rishabh Chandra. *Prakrit Proper Names*. Ahmedabad: L. D. Institute of Indology, 1970.

Mullin, Robert Bruce. *Miracles and the Modern Religious Imagination*. New Haven: Yale University Press, 1996.

Preciado-Solis, Benjamin. *The Kṛṣṇa Cycle in the Purāṇas*. Delhi: Motilal Banarsidass, 1984.

Ratnachandraji Maharaj, Shatavadhani Jain Muni Shri. *An Illustrated Ardha-Māgadhī Dictionary, with Sanskrit, Gujarati, Hindi and English Equivalents, References to the Texts and Copious Quotations*. 5 vols. Delhi: Motilal Banarsidass, 1988.

Ratna Prabha Vijaya, Muni. *Śramaṇa Bhagavān Mahāvīra: His Life and Teaching*. 5 vols. (reprint; first published 1948–50). Delhi: Parimal, 1989.

Reichenbach, Bruce. *The Law of Karma*. Honolulu: University of Hawaii Press, 1990.

Sāgarānanda Sūri Jī Mahārāja, Ācārya, and Muni Jambuvijayajī, eds. *Sthānāṅga Sūtram and Samavāyāṅga Sūtram*. Delhi: Motilal Banarsidass, 1985.

Śāntisāgara. *Kalpakaumudī* [*Kalpa Sūtra* commentary]. Navyanagar: Śvetāmbara Śrī Ṛṣabhadevajī Keśarīmalajī Foundation, Śrī Jainānanda Printing Press, 1936.

Shastri, Devendra Muni. *Bhagavān Ariṣṭanemi aur Karmayogī Śrī Kṛṣṇa: Ek Anuṣīlan*. Udaipur (Rajasthan): Sri Tarak Guru Jain Granthalaya, 1971.

Singh, Ramjee. "Some Reflections on the Problem of Omniscience and Freedom." *Jaina Antiquary* 24 (1964): 28–32.

_______. *The Jaina Concept of Omniscience*. Ahmedabad: L.D. Institute of Indology, 1974a.

———. "The Concept of Omniscience: Some Misconceptions and Clarifications." *Jaina Antiquary* 27.1–2 (1974b): 8–19.

Sukhlalji Sanghvi, Pandit. "Dharmavīr Mahāvīr ane Karmavīr Kṛṣṇa." In *Darśan ane Ciṃtan*, vol. 1. Ahmedabad: Pandit Sukhlālji Sanmān Samiti, 1957, 239–73.

Tapasyananda, Swami, trans. *Śrīmad Bhāgavata Purāṇa: The Holy Book of God*. Madras: Sri Ramakrishna Math, 1981.

Vaidya, P. L., ed., and Devendra Kumar Jain, trans. *Mahākavi Puṣpadanta's Mahāpurāṇa*, vol. 5. Delhi: Bhāratīya Jñānpīṭh, 1970.

Van Buitenen, J. A. B., trans. *Mahābhārata: 2. The Book of the Assembly Hall, 3. The Book of the Forest*. Chicago: University of Chicago Press, 1975.

Vijayendrasūri, Jainācārya Śrī. *Abhidhānarājendraḥ: Prakrit Māgadhī Sanskrit*. New Delhi: B. R. Publishing, 1985.

Wilson, H. H., trans. *Vishnu Purāṇa*. Calcutta: Panthi Pustak [orig. 1840], 1961.

Winternitz, Maurice. *A History of Indian Literature*, vol. 1. Delhi: Motilal Banarsidass, 1981.

Chapter 10

Epiphany in Rādhā's Arbor

Nature and the Reform of Bhakti in Hariaudh's Priyapravās

Valerie Ritter

In 1914, Ayodhyāsiṁh Upādhyāy 'Hariaudh,' a tax officer in a district near Varanasi, and well-known Braj Bhāshā poet, published an epic-length poem entitled *Priyapravās* (The Sojourn of the Beloved). It was named for the episode in Krishna's biography when he left his home in Vrindāvana for Mathurā at the evil king Kaṁsa's invitation, and resides there while the residents of Braj long for his return and worry about his welfare. *Priyapravās,* a harbinger of some characteristics of later modern Hindi literature, quickly became part of the modern Hindi literary canon, and remains part of the syllabi of many Hindi literature courses in India. The work was conceived as a *mahākāvya* in modern Hindi, and toward this purpose, it was written in Sanskrit meters, and its contents were clearly inspired by the long poetic works of classical Sanskrit poet Kālidāsa, and based upon the deeds of Krishna as put forth in the *Bhāgavata Purāṇa*. At the same time, the subject matter evoked Braj Bhāshā *bhakti* and *rīti* (or courtly) poetry on Krishna and Rādhā.[1] In matters of language, Hariaudh subscribed to the agenda of the Hindi movement of the late nineteenth century, which promoted the use of the Nāgarī script, and sought to reidentify the Hindustani lingua franca with Sanskrit, to the exclusion of the other basic strain of its linguistic heritage, Urdu.[2] This agenda was carried out in a political atmosphere of Hindu-Muslim tension, and a nationalist movement that increasingly defined itself as Hindu. Braj Bhāshā, a literary dialect of Hindi used pan-regionally in devotional and courtly poetry, had come into disfavor as a literary medium, due to its distance from common speech, Kharī Bolī, and its association with erotic poetry concerning the love relationship between the *nāyaka* and *nāyikā*, hero and heroine of the *śṛṅgāra rasa*, who had become identified with Krishna and Rādhā.

The problem posed for the colonial intelligentsia by the eroticism in the Krishna-bhakti tradition has been well documented. Braj Bhāshā was accused of being unmasculine, and the erotic topics of Krishnaite bhakti and courtly literature deemed improper.[3] Decades earlier, a sex scandal plagued the Vallabha sect, leading to the Maharaj Libel Case, which inspired much defensiveness among Vaishnava Hindus confronted with Victorian British legal circumspection of theology concerning Krishna's physical love with *gopīs*.[4] In 1886 the famous Bengali novelist Bankimcandra Chattopadhyay wrote a treatise in defense of the "heroic" Krishna, rejecting the god's sexual exploits as "medieval accretions."[5] The bourgeois *bhadralok* in Bengal rejected certain forms of popular culture considered to present unseemly sexual portrayals of Krishna myth.[6] Likewise, the idioms and images of romantic love that infused the Rādhā-Krishna myth were rejected by many early modern Hindi authors in the construction of "modern literature." In short, it was a period of identity crisis for those who were steeped in previous literary and religious traditions of Braj poetry and Krishna bhakti, but who also wanted to create a "modern" Hindi literature, comparable to that of nineteenth-century England or Bengal.

Hariaudh and his *Priyapravās* arose out of the hotbed of Hindi literary canon formation, as Hindi literature was becoming an industry, due to new textbook demands and writers with missionary intentions to promote a Sanskritized Hindi style. However, the Hindi movement's task was not only to produce the modern literary canon, but also to edit and represent a canon of early Hindi poetry, much of it bhakti poetry, through a modern lens, and with a particularly Hindu slant. Hariaudh was one of the editors for the Nāgarī Pracāriṇī Sabhā's *Sūr Sāgar*, and as such was at the center of this larger project to create a standardized textual canon for Hindi.[7] Hariaudh considered himself a *rasik*, a connoisseur of the traditional poetic arts, and he was not particularly invested in English-language literature, having studied English for only six months as a youth. He also identified himself as both Hindu and Sikh, and his persona as a poet later became linked somewhat with his Sikh apparel and santlike social reformism.

Priyapravās was first published in 1914 by the well-known Khaḍgavilās Press in Patna,[8] and later in Vārānasī.[9] The text was revised at least twice, and the latter revision has been continually mass produced since 1941. By 1997 it had gone through twenty-four printings. It has been part of college syllabi and widely excerpted in readers for lower levels. Although ostensibly written in a Khaṛī Bolī, spoken-style Hindi, *Priyapravās* was a difficult text, its language Sanskritized and its Khaṛī Bolī traits altered by the complex Sanskrit meters in which the work was written. It seems that *Priyapravās* was written expressly to be a text, separate from its predecessors, the essentially oral medieval Hindi poetries. Its revision of bhakti distanced it from the oral heritage of Krishna poetry, and its evocation of Sanskrit invoked a "textuality" that Orientalism glorified. While *Priyapravās* recalled an oral precedent in Braj poetry and song, it ultimately rejected it. Instead it embraced iconic Sanskrit texts: Kālidāsa's *Meghadūta*, the *Bhāgavata Purāṇā*, and the Bhagavad Gītā. It was substantially different from previous poetic renderings of Krishna mythology, and it is remembered for its metrical virtuosity, its description of nature, and perhaps primarily, its new "respectable" Rādhā. In a sense, *Priyapravās* was a literary commodity made to order for the rhetoric of modernity in Hindu nationalist India.

Hariaudh's experiment with literary modernity involved, firstly, a recasting of the carnal relationship between Rādhā and Krishna. Krishna in *Priyapravās* is a *mahāpuruṣa* (a great man), a historical figure who lived in the natural world of post-Enlightenment rationalism, and who was an exemplar for mankind. Hariaudh explained in his introduction:

> It is not favored by people of modern opinions, [to] go on writing line after line that god Śrī Krishna is *brahma*, and at the time of writing about his deeds . . . , make him the agent of such actions which even a man of common opinion would abhor. I . . . have outlined the biography of Krishna in a way with which modern people, also, may be able to agree.[10]

Along with this, Hariaudh dispensed with the usual Rādhā, the lovelorn gopī of centuries past. Instead, at the climax of the poem, Rādhā explicitly rejects the sensual solipsism of *viraha*, swears herself to virginity, and dedicates herself to the "true bhakti" of social service. This chapter will closely examine passages from *Priyapravās* that demonstrate Hariaudh's alternative vision of the Rādhā-Krishna relationship, which entailed altering the traditional representations of love for Krishna. The alterations performed in *Priyapravās* exploit the connection between śṛṅgāra rasa and the objects of nature, such that a chaste and socially useful love emerges from Rādhā's pains of viraha.

In *Priyapravās*, Krishna and Rādhā are engaged to be married, but there has not been, and will not be, in this work, any sexual consummation between them. The familiar evocations of Rādhā as a *virahiṇī* during Krishna's absence are augmented with an entirely different characterization of Rādhā, akin to that of other self-sacrificing female mythological personae, such as Sītā, who are supremely dedicated to the welfare of their husbands (*pativratā*) and endure hardships on their behalf. This saintly Rādhā is portrayed in specifically "modern" terms, as she is educated, and dedicated to altruism for the benefit of society. She is clearly modeled on an idea of the modern that included the value of formal education of women, and their employment in certain professions. She is a figure that resonates with various and richly established aesthetic categories, but at the same time, is substantially rewritten as an exemplar of civic virtue.

"Rādhā" has been widely known in literature and religious practice as the gopī (cowherdess) of the region of Braj with whom the philandering Krishna had his primary love relationship.[11] The *Gītagovinda,* a highly popular and influential Sanskrit poem by Jayadeva, thought to have been composed in the twelfth to thirteenth centuries CE, was the first to focus extensively on Rādhā, in a manner evocative of the courtly nāyaka and nāyikā (hero and heroine) of Sanskrit poetry. Rādhā's presence in poetry and her theological importance increased with the growth of the Caitanyite sect of Vaishnavism in Bengal, which saw the integration of poetic theory of the śṛṅgāra rasa (the erotic sentiment) and its taxonomies of the nāyaka-nāyikā with theology concerning the love of Rādhā and Krishna.[12] This and other Krishnaite sects proliferated during the "bhakti movement," in which Rādhā and the gopīs generally became an object of devotional focus.[13] Krishna's homeland region of Braj became a center of pilgrimage for devotees of Krishna and Rādhā, and the dialect of this region, Braj Bhāshā, became elevated to a pan-regional vernacular language of courtly poetry. In Braj-dialect Hindi literature (as well as other languages), Rādhā continued her double life as both a simple gopī and a sophisticated lover (*nāgarī*) of Krishna, in poetry comprised of both popular devotional lyrics and courtly poetry. From the eighteenth century, the ambigous moral status of Rādhā and the gopīs was under examination, as debate flourished over her status as either a *svakīya* (i.e., married to Krishna) or *parakīya* (married to another man), both classifications from *nāyikā-bheda*, the taxonomy of heroines.[14] In light of this and the continuing problematic nature of Rādhā's moral status in theology and discourse of the nineteenth century, Hariaudh's *Priyapravās* might be considered a further attempt to portray Rādhā as a more proper svakīya.

Rādhā remained a relevant figure for an early-twentieth-century literary work, not only because of her established presence in both classical and popular devotional poetry, but also because of her linkage with women of dubious character, the courtesanlike nāyikās and the parakīya women of Krishna theology and courtly poetry. She was a fit object of the particular agendas of movements for social reform and nationalism in this era, which were fundamentally concerned with ameliorating the status of women (usually in dialogue with colonial critique) and ostensibly edifying women as symbols of Indian cultural identity. While she represented an undesirable "erotic" element of Hindu religious tradition, her reformulation as an iconic "modern woman" could function metonymically for the uplift of Indian women, and thereby contribute to the rhetoric for the cause of Indian self-rule.

Hariaudh's Rādhā was an instrumentalized icon, embodying the usefulness she preached. Here Hariaudh took up the ideas of didactic, socially utilitarian literature that many Indian authors had begun to create in the nineteenth century.[15] While authors accepted the premise that utilitarian literature might reform the ills of Indian society, there was also an urge to positively (though defensively) represent Indian culture in the face of colonial misunderstanding and use realistic, moralistic fiction to express distaste for the acceptance of Western standards of behavior. A didacticism mixed with cultural pride became a defining trait of this era. Works such as Hariaudh's *Priyapravās* and many other poems, novels, and short stories, might be interpreted as culturally defensive works, which present highly idealized characters and exhort the reader (implicitly or explicitly) to emulate the moral standards and deeds presented therein, or avoid the pitfalls of immorality. It is perhaps also significant that literary works began to be prepared for a new audience of female readers, further necessitating the censorship of "licentious" material from indigenous literary traditions, and necessitating idealized and didactic content in the interest of instructing the mothers of the nation. It seems obvious that *Priyapravās* would have been used in the educational texts for girls, having didactic and supremely chaste contents, and at that time being a genre in demand.[16] The character of Rādhā in *Priyapravās* underwent a similar alteration to that of the language of the text: she was "purified" of aspects of her character newly deemed inappropriate, and reinfused with other elements. These elements were not only those of "classical Sanskrit" literature, but also elements of Western social utilitarianism, mixed with Wordsworthian (or most possibly, Tagorean)[17] sentiments concerning the divine within nature. Hariaudh's Rādhā might be considered a literary solution to the theological problems posed by the Rādhā of traditional literature.

The Description of Rādhā

The description of Rādhā (4.4–8) is one of the most oft-cited portions of the text, in anthologies and in literary criticism. These five verses are some of the most Sanskritized in the entire work, and it may be significant that the introduction of Rādhā was written in such a high register of Hindi, far afield from Braj bhakti songs.

The verses are not overly radical in their description of Rādhā. Only one of these verses is explicitly "modern" in perspective. The first three verses of this passage are very much in keeping with the precedents for describing Rādhā or any high classification of nāyikā, that is, ideally beautiful and skilled in the female arts.[18]

> A garden of beauty, a little bud almost bloomed, her face a reflection of the full moon,
> Having delicate limbs, a pretty laugh, full of *rasa*, an embodiment of art and sport,
> Like a priceless jewel of an ocean of splendor, full of charm and play,
> There was the full image of sweetness of the doe-eyed one, the soft-spoken one, Śrī Rādhā. (4.4)

> Skilled in the many mannerisms of emotion and its causes, filled with amusement,[19]
> Skilled in the casting of glances with the flirtatious rolling [of her eyes], a pundit of eyebrow gestures,
> Excelling in playing musical instruments with pleasure, adorned with adornments,
> Rādhā [was] a beauty, big-eyed, swinging with joy. (4.6)

> She used to redden her lotus-feet, ornament[ing] the surface of the earth,
> The redness of her lips made the *bimba* and the coral-tree seem less lovely,
> The excellence of her lotus-face, blooming with joy, was the foundation of beauty,
> Rādhā's desirable and lovely beauty was the entrancer of Kāma's wife Rati. (4.7)

This description clearly evokes the nāyikā of Sanskrit and Braj courtly poetry. Hariaudh does not shrink from a conventional and somewhat sexualized description of Rādhā, using terms such as *kāmanīya* (desirable), and attributing skills to her such as *hāva-vibhāva* (flirtatious gestures). The passage does not deny the standard, sexual Rādhā, but is not as explicit and thorough as the *nakha-śikha* (toe-to-head) body descriptions found in Sanskrit and Braj poetry.[20] Her talents are those associated with the highest classes of heroines in Sanskrit *kāvya* and courtly Braj literature generally, as she has the skills of a courtesan, such as hāva-vibhāva, alluring and coquettish gestures that are the *anubhāva*s (indications) of the emotion of passion, (*bhāva* of *rati*).

Rādhā is not unfamiliar at this point in the text, but the transition attempted by Hariaudh becomes baldly apparent in the next verse.

> Well dressed and well ornamented, full of virtues and everywhere respected,
> Engrossed in helping sick and elderly people, dedicated in thought to the pure *Śāstra*s,
> Steeped in goodwill,[21] of incomparable heart, nurturer of pure love,
> Was Rādhā, of good soul, with a happy face, as if a jewel of the race of women. (4.8)

The language remains consistent, in its highly Sanskritic style, but the content is somewhat startling. While previously described in merely physical terms, and with some indication of a pleasant personality, here Rādhā is ascribed civic virtues, in helping the sick and elderly, "steeped in goodwill." The love that she promotes is *satprema*, pure or true love. While satprema is not antithetical to Vaishnava theology about Rādhā, it connotes a chaste love, which is Hariaudh's point here. In this verse, Rādhā has become an exemplary model for the audience of *Priyapravās*, which would have heard hortatory speeches concerning such social service often. Interestingly, Rādhā remains loving and emotional, but she is described in terms punctuated with the prefix *sat* (pure), perhaps disassociating Rādhā from her previous licentious past: "*sadvastrā-sadalaṅkṛtā* . . . *sacchāstra cintāparā* . . . *sadbhāvātiratā* . . . *satprema-saṃpoṣikā* . . . [well dressed . . . well ornamented (or 'of pure dress . . . having pure ornamentation') . . . devoted in thought to the pure *Śāstras* . . . steeped in goodwill . . . nurturer of pure love" (4.8).[22]

The ambiguity of the text concerning Rādhā's identity is most clear in the instance of the phrase *krīṛā-kalā-puttalī*, which could have a range of meanings. The components of the compound are (in their semantic order): (1) *puttalī*: doll/embodiment/lovely woman (= "apple" [lit. "pupil"] of the eye); (2) *kalā*: art; (3) *krīṛā:* sport/entertainment/pleasure. In one interpretation, this compound could be translated as "an embodiment of art and sport"; yet another, contrasting translation is also possible: "doll for the art of pleasure," implying suitability for, or perhaps skill in, amorous physical acts. Hariaudh therefore did not altogether refrain from using terms that might sexualize Rādhā in the traditional fashion, but he used them judiciously, so that such terms of description might be interpreted in a "modern," "moral" framework as well. Although the "erotic" nature of the previous Rādhā was not considered vulgar per se by insiders of Krishna worship, this passage, and the text as a whole, demonstrates that for a writer such as Hariaudh, the paradigm of an idealized lover of god had shifted. In *Priyapravās*, in these few verses, the strangeness of such a shift is presented in high relief.

Epiphany

Peter Gaeffke, a historian of Hindi literature, wrote succinctly that Hariaudh's Rādhā was "converted into a social worker."[23] This "conversion" is an event that occurs in the sixteenth *sarga*, in which Rādhā responds to Uddhava's message from Krishna. In this lengthy passage (16.49–136), Rādhā delivers several different yet linked expositions. Firstly, she discusses the difference between infatuation (*moha*) with forms and love (*praṇaya*). Secondly, she offers an explanation of her new, positive vision of Krishna in nature. Thirdly, she gives an explanation of the differences in perception according to the *guṇa*, or quality, possessed by the perceiver, as put forth in Sāṁkhyā philosopy. Lastly, she puts forth a redefinition of the conventional nine types of bhakti as particular types of altruistic "good works," having as their concern the welfare of the world.

These elements are set forth in a manner that suggests the presence of particular progressive and/or "Western" ideas, rederived, as it were, out of the philosophical concepts of the Bhagavad Gīta and Vaishnavism generally. I would characterize this passage as "Rādhā's epiphany" because it is a moment in which the absent Krishna becomes manifest to Rādhā, and another, "true" meaning of the practice of bhakti becomes clear to her. Although this is the fruition of Rādhā's progressivism, still she intersperses her speech with humble references to her womanhood, reminding the reader of the simple village girl Rādhā of folk culture, and perhaps implying the ability of Indian "folk" to embrace such ideas themselves.

This passage describes the "conversion" of her character from an excitable woman to one who finds peace through communion with nature, much like a "modern poet." As she states in the midst of this monologue:

> Having looked at the beauty of lotuses or a risen moon with
> my eyes,
> Or heard with my ears the sweet song of the birds,
> I was agitated. Now I find happy peace;
> I find them like the feet, face, [and] sound of the flute of the
> beloved. (16.102)

This vision is in stark opposition to the reaction of the medieval gopīs to Uddhava's message, for whom nothing is equal to the embodied Krishna,[24] and contrary to previous characterizations of Rādhā, in which Rādhā finds peace only in Krishna's embrace. Hariaudh effected this transformation of Rādhā in her own voice, as she affirms her sensual nature, links the senses to nature itself, and then explains her elevated, *sātvik* perception with which she perceives the body of Krishna in the landscape. Rādhā's speech of eighty-seven verses far surpasses Krishna's message given by Uddhava, both in length and in erudition, and it bears a resemblance to a *guru-pravacan* (a sermon by a religious teacher) such as one might find at a religious center in North India. Through this passage, Hariaudh's Rādhā encompasses an earthy sensuality, social concern, and a monistic transcendentalism in one chaste personality. In her epiphany, nature functions as a link between conventional and experimental literary modes, between Sanskritic and perhaps British Romantic literary associations, and between bhakti and social service. The passage is notable for Rādhā's merging of a classical description of nature with modern civic utility, resulting in the forging of a modern poetic voice out of the expression of viraha.

Krishna's message, delivered in ten verses by Uddhava, contains the basis for Rādhā's subsequent epiphany, which elaborates upon Krishna's message, intellectually and poetically. Krishna's companion Uddhava, having heard the lamentations of all of the other Brajvāsīs, arrives at Rādhā's side and gives the message from Krishna (16.37–46). Krishna's message is given in the *mandākrāntā* meter, the same meter as Rādhā's following epiphany, and the same meter as that of the *pavandūtī* episode above. At first, Krishna expresses his sadness at his separation from Rādhā and his pain in this separation:

> When loving hearts meet and become one,
> Why has God separated their bodies like this?
> How is it that a great mountain has come between them,
> When the two lovers were ever mixed like milk and water?
> (16.37)

He expresses his grief in a manner reminiscent of the *yakṣa* of the *Meghadūta*, who cannot find his beloved in any element in nature.

> Helpless from [my] longing, I look often at the sky, the earth,
> the trees,
> The stars, the faces of men,
> O beloved! I do not get any such suggestion[25] from anywhere
> That would give peace to my heart, nervous from worry. (16.49)

This mirrors other classical instances of men looking for, and not finding, their beloved in elements of nature. As in the *Meghadūta*, the yakṣa speaks:

> I see [your] limbs in creeper-vines, [your] glance in the startled look of the deer,
> The luster of [your] face in the moon, [your] tresses in the peacock's mass of feathers
> The play of [your] brows in the gentle ripples of the river,
> O! Nowhere, in any one thing, is your likeness, O cruel one.[26]

This vision of nature in viraha, and the search for signs of the beloved in nature in the state of viraha, later becomes a key component of Rādhā's epiphany. This verse of Krishna's message thus foreshadows the poetic sleight of hand that will justify Rādhā's theology in her epiphany. Krishna states that "the desire for the benefit of the world (*lipsā jagata-hita*) is . . . delightful," and "the desire to offer oneself is more beautiful" than desires for happiness or even the desire for *mukti* (16.41). He continues, stating that doing the usual *tapasya* (self-denying austerities) is merely self-interest, and that performing service for people and the world is true self-sacrifice. Here he uses the term *sevā* (service), a term used for the performance of ritual worship of gods and for the selfless performance of tasks for one's elders or superiors.

> He who is engrossed in austerities by the desire for *mukti*
> Is self-interested, [we] can't say that he is self-sacrificing (*ātmatyāgī*).
> He to whom the benefit of the world and service of people (*jagata-hita au loka sevā*) is dearer than life,
> O Dear, he is the true self-sacrificer of the world. (16.42)

The obtainment of the happiness born of service for creatures (*prāṇī-sevā*) is equal to the holiness of the Ganges River (16.43.1–2). The benefit of the world is intoxicating (*mughdakārī*), as are the attractive powers in things that are enjoyed. While there are impurities or sins (*kaluṣa*) in these attractive powers, there is an *alaukik* (otherworldly, divine) peace in service (16.44). He states that all creatures of the world desire their own happiness, but he who, by means of offering himself (*ātma-utsarga-dvārā*), is not in the power of this desire, has achieved his human purpose (literally, "his coming-into-the-world is successful") (16.45). He concludes that *sātvik* work (*sātvikī-kārya*) alone is meritorious, and that he who is beyond self-interest is a helper of all beings (*sarva-bhūtopakārī*) (16.46). The rejection of ascetic disconcern with this world in favor of social action was a common theme in India at this time, and as such, Hariaudh's Krishna illustrates this type.

Rādhā thanks Uddhava, and begins her lengthy treatise, agreeing with, and explicating, these very ideas. To this purpose, Rādhā explains her commitment to being a sarva-bhūtopakārī with a philosophical exposition. In the process, she explains the difference between love and infatuation or lust as a difference in personal perception. Rādhā's pontification on perception is the most extended passage on a philosophical subject in the entire work. Up to this point, long monologues are lamentations given "in character," and often recounting the deeds of Krishna, a common literary motif. The beginning part of Rādhā's monologue on the difference between love and infatuation (16.49–74) is markedly different. The effect of this part of the passage is not unlike that of the Bhagavad Gītā within the narrative of the *Mahābhārata*, in the sense that it breaks away from the "action" with an explanation of a philosophical/religious matter. Indeed, the comments of Rādhā therein are similar to some of the Bhagavad Gītā concerning the world of illusion and later on, the guṇas.[27]

Appropriate to her character, her intellectual treatise is premised by an assertion of her human and female identity, as one who is enchanted by forms: "I am a woman, having a volatile heart, [and] I am deprived of love. / If I am distressed, heartbroken, disturbed, what is surprising about that?" (16.50.3–4). But despite her viraha, she says, "I remain detached mostly, I am perpetually restrained" (16.56). Rādhā describes her desires as natural, but delusional. Rādhā then elaborates on the philosophical basis for her restraint, the understanding with which she will stem the passions that arise from viraha, passions that derive ultimately from her attachment to the material world, a quality that perhaps epitomizes her femaleness.

As Rādhā's speech becomes more abstract and erudite, the verses become considerably more difficult, in terms of the grammatical relations of elements, and the usage of some terms. She addresses attachment and infatuation via the senses like a veritable pandit, including one verse that may even make obscure reference to the nāyikā-bheda system of classification of heroines from the rhetoric of classical Sanskrit and its Braj Bhāshā counterparts. This verse provides a succinct example of the intellectual acrobatics of this long-winded section of Rādhā's monologue.

In an awakened[28] heart the enchantment, which by means of
beautiful form[s],
Is pervasive in the world, of which there are many beautiful
acts,
That [world] usually gives birth to an infatuated state in people.

> That is the field of play of the mind, [that enchantment] is delusion and perplexity. (16.57)

Rādhā asserts that true love is based in the intellectual and the moral: "The root form of this love is the workings of the mind. / They become authoritative (*samadhikṛt*) when [made] by the good qualities of the person" (16.61.1–2). "So many emotions arise . . . / In which there is usually the delusion of love, under the influence of infatuation. / [These emotions] are not love, nor are they appropriate" (16.65.1–3). Rather, "wise men have given the name of love to the following qualities: being without hope for merit, [having] the beauty of good respect, or [being] engrossed in dharma" (16.66).

With Rādhā as his proxy, Hariaudh is reassessing the meaning of love for Krishna on the part of *saguṇa bhakta*s, for whom attraction to forms is a means to the divine. Hariaudh is not exactly disposing of the saguṇa method of loving Krishna; rather, his Rādhā is buttressing her new chaste identity with philosophy. The erasure of the erotic[29] from the Rādhā-Krishna relationship necessitated such a reexplanation of Rādhā's love for Krishna.

Rādhā subsequently launches into a description of her newly transformed personal vision of Krishna. Rādhā prefaces this section of her monologue with a statement linking her capability of this vision with being a lovelorn woman, even as she evokes the voices of these males in viraha. As before, she admits her humble status in preface to the more surprising verses that follow.

> There are many girls in Braj who are infatuated.
> They are all dyed by the color of love of Śyāma.
> I believe that among them, most are drowned in great delusion.
> Even so, all of them are generally mere travelers[30] on the path of love. (16.75)

> I have this very state [of infatuation] also; why would I forget about Śyāma?
> How would I extract from my heart the wonderful dark divine image? (16.76.1–2)

Although she characterizes herself as simply a gopī, Rādhā then launches into a classically allusory description of her vision of the landscape that both defies and supports this identity. Rādhā perceives the body of Krishna in the landscape, in the objects of nature, through the natural objects of Sanskritic poetic comparison. She transposes the usual sensual similes for Krishna's body and finds the *darśana* and actual physical presence of Krishna, seemingly in counterpoint to Krishna's lament in the manner of the *Meghadūta*'s yakṣa. This results in the dislocation of Rādhā's sensual experience of Krishna, the stock and trade of earlier poetry, and the relocation of the field of worship to this physical world. Nature thus becomes a source of multivalent tropes, which can be read in a Sanskritic frame, yet can also be interpreted as a logical force in her subsequent exposition of bhakti as good works in the world.

Natural metaphors for idealized bodies are conventional in Indian literature. These metaphors were commonly related to a perspective that highlighted the attractive and pleasing qualities of the poetic subject, often in a sexual manner. These common *upamānas* (objects of comparison) might also function as *uddīpanas* (stimulants) to the śṛṅgāra rasa—for example, creeping vines on a tree and so on. In the case of Rādhā and Krishna, this would not be surprising, as their relationship is inherently sexual. As an example, one might consider these verses from the *Gītagovinda*, the highly influential twelfth-century Sanskrit text that first elaborated upon the theme of Rādhā as Krishna's favorite gopī lover: "The soft black curve of [Krishna's] body was wrapped in fine silk cloth, / Like a dark lotus root wrapped in veils of yellow pollen," or "[Rādhā's] passion rose when glances played on his seductive face, / Like an autumn pond when wagtails mate in lotus blossom hollows."[31] Or this, a verse from Vidyākara's eleventh-century anthology of Sanskrit poetry: "The *romāvalī*'s[32] thick stem supports / a pair of lotuses, her high and close-set breasts, / on which sit bees, the darkening nipples."[33] The common use, in Sanskrit literature generally, of epithets and descriptive compounds using terms of comparison such as creeper vines, lotuses, birds, and deer, further supports the argument that flora and fauna are paramount in classical poetic description. Courtly poetry in Hindi also relied heavily on this trait of Sanskrit poetic tradition. In her epiphany, Rādhā refers to the established association of elements of the natural world with idealized bodies.

In contrast to the mad visions of Kālidāsa's yakṣa and the lonely Rām, her vision of the beloved in nature is positive, and ultimately serves to explain Krishna's exhortations to social service. Her train of thought begins with Krishna's moonlike face: "When the full moon of Kārttika comes and is risen in the sky, . . . The memory of my darling's radiant little face comes [to me], even today" (16.78). If she "look[s], enchanted, at the cluster of flowering flowers," then her tearful eyes see "the beautiful[34] splendor of the exquisite hands and wonderful feet" of Krishna (16.79).

Whenever I look at the sky, inlaid with stars,
Or when lines of happy cranes appear in the clouds,

Then I become elated, I have such a constant thought,
As if the chest of Śyāma appears, shining [with his] pearl necklace. (16.80)

The blooming twilight appears like the loveliness of the supreme Beloved.
I find in the body of the night the reflection of Śyāma's color.
Dawn comes every day colored with love.
A luster like his face is found in the sun. (16.84)

I find the exquisiteness of his locks in a garland of bees.
[I find] the beauty of his eyes in wagtails and deer.
Both [his] arms [I] remember when I see a young elephant's trunk.
I found the radiance of [his] nose in the beak of a pretty parrot. (16.85)

The glimmer of his teeth appears to me in pomegranates.
In red *bimba* fruits gleams a redness like his lips.
I see the beauty of his two thighs in banana-trees.
A graceful exquisiteness like his ankles appears in roses.[35] (16.86)

Intoxicating the eyes, a very joyful blueness like [that of] his body
Shines in the lap of the rare blue vault of the sky.
Beauty in the earth, *surasa*[36] in water, in fire the divine light,
Often appears like my darling dear boy. (16.87)

Her visionary state includes aural and physical elements as well, as she finds "in the calling of the birds / The sweet strains of the . . . flute of the most beloved" (16.88), and "when the soft wind . . . touches" her body, she is conscious of "the touch of Śyāma's lovely hands" and the fragrance of his face (16.81). Overall, this passage is an enumeration of natural objects, flora and fauna, in her line of vision and in her physical experience, which were almost all poetically familiar to the reader from the metaphors of Sanskritic poetry.

The twilight and the sun, the elephant, the parrot, the swarm of bees, the pomegranate, and other plant life all show themselves to her and affect her as if they are the body parts of her Beloved; they do not serve as directly descriptive comparisons for Krishna's body. Hariaudh's Rādhā does not compare Krishna's body to natural objects, but rather, the direction of the comparison is reversed, and the object of the metaphors become identified with their subject. Rather than offering a description of Krishna that denotes his desirability to Rādhā, this passage disembodies Krishna, and deconstructs his fundamental carnality, by identifying his body parts with the concrete objects with which they might be compared.

This passage might be described as a *mālā*, (garland) of *rūpakas* (metaphors, identifications) and similes (*upamās*).[37] This mālā of identifications and comparisons may be likened to the *tattvapahnava* rūpaka, in which the real subject of the comparison is denied and the object affirmed in place of it.[38] The tattvakhyāna upamā may also be a relevant term, meaning "literal description," "in which the similitude is assumed to lend itself to a confusion, so that one is obliged to identify the subject and object." Gerow illustrates this term with the apt quotation from Daṇḍin, "That is no lotus, that is a face; those are not bees, they are eyes."[39] It may be worthwhile to refer to a later term, *pratīpa upameya* (inverse simile), in which the object (upamāna) is made into the subject (upameya) (e.g., the lotuses look lovely like your eyes).[40] However, it should be noted that none of these definitions exactly match what takes place in this monologue: no explicit denial of the reality of Krishna's body, or the objects of nature, occurs here. There is less comparison than positive literal identification of Krishna's body with the elements of the landscape. Additionally, while this passage may derive from a Sanskritic precedent of the confusion of the perceptions in the state of viraha, Rādhā's identification of natural elements and the body of Krishna seems intentional, not the result of confusion or madness. Considering her monologue as a whole, it is clear that Rādhā implies the superiority of her perspective to conventional Hindu religiosity, which suggests that she is intentionally putting forth an alternative religious philosophy, which denies the usual conception of Krishna's body. Her vision seems rather to be a revelatory insight that allows her to perceive Krishna conventionally but in transcendental, disembodied terms. As these object "show" or "reveal" an immanent beloved, the quality of the poetry changes from one of sensual description, to the discernment of an abstracted divine body in nature.

That is not to say that Krishna is bodiless, however. The scented flower breath and the touching wind preserve the aspect of "dalliance" of the Rādhā-Krishna relationship but transmute it into an interaction that avoids overt eroticism. While she "remembers" his body in the manner of classical Sanskrit poetry,[41] overall Krishna's body has become something "found" and "shown to [her]": *"pāī jātī"* and *"mujhe dikhāte haiṃ."* This passage resembles the British Romantic ideal of the individual inspired poetic voice, that perceives the divine through the conduit of nature,[42] yet the passage also remains firmly within the Sanskritic poetic framework, in which such natural objects might suggest erotic union, or be the upamāna of bodily description.

While the reversal or mutual identification of the metaphorical object and subject was therefore not an original literary device, it must have been useful for a poet who sought to convert the erotic nature of love in bhakti and rīti poetry into a literary aesthetic, in sync with current ideas of modernity. As will become clear below, such an idiom was also useful for an argument to convert Krishna devotion into a dedication to social ideals.

Rādhā concludes, addressing Uddhava directly, in defense of the validity of her vision, as one not of lovesickness, but having a more profound import:

> You must be troubled at hearing my words.
> You will think that I become helpless, am drowned in great infatuation,
> [But] it's true [that] I am infatuated not for the sake of my own pleasure.
> Safely [*saṃrakṣā*], I am industriously [*sayatnā*],[43] because of my feeling, on the path of love.[44] (16.89)

Rādhā then explains that attraction to forms, and desire for Krishna, is only natural: love for Krishna is as natural as "sweetness in sugarcane" or "color in a flower petal"[45] (16.90). However, she then elaborates this statement with the caveat that the senses are differentiated among the perceivers. Perceptions are affected by the essential nature of the perceiver, characterized as one of the three guṇas.

> Beautiful trees shine with the voices of birds.
> The scientist finds the lesson of the love of supreme lord;
> The tastes for killing of the hunter become even stronger.
> Thusly, in the listening of both of them there is great difference. (16.96)

Rādhā perceives an imperative to use the senses and desires, and to actively color (or dye) them, with the pure attitude of the sātvik guṇa, the quality of virtue and purity that is associated with colorless*ness*. Here Hariaudh has twisted the famous metaphor attributed to the poet-saint Mīrābāī, "dyed in the color of the dark one," to express a new kind of devotionalism, intentionally drained of erotic passion.

> The tongue, the nose, the ears and eyes are of the body.
> How will they abandon their nature, why would they abandon their work?
> How can the desires of the heart be calmed? Therefore I
> Dye them everyday in the *sātvikī* mode. (101)

Here, as quoted above, she states that what once agitated her now gives her peace, as she finds lotuses, the moon, and the birdsong, "like the feet, face, [and] sound of the flute of the beloved" (16.102).

> Like this, that which is divine and lovely in the earth and sky,
> When I touch, hear, see, and listen to them,
> Then I am happy among them, having found, because of feeling,[46] Śyāma's
> Wonderful beauty, the greatness of his virtues, [and] the equivalence of all of his limbs [in them]. (16.103)

In the last line, she sees the *aṅga saṁbhūta sāmya*, the likeness or equivalence between Krishna's limbs and the objects in the world. From this perception, Rādhā was transformed: "The heart-conquering love of the world awoke in my heart / I saw the supreme lord in my very own lord-of-my-life (husband/lover)" (16.104).

> However many various things are found, in them all,
> When I see the beloved in the countless colors and shapes,
> Then how can I not love them all with all my heart?
> Like this the love of the world awoke in my heart.[47] (16.105)

Thus Rādhā speaks not for renunciation of the sensual world—for sensuality is natural, the biologically prescribed work of our anatomy—but for a "renunciative heart" that remains vital in the world, paradoxically colored with pure sātvik cravings (100). This perception is what leads her to a universalistic love of the world, identified with love for Krishna.

Rādhā then humbly points out that she is unqualified to fully understand religious truths:

> That which doesn't come into the heart of the people, that is beyond the intellect,
> That is not made of the field of feelings, that is always imperceptible,
> In which there is not the method of the thinkers, that is beyond the senses,
> What that is, how might I, an ignorant woman, know that? (16.106)

The language of this verse invokes Rādhā's gender, through the use of the pronoun *so*, avoided in the formal speech of the bulk of *Priyapravās*, and through the reference to herself as ignorant, and *abalā*, "a weak one" (*so kyā hai, maiṁ abudha abalā jān pāūṁ use kyoṁ*). Rādhā then recapitulates the philosophical message of the Gītā, that Krishna is truly beyond the sensory world, but she interprets it in concrete terms: his body parts are found in natural objects and hence are identified with all the beings in the world. Here she seems to be referring to verses 13.13–14 of the Gītā, describing *brahma*,[48] which Rādhā alludes to and glosses as follows:

> It is said in the *Śāstras* [that] the heads and eyes of the Lord
> Are countless in their reckonings, and [he has] many feet and hands also.
> This being the case, even so, without a face, eyes, a nose, etc.,
> He touches, eats, hears, sees, and smells. (16.107)
>
> Thinkers have told his beautiful secret like this:
> All of the beings of the world are the *mūrti*s of him
> His eyes and other sense organs are innumerable.
> Therefore that soul of the world (*viśvātma*) has innumerable eyes and other sense organs. (16.108)
>
> All the senses of the body are made useless without living beings.
> Because of this, [it follows that] another power does the work of the senses.
> That is not the nose, nor the eyes or tongue, etc. [but] a part of God.
> Being without a nose and other sense organs, therefore, he smells, etc. (16.109)
>
> In stars, in the destroyer of darkness [the sun], in the flash of fiery lightning,
> In various jewels, various gems, there is his radiance.
> In the earth, water, wind, the sky, in trees, in birds,
> I find [his] pervasive, celebrated greatness in the world. (16.110)

Her interpretation is both more concrete than the Gītā and more abstract than that of the usual gopī, as embodied by the gopīs of Nand-das's *Rāsapañcādhyāyī*, who refute Uddhava's message with resolute claims of the bodiliness of Krishna, typified by the question Then who stole the butter?

Following the shift of Krishna's mūrti to the living world, the practice of bhakti is also transformed into serving the world. A universal moral code is attached to Krishna bhakti proper and then explicitly defined as good works, turning on the concept of sevā. The nine types of bhakti are reinterpreted as acts of personal compassion and social service, because the living world and Krishna are interchangable: "The world is pervasive in the beloved, in the world is the beloved. / In this way, I saw the lord of the world in Śyāma" (16.112).

> There is the bhakti of the beloved [which is] *sādhana*, of one's own beloved,
> Of the form of the life-breath of the life of the world [brahma],
> Of one's own father and mother, and guru, etc.
> That [sādhana] bhakti, [done] without desire, is greatly desirable. (16.114)

Rādhā prefaces her explanation of the types of bhakti with a bald statement of the superiority of her perspective over the conventional understanding of saguṇa bhakti: "If someone makes a mūrti, fashioned from the imagination, / And serves its feet . . . , / That will not be equal, in the view of intelligence [*buddhi dṛṣṭi se*], / To worshiping the feet . . . of [God] himself" (16.116). She thereby implies a rejection of the use of images in worship, but then subsequently transfers the image to the world, thus proving that bhakti consists of service in the world, which she perceives as the body of Krishna: "The soul of the world (*viśvātmā*) that is the supreme lord, is his very forms. / All of the creatures, rivers, mountains, creepers, vines, and various trees—Protection [and] worship of them, proper effort on their behalf, reverence, and service" is the bhakti that is "best of all" (16.117).

> To listen to all of the words of the afflicted and oppressed with one's heart,
> [To the words of] sick people, distressed people, and [the words] of reformers of the people,
> To listen to the recitation of the pure *Śāstra*s, to listen to the words of virtuous people,
> Is considered the bhakti named *śravaṇa* among gentlemen. (16.118)

Rādhā then redefines *kīrtana*, singing devotional songs, as a method to awaken the sleeping, bring light to the "dark and fallen," put the erring on the right path, and promote knowledge (16.119). She then explicitly links the attitude of bhakti to the political, social world:

> To bow down before scholars, one's own elders, and patriots,
> Wise men, charitable men, the virtuous, the all-brilliant,[49]
> Self-sacrificing wise people, [and] holy images of god
> Is the bhakti of the lord called *vandanā*. (16.120)

Dāsatā is redefined as being "engrossed in service," and specifically to "lift up the base fallen castes" (16.121). She goes on to equate *smaraṇa* with "remembering the troubles of the poor," "helpless widows," "orphans and dependents," and doing "good works" (16.122). She describes *ātma-nivedana* with "driving away . . . sorrow" of those "fallen into . . . adversity" (16.123). *Arcanā* is interpreted as giving solace to the frightened, suffering, and ignorant, to "give . . . medicines to those in pain, / . . . water to the thirsty, food to the hungry" (16.124). "To deal with each thing [in the world] with good intentions, / To be honest and kind" is *sakhya* bhakti (16.125). *Pāda-sevana* is directed toward caste, and evokes the Vedic myth of *puruṣa*: "That mass of beings, which is fallen down, as if the feet of the body of society/ Because of . . . their karma, / To give them shelter and dignity through efforts[50] is [*pāda sevana*]"(16.126). The true bhakta gives medicine to the sick, food to the hungry, and shelter to widows and orphans, and acts as a steward of the earth itself. The conceptual framework of the ninefold bhakti is found in the *Bhāgavata Purāṇā*,[51] and elaborated in Caitanyite Vaishnava theology, as well as in the writings of Nānak.[52] These verses by Hariaudh not only elaborate a concept taken from the Gītā, but particular elements evoke the rhetorical methods of the hymns of Nānak. Namely, in 16.118.3, a fulcrum structure is found, in which the verb is placed in the middle and functions in reference to the preceding and following words: *Sacchāstroṁ kā śravaṇa sunanā vākya satsaṅgiyoṁ kā*.[53]

Rādhā closes her monologue with a climactic vow: "I should not forget the command of the beloved, and [if] I were be useful to the world, / My vow of celibacy (*kaumāra-vrata*) in the world would be fulfilled completely" (16.135). Hence, the modus operandi of the Rādhā of bhakti and rīti poetry has changed almost completely. Rādhā defines her relationship to Krishna as not primarily sexual, but one of serving God. Her vow of celibacy, to remain unmarried, requires service in the world. Her previous wifely energy to perform sevā for her husband is now directed toward the "real" world, which is identified with Krishna himself.

In this revision of the ninefold bhakti, Hariaudh was obviously influenced by reformist religious movements, among which Swami Vivekānanda's Rāmakrishna Mission is a famous example. Vivekananda had identified karma yoga as the path of good works, selfless service to one's fellow man. His idea was based upon the Vedantic identity of the individual *ātman* with universal *brahman*: "The saint sees the Self in all beings and in that consciousness devotes himself to service."[54] From the beginning of his religious leadership in 1886, he supported progressive social causes of the day and created mission centers serving the sick, orphans, and wayward women.[55] Social service is thus the concrete corollary, or praxis, of monistic Vedanta philosophy. The work of service, done for the sake of itself, will lead to the knowledge of Brahman. However, social service does not supersede this philosophical goal, but rather is a method of realizing oneness in the concrete world, thereby leading to the philosophical realization that is beyond action:

> The knowledge of *Brahman* is the ultimate goal—the highest destiny of man. But man cannot remain absorbed in *Brahman* all the time. When he comes out of It, he must have something to engage himself. At that time he should do such work as will contribute to the real well-being of people. . . . Some attain to the knowledge of *Brahman* by means of unselfish work. This is also a means, but the end is the realization of *Brahman*.[56]

Therefore oneness of self and universe was the theoretical basis of this equation of service and religion. Social service became a sort of devotion for modern religiosity and the basis of a new sort of asceticism. The familiar concept of "sevā," in the past reserved for deities and gurus, was reinterpreted in light of social positivism and funneled into the new administrative unit of the "mission." The Brahmo Samāj and the Ārya Samāj, in varying degrees and with varying agendas, also supported such activities, and also notably rejected the use of images, as Rādhā seems to imply in *Priyapravās* 16.116.

Aside from the parallels in other historical movements, it is perhaps possible to deduce a shift in poetic and religious aesthetics in *Priyapravās,* linked indirectly to British Romanticism. Rādhā cites a "vision of intelligence" that is capable of transforming the world into *līlā* through emotion, and that entails recognizing "true" Krishna bhakti, more profound than common religiosity. This position seems to indicate a rationalism that is enacted through emotion, perhaps *sadbhāv*, perhaps Romantic "feeling." Indeed, Rādhā's privileged vision, and her particular vision of God in the landscape, suggest the poetic precepts of British Romantic poetry of the unity of nature, God, and the human perceiver, as well as the poet's mystical vision of this universal connection in the landscape. Furthermore, the work as a whole implies the Romantic/Orientalist trait of resuscitation of a glorious ancient past for the purpose of future regeneration, political and moral. The intense classical referencing in *Priyapravās,* combined with its strictly modern political message of civic brotherhood as the core of religiosity, suggests such an influence. Hariaudh's participation in the movement to write in Kharī Bolī at all is ultimately linked to the Romantic ideals of writing in simple language which mirrored democratic revolution in the West.[57] There is no clear connection between *Priyapravās* and British Romanticism per se, though the strong possibility exists of such a literary influence, and perhaps even conscious reference. Whether the alleged "Romanticism" of Rādhā's perspective is a direct reference to English poetry or Bengali, it is impossible to know. At any rate, Rādhā's perspective diverged starkly from previous literary characterizations of the *virahin/virahiṇī*, and of the "old" Rādhā of medieval literature and popular devotion. It is possible that *Priyapravās* is thus interculturally "intertextual," built upon selected components and absences in the Indian literary tradition, and in reference to ideas of the function of literature, introduced through colonialism. It might be surmised that the use of such elements amenable to Romanticism constituted a part of Hariaudh's attempt to write a "modern" *mahākāvya*.

Rādhā in *Priyapravās* and the Linkage of Gender and Nationalism

Did Hariaudh intend for Rādhā to be perceived, and perhaps emulated, as a gender-specific role model? The Rādhā of *Priyapravās*, as the fictive creation of an upper-caste male, fits well into Partha Chatterjee's assessment of a "nationalist resolution of the women's question." Chatterjee characterizes this phenomenon as the oppressive resolution of the problem of "the women's question" (i.e., how to better the status of Indian women without "westernization"), inflected as it was by colonial legislation on behalf of Indian women, through use of the false binary essentialisms of spiritual and material, home and the world, and feminine and masculine in nationalist rhetoric. Women, as representatives of the spiritual and the inner, private sphere of the home, bore the burden of supporting an Indian cultural identity, which had contradictory consequences for women's emancipation as citizens of the Indian nation-state:

> the 'spirituality' of her character had also to be stressed in contrast with the innumerable surrenders which men were having to make to the pressures of the material world. . . . associating the task of 'female emancipation' with the historical goal of sovereign nationhood, [patriarchy] bound them to a new . . . subordination.

Like the women of which Chatterjee writes, Hariaudh's Rādhā also bore this burden of Indianness, which was manifested in spiritual purity, and tied to nationhood. As a literary figure, Rādhā served the purpose of re-representing Indian identity at many levels, as a metonym for Indian women, Vaishnavism, and classical and popular Indian literatures.

Furthermore, as the representation of what was deemed "obscene" in colonial discourse, Rādhā's reformation takes the form described generally by Chatterjee as the Satī-Sāvitrī-Sītā construct:

> . . . an inverted ideological form of the relation of power between the sexes: the adulation of woman as goddess or mother. It served to emphasize . . . the "spiritual" qualities of self-sacrifice, benevolence, devotion, religiosity, etc. . . . making it possible for her to go out into the world under conditions that would not threaten her femininity. In fact, the image . . . served to erase her sexuality in the world outside the home.[58]

Although it is not within the scope of this chapter to discuss the origin of the false essentialisms Chatterjee identifies, it will be sufficient to note the degree to which Rādhā in *Priyapravās* expresses such dichotomies, such a state of being symbolically "loaded," and such rhetorical concepts of "middle-class nationalism." Hariaudh's Rādhā resides at home, while Krishna is "abroad" in the city working for the good of the people. She functions in the public sphere, but only of the village, in the "inner quarters" of the public world. Hariaudh's Rādhā is decidedly not urban. She remains in the home territory, doing concrete work of social uplift, while Krishna deals with the world of politics and power. Rādhā goes beyond the home, but not much farther, and within particular parameters. She remains "only a woman," a good daughter and citizen of Braj.

The concept of sevā, "service" performed for a god and for one's husband, is a key factor in interpreting the meaning of Rādhā in *Priyapravās.* As a visionary spiritual leader of sorts, self-sacrifice forms the core of the theology she espouses. Her *kaumāra-vrata* allays the fear of miscegenation associated with the sexual freedom of the modern/westernized woman. While unmarried, her marriage to a man is substituted with marriage to an ideal of sevā in the world, preserving her propriety. Bhakti has thus been abstracted into sevā for a husband who is the greater polity, and implicitly, the nation. While India is often anthropomorphized as Mother India, here India appears as Rādhā's *pati* (husband, or lord).

Hariaudh's Rādhā can be read as part of a nationalist resolution to the women's question, as a chaste female with a penchant for social work, an integration of the new "working woman" of the middle class into a traditional/national framework of motivation and use. She can also be simply the female corollary to the equivalence of the social world or polity to the male pati. However, she might also be considered the personal mouthpiece of Hariaudh, in which case the significance of gender in the work's implied nationalism might be subsumed in the conventional use of the female voice in bhakti poetry. The identity of Rādhā's philosophy with that of Hariaudh's seems obvious. Rādhā is not only a *paṇḍitā* of eyebrow gestures—her speech in the sixteenth *sarga* is veritably the speech of a Brahmin pandit like Hariaudh. Furthermore, it is conventional knowledge that the composition of *Priyapravās* resulted from Hariaudh's own experience of viraha after the death of his wife in 1904. Hariaudh himself is linked to Rādhā not only through pandithood, but the *sātviktā* with which both character and poet are known. His use of the "gendered" voice of Rādhā is a familiar device, at any rate, in bhakti poetry, in which expressing the emotions of a gopī is a devotional stance.

Rādhā thusly might constitute a gender-neutral exemplar, although still idealizing wifely humility, devotion, and passion toward the husband/world. In a parallel argument, Ashis Nandy has suggested that Gandhi drew upon a gendered nationalism that expressed *klībatvam* (lit. "neuterness"), to the extent that he presented an androgynous model of virtue. Refuting the binary attributes of male/female as they extended in discourse to colonizer/colonized, he held up female fortitude, self-sacrifice, and self-control as the model of national character for men and women.[59] Like Gandhi, Hariaudh likely found the androgynous model of Rādhā perfectly acceptable, and perhaps resonant with preceding religious practices of men imagining themselves as Rādhā, the lover of Krishna. In this vein, we might consider that Hariaudh's Rādhā is not a model merely for women, but for the entire populace of India, and she functions as a gendered exemplar, but not necessarily as a female exemplar.

Conclusion

Priyapravās, and its "modernity," may be characterized by the absence of several elements of the well-known mythology of Rādhā and Krishna, and the absence of elements of language itself. Rādhā must necessarily be regarded through the lens of her past self, now erased and "written over." While the audience may not have considered Rādhā's sexuality as anything other than her right by divine ordinance, the elision of this aspect from her character draws attention to it. The *lack* of the old, desirable Rādhā is the root of her modernity. This absence is mirrored by the lack of Krishna that is the premise and the ultimate conclusion of the poem. The sense of lack is repeated at the linguistic level, where much of the Hindustani lingua franca is elided for a "pure"

Hindi. Images and feelings are separated from their original referents, redirected away from concrete mythology to the more real this-world.

"Feeling," the bhāva of Vaishnava discussion of the experience of rasa, and nature, replete with its Sanskrit vocabulary of images, are reinvented as discursive topics themselves. Regardless, the memory of religious bhāva and the uddīpanas and upamānas of Sanskritic poetry persist, as does the memory of the "real" Rādhā, in the face of the "realistic" Rādhā presented in *Priyapravās*. Bhāva remains the method of creating "līlā," but this time a utopian one. Furthermore, Hariaudh's use of Rādhā as a didactic, exemplary figure may have been linked somewhat to the devotional practice of striving to inject oneself into the eternal ongoing Krishna līlā through self-identification with the characters of Krishna līlā. The presumed effect of didactic literature—inspiring like behavior in the receptor—and the devotional practice of self-identification of the receptor with the mythical consort of Krishna—here overlap. Both literary practices could be considered functional here, to some degree. Hariaudh's intent can be read ambiguously as including the intentions of both devotional and didactic literary genres.

While the critical reception of *Priyapravās* since its publication has generally been one of admiration, there is also consensus that Hariaudh's revision of myth is strange, against the grain of both conservative Brahmanical Hinduism as well as the living religious practices of Hinduism. Indeed, *Priyapravās* has not succeeded in effecting any real change in conceptions of Rādhā; this was likely never Hariaudh's intent. However, Hariaudh's vision of Rādhā did represent certain nationalist ideals, and nationalist aesthetics, that persisted through Independence, if not to the present day. The fact that this work was written explicitly for the development of a modern Hindi literary canon and was destined for future consumption by Indian citizens in government-endorsed and subsidized educational curricula, also suggests a relation between the aesthetic characteristics of *Priyapravās* and the goals of nationalism. Examining *Priyapravās* in terms of possible linkages between social/political reform, religious change, and particular literary tropes may elucidate an aesthetic concomitant of the cultural changes sweeping through the districts of India at the beginning of the twentieth century.

Hariaudh's *Priyapravās* documents the unusual outcome possible in the translation of a subject of "religious literature" into "modern Indian literature," as it appropriated aspects of a religious and poetic tradition for its new purpose. It was a representative artifact of its era, providing a window into a poignant moment of cultural revision. It is odd, and its oddity to us arises from its unique set of epistemological circumstances, its situation of being embedded in previous poetic referents while foraying into another set of meanings and desires. Nature, the divine, and the social imperative combine in this literary work, such that it creates a strange, slightly altered poetic landscape, where the psychology of viraha and the epiphanous voice of the modern, political poet merge in the setting of Rādhā's arbor.

Notes

This chapter is drawn from chapter 4 of my Ph.D. Dissertation, "Useful Absences and the Nature of the Modern: Ayodhyāsiṁh Upādhyāy 'Hariaudh' (1865–1947), his *Priyapravās* (1914), and Hindi Poetry" (University of Washington, 2001). I would like to thank several people who have helped me with this project: Drs. Michael Shapiro, Sagaree Sengupta, Heidi Pauwels, Frank Conlon, Leroy Searle, Robert Hueckstedt, and Geoffrey Heeren.

1. This name will be spelled as "Rādhā" to conform with the style of this volume.

2. This agenda was epitomized by the Nāgarī Pracāriṇī Sabhā [Society for the Promotion of Nāgarī], of which Hariaudh was a member. An account of the Hindi-Urdu controversy is beyond the scope of this chapter. For further information, see Christopher R. King (1994), and Vasudha Dalmia (1997), chapter 4, and for a linguistic perspective, Colin P. Masica (1993 [1991]), 27–30.

3. Christopher King (1994), 36.

4. See David L. Haberman (1993), 44–70.

5. Bankim Chandra Chatterjee, *Krishna-Charitra* (1991 [1892]). In the words of Ashis Nandy (1983), 23–24, "Bankimchandra did not adore Krishna as a child-god or as a . . . sexually playful . . . adolescent. . . . His Krishna was a respectable, righteous, didactic, 'hard' god, protecting the glories of Hinduism . . . [and] who would not humiliate his devotees in front of the progressive Westerners." See also "The Myth of Praxis: construction of the figure of Krishna in the Krishnacaritra," in Sudipta Kaviraj (1998 [1995]), 72–106.

6. See Sumanta Banerjee (1989).

7. He became a member of the editorial committee as a replacement for his late friend Jagannāth Dās "Ratnākar," former court poet of Ayodhya.

8. The major literary press of Bihar in the late nineteenth and early twentieth centuries, with which interested British civil servants also had connections. Notable among them was the Irish scholar and civil servant Sir George Grierson (1851–1941), who conducted the Linguistic Survey of India 1898–1928, and through whom Hariaudh received public recognition for his prose works published at the press.

9. As of ca. 1940, Hariaudh transferred publishing rights to the Hindī Sāhitya Kuṭīr [Hindi Literature Cottage], a publisher of educational and devotional texts.

10. Hariaudh (1941 [1914]; 23d printing, 1993), 23.

11. For a detailed history of the figure of Rādhā in earlier literature, see the introduction by Barbara Stoler Miller in Jayadeva (1977). See also the comprehensive collection of essays on Rādhā in John Stratton Hawley and Donna Marie Wulff, eds. (1982).

12. The works of Rūpa Goswāmin are famous in this regard. See chapter 4 of Sushil Kumar De (1961).

13. Two definitive works on these developments include A. W. Entwistle (1987) and Edward C. Dimock (1989).

14. Sushil Kumar De (1961), 349 ff., and A. W. Entwistle (1987), 57–58.

15. Colonial administration actively encouraged such "useful" literature through the administration of competitions and prizes. Many of such works were directed toward women. See Susie Tharu (1994), 167 ff; and C. M. Naim (1984), 290–314. Discussion of didactic novels can be found in any history of the development of prose literature in Indian languages.

16. For information on the already established market for "women's literature" in Hindi, see Vasudha Dalmia on Hariścandra's women's magazine *Bālābodhinī* and didactic literature for women in general (1997), 245–51. Hindi was a relative latecomer to this genre.

17. Rabindranath Tagore (1861–1941), 1913 Nobel laureate who is considered by many to be the greatest Bengali poet.

18. The translations given here are of the vulgate text of 1941 published by the Hindī Sāhitya Kuṭīr. I will mention variants in the previous editions as warranted in the discussion here. For detailed notes on the textual variants between the first (1914), second (1921), and vulgate (1941) editions, and grammatical issues, please see the appendix of Valerie Ritter (2001).

19. Or "fragrance."

20. The *nakha-śikha* genre, however, was also exploited by Hariaudh in *Rasakalas*: *Ras-sambandhī anūṭhā kāvya-granth* (1933; reprint, 1964). As in *Priyapravās*, the subject matter was altered with exemplary and didactic contents. The *nakha-śikha* became a symbol of the decadence and limited nature of Braj poetry for the Chāyāvād poets (see Karine Schomer, 1982), 89–115.

21. *Sadbhāva*: goodwill, pure feeling. A term now used for political goodwill between communities or nations; possibly this connotation existed in the original text.

22. Dr. Robert Hueckstedt has drawn my attention to somewhat similar castings of the nāyikā as morally worthy in Bāṇa, but I would argue that Hariaudh's portrayal of Rādhā here stems from nineteenth-century literary motivations.

23. Peter Gaeffke (1978), 23.

24. Exemplified by Nanddas (1973).

25. *Dhvani,* I take here as "suggestion." This could refer to sound, if this verse refers to Krishna asking these elements of nature about Rādhā, which is standard behavior in viraha.

26. *Uttarameghaḥ*, verse 44, Kālidāsa (1993 [1969]), 167. This is my translation from the text as printed in Kale's edition, with reference to his translation.

27. The popularity of the Gītā in Hindu nationalist movements may be of note here. At any rate, these concepts were part of generic Vaishnavism and Hinduism.

28. *Udita*: arisen; spoken; a type of nāyikā (*uditayauvananāyikā*: a young heroine having recently "arisen" youth or breasts) who is still part girl. I have chosen "awakened" in order to convey the sense of recently matured. The term "udita" is used elsewhere in the work in reference to the risen moon, etc., so here it is at least metaphorical. It is intriguing to consider that it may be an obscure reference to a class of nāyikā, which class is followed in age by the *mugdhā*. The term *mughdatā* (infatuated state) in line 3 of this verse might be a reference to this. It is possible that this verse thus refers to nāyikā-bheda theory in its explanation of infatuation.

29. My usage of the term "erotic" here is problematic. Suffice it to say that the conventional idea of "the erotic," with its connotations of lasciviousness, was part of the Victorian zeitgeist, but is problematic in reference to Rādhā-Krishna religious traditions. The term "sexual" is similarly problematic in this context.

30. Or "adherents."

31. Jayadeva (1977), 120.

32. *Romāvalī*: a line of hair extending from the pubic area up the trunk of the body.

33. Author unknown, in Vidyākara (1965), 16.434.1–3.

34. More precisely, *sarasa*, "possessing *rasa*."

35. "Mānav" [Viśvambhar] in *Priya-Pravās kī ṭīkā* remarked on this strange simile, and the use of the Persian word *gul* for "flower" (1968), 424.

36. Literally, "beautiful *rasa* [juice, etc.]"

37. Perhaps the term *utprekṣā* might also be applied here. See Edwin Gerow (1971), 131 ff.

38. Edwin Gerow (1971), 249.

39. Edwin Gerow (1971), 156.

40. See the text and translation of this verse in excerpts of the seventeenth-century *Bhāṣā-Bhūṣaṇ* by Jaswant Simha in Rupert Snell (1992), 151. Compare also the definition of a *pratāpa* in Edwin Gerow (1971), based on Rudraṭa's *Kāvyālaṅkāra* (mid-ninth century) and Mammaṭa's *Kāvyaprakāśa* (late eleventh century) which is slightly different.

41. For extensive examples of Sanskrit lyric poetry framed as the remembrance of physical union, see Bilhaṇa (1971).

42. The presence, popularity, and influence, overt or otherwise, of English Romantic poetry in India in the late nineteenth and early twentieth centuries, both in English and in translation, are well known. I speak here generally of the subjective and quasi-mystical voice of the Romantic poet, à la Wordsworth and Coleridge, et al., who look upon nature and perceive signs of the divine. A fuller discussion of the question of literary influence takes place in chapter 5 of Valerie Ritter (2001).

43. *Sayatnā . . . hūṁ*. Compare with Brian A. Hatcher (1996) as "with care, lovingly" and also "industriously."

44. *Praṇaya*. This may perhaps have somewhat chaste connotations, relative to other words for love used in Krishna literature.

45. This type of appeal to biology for an explanation of the emotions of *śṛṅgāra* is found also in the preface to Hariaudh's *Rasakalas.*

46. *Bhāvataḥ.* Cf. 16.97, in which the world can be transformed into *līlā, bhāvoṃ se.*

47. Mānav, 429, comments: "This is also the point of view of the Sufis and *bhaktas,*" in regard to love as mode of operation in the world.

48. "*Sarvataḥ pāṇipādaṃ tat sarvato' kṣiśiromukhaṃ / sarvataḥ śrutimalloke sarvam āvṛtya tiṣṭati / sarvendriyaguṇābhāsaṃ sarvendriyavivarjitaṃ / asaktaṃ sarvabhṛccaiva nirguṇam guṇabhoktṛ ca*" (13.13–14). Text as given in *Bhagavadgītā or The Song Divine* (1996 [1943]).

49. This term *tejasvīyoṁ* (here apparently in the plural oblique) likely refers to reformists, nationalists, or other public leaders.

50. It is unclear whether this means the people will be uplifted "through [their own] industry," or whether this is an adverbial phrase modifying "to give," "energetically, zealously." The commentaries take the latter interpretation.

51. *Bhāgavata-Purāṇa* 7.5.23: *śravaṇaṃ kīrtanaṃ viṣṇoh smaraṇaṃ pādasevanam / arcanaṃ vandanaṃ dāsyam sakhyaṃ ātmanivedanam. Śrimadbhāgavatapurāṇa-mahāpurāṇa* (1951).

52. The nine types of bhakti given here are elaborated in Caitanya's and Jīva Goswamin's exposition of the eleven types of *vaidhī* bhakti (i.e., deriving from the injunctions of the *śāstras*). See Sunil Kumar Das (1985), 157, and Sushil Kumar De (1961), 369 ff. Das explains that Nānak takes Naodā bhakti (ninefold bhakti) as a separate class and reinterprets it "by purging it of the outward ritualistic performances" (1985), 327. Hariaudh's Sikh background may have been a factor in his reworking of the ninefold bhakti in *Priyapravās.*

53. I am grateful to Dr. Michael Shapiro for pointing out this particular "fulcrum" semantic structure in Nānak. The term "satsaṅg" in this line also resonates with Sikh theology generally.

54. Swami Vivekananda (1969), 113.

55. Kenneth W. Jones (1994 [Indian edition]), 43.

56. Swami Vivekananda (1969), 197–98

57. For information in addition to my generic characterizations of Romanticism, refer to "Romanticism" in *The New Princeton Encyclopedia of Poetry and Poetics* (1993), and the classic *The Mirror and the Lamp,* by M. H. Abrams (1958).

58. Partha Chatterjee (1989), 248–49.

59. Ashis Nandy (1983), 52 ff.

References

Abrams, M. H. *The Mirror and the Lamp*. New York: Norton, 1958.

Banerjee, Sumanta. "Marginalization of Women's Popular Culture in Nineteenth-Century Bengal." In *Recasting Women: Essays in Colonial History*. Kumkum Sangari and Sudesh Vaid, eds. Delhi: Kali for Women, 1989, 127–79.

The Bhagavadgītā or The Song Divine (With Sanskrit Text and English Translation). Jayadayal Goyandaka, ed. and trans. (translated to English by anon.). Gorakhpur: Gita Press, 1996 (orig. 1943).

Bilhaṇa. *Phantasies of a Love-Thief: The Caurapancasika Attributed to Bilhaṇa.* B. S. Miller, ed. and trans. Studies in Oriental Culture, no. 6. New York: Columbia University Press, 1971.

Chatterjee, Bankim Chandra. *Krishna-Charitra.* Translated from the Bengali and with an introduction by Pradip Bhattacharya. Classics of the East Series. Calcutta: M. P. Birla Foundation, 1991 (orig. 1892).

Chatterjee, Partha. "The Nationalist Resolution of the Women's Question." In *Recasting Women: Essays in Colonial History.* Kumkum Sangari and Sudesh Vaid, eds. Delhi: Kali for Women, 1989, 233–53.

Dalmia, Vasudha. *The Nationalization of Hindu Traditions: Bharatendu Hariscandra and Nineteenth-Century Banaras.* Delhi: Oxford University Press, 1997.

Das, Sunil Kumar. *Śrī Caitanya and Guru Nānak: A Comparative Study of Vaiṣṇavism and Sikhism.* Calcutta: Rabindra Bharati University, 1985.

De, Sushil Kumar. *Early History of the Vaiṣṇava Faith and Movement in Bengal from Sanskrit and Bengali Sources.* 2d edition. Calcutta: Firma K. L. Mukhopadhyay, 1961.

Dimock, Edward C. *The Place of the Hidden Moon: Erotic Mysticism in the Vaiṣṇava-sahajiyā Cult of Bengal.* Chicago: University of Chicago Press, 1989.

Entwistle, A. W. *Braj: Centre of Krishna Pilgrimage.* Groningen: Egbert Forsten, 1987.

Gaeffke, Peter. *Hindi Literature in the Twentieth Century.* A History of Indian Literature, vol. 8, fasc. 5, Jan Gonda, ed. Weisbaden: Otto Harrassowitz, 1978.

Gerow, Edwin. *A Glossary of Indian Figures of Speech.* The Hague: Mouton, 1971.

Haberman, David L. "On Trial: The Love of the Sixteen Thousand Gopees." *History of Religions* 33, 1 (Aug. 1993): 44–70.

"Hariaudh" [Ayodhyāsiṁh Upādhyāy]. 1914. *Priyapravās: bhinnatukānt kavitā kā ek Hindī mahākāvya.* Bankipore: Khaḍgavilās Press. 1941. Revised and expanded new edition, Banaras: Hindī-Sāhitya-Kuṭīr, 1993.

———. *Rasakalas: Ras-sambandhi anūṭhā kāvya-granth.* Patna: Pustak Bhaṇḍār, 1931. 4th printing, Varanasi: Hindī-Sāhitya-Kuṭīr, 1964 [reprint, 1944; 3d printing 1950].

Hatcher, Brian A. *Idioms of Improvement: Vidyāsāgar and Cultural Encounter in Bengal.* Calcutta: Oxford University Press, 1996.

Hawley, John Stratton, and Donna Marie Wulff, eds. *The Divine Consort: Rādhā and the Goddesses of India.* Berkeley: Graduate Theological Union, 1982.

Jayadeva. *Love Song of the Dark Lord: Jayadeva's "Gītagovinda."* Translated and introduction by Barbara Stoler Miller. New York: Columbia University Press, 1977.

Jones, Kenneth W. *Socio-Religious Reform Movements in British India.* The New Cambridge History of India, vol. 3, no. 1. Cambridge: Cambridge University Press, 1994 [Indian edition].

Kālidāsa. *The Meghadūta of Kālidāsa: Text with Sanskrit Commentary of Mallinātha, English Translation, Note, Appendices and a Map.* M. R. Kale, ed. and trans. Delhi: Motilal Banarsidass: 1993 (1969).

Kaviraj, Sudipta. *The Unhappy Consciousness: Bankimchandra Chattopadhyay and the Formation of Nationalist Discourse in India.* Delhi: Oxford, 1998 [1995].

King, Christopher R. *One Language, Two Scripts: The Hindi Movement in Nineteenth-Century North India.* Bombay: Oxford University Press, 1994.

"Mānav" [Viśvambhar]. *Priya-Pravās kī ṭīkā.* Allahabad: Lokabhāratī Prakāśān, 1968.

Masica, Colin P. *The Indo-Aryan Languages.* Cambridge Language Surveys. Cambridge: Cambridge University Press, 1993 (1991).

Naim, C. M. "Prize-Winning Adab: A Study of Five Books Written in Response to the Allahabad Government Gazzette Notification." In *Moral Conduct and Authority.* B. Metcalf, ed. Berkeley: University of California Press, 1984, 290–314.

Nanddas. *The Round Dance of Krishna and Uddhav's Message.* R. S. McGregor, trans. London: Luzac, 1973.

Nandy, Ashis. *The Intimate Enemy: Loss and Recovery of Self under Colonialism.* Delhi: Oxford University Press, 1983.

The New Princeton Encyclopedia of Poetry and Poetics. A. Preminger and T. V. F. Brogan, eds. New York: MJF, 1993.

Ritter, Valerie. "The Language of Hariaudh's Priyapravās: Notes toward an Archaeology of Modern Standard Hindi." *Journal of the American Oriental Society* (forthcoming).

———. "Useful Absences and the Nature of the Modern: Ayodhyāsiṁh Upādhyāy 'Hariaudh' (1865–1947), His *Priyapravās* (1914), and Hindi Poetry." Ph.D. Dissertation, University of Washington, 2001.

Schomer, Karine. "Where Have All the Rādhā's Gone? New Images of Woman in Modern Hindi Poetry." In John Stratton Hawley and Donna Marie Wulff, eds. (1982), 89–115.

Snell, Rupert. *The Hindi Classical Tradition: A Braj Bhāṣā Reader*. SOAS South Asian Texts Series. New Delhi: Heritage, 1992.

Śrīmadbhāgavatapurāṇa-mahāpurāṇa. 2 vols. Gorakhpur: Gita Press, 1951.

Tharu, Susie. "The Arrangement of an Alliance: English and the Making of Indian Literature." In *Rethinking English: Essays in Literature, Language, History*. Svati Joshi, ed. Delhi: Oxford University Press, 1994.

Vidyākara. *An Anthology of Sanskrit Court Poetry: Vidyākara's "Subhāṣitaratnakoṣa."* Daniel H. H. Ingalls, trans. Harvard Oriental Series, no. 44, Daniel H. H. Ingalls, ed. Cambridge: Harvard University Press, 1965.

Swami Vivekananda [Narendranath Datta]. *The Complete Works of Swami Vivekananda*. Mayavati, ed., vol. 13. Calcutta: Advaita Ashrama, 1969.

Contributors

JEROME H. BAUER is Lecturer in Religious Studies at Washington University in St. Louis, MO, where he teaches courses in South Asian, American, and comparative religions. His teaching interests also range from miracles to fantasy to cooperative living to fundamentalisms in Hindu/Jain and Christian/pagan traditions. He is currently developing teaching and research interests in medical humanities, yoga, Ayurveda, and Sanskrit culinary texts. Recent publications include four articles for *South Asian Folklore: An Encyclopedia* (2003), on Dohada, Kalpa Sutra, Purana, and karma. He is also an active organizer of community events.

GUY L. BECK teaches courses in Hinduism, Asian Religions, and Religion and Music in the Religious Studies Program at Tulane University, New Orleans, LA. His book *Sonic Theology: Hinduism and Sacred Sound* (1993) explores the theological and philosophical basis for the use of sound and music in Hindu religious practice. He holds an M.A. in Musicology and a Ph.D. in Religion from Syracuse University, and has also studied vocal music in India for six years, releasing a CD in 1999 entitled *Sacred Raga*. In 2001, he was a Visiting Fellow at the Oxford Centre for Hindu Studies, Oxford University (U.K.), where he taught Hinduism and Music and conducted research, sponsored by the Infinity Foundation, on the Indian influences on Western religious and musical traditions. He has also published articles on the Bhakti traditions of Krishna, and Vaishnava temple worship. In addition to Asian studies and music, his research interests include comparative religion, ritual studies, and esotericism. Recent projects include an edited volume on music in world religions and a CD archive of Vaishnava devotional music recorded in Vrindaban (North India) during a Fulbright Senior Research Grant.

GLEN ALEXANDER HAYES is Professor of Religion at Bloomfield College in Bloomfield, NJ. He received his Ph.D. in History of Religions in 1985 from the University of Chicago Divinity School. His dissertation examined body symbolism and cosmology in medieval Tantric traditions of Bengal. Author of numerous essays on the Vaishnava Sahajiyā traditions of Bengal, he has also published translations of Bengali Tantric yoga texts in *Religions of India in Practice* (1995) and *Tantra in Practice* (2000). Recently he explored the use of metaphor in Vaishnava Sahajiyā traditions in an essay in *Yoga: The Indian Traditions* (2003). A contributor to *The HarperCollins Dictionary of Religion* (1995), *The Encyclopedia of Women and World Religions* (1999), and *The Encyclopedia of Holy People* (2004), he is currently co-editing and writing a chapter for *In the Flesh: Eros, Secrecy and Power in the Tantric Traditions of South Asia,* with Hugh B. Urban and Paul E. Muller-Ortega (2004). In addition to his specialization in medieval Bengali Yoga and Tantra, his research interests include contemporary metaphor theory and cognitive linguistics. He also serves as Chairperson of the Steering Committee of the Society for Tantric Studies.

JUNE MCDANIEL is Professor of Religious Studies in the Department of Philosophy and Religious Studies at the College of Charleston, Charleston, SC, and has been Director of the Religious Studies Program for six years. Her Ph.D. was from the University of Chicago, in History of Religions with a focus on the religions of India. Her areas of research are Hinduism (especially Bengali Bhakti and popular folk traditions), mysticism and religious experience, psychology and religion, women's roles in religion, fieldwork issues, and the cross-cultural study of religious ecstasy. Her books include *The Madness of the Saints: Ecstatic Religion in Bengal* (1989), *Making Virtuous Daughters and Wives: An Introduction to Women's Brata Rituals in Bengali Folk Religion* (2003), and *Offering Flowers, Feeding Skulls: Popular Goddess Worship in West Bengal* (2004).

ANNE E. MONIUS is a historian of religions specializing in the religious traditions of South Asia. She taught at the University of Virginia for five years before joining the faculty of the Harvard Divinity School in 2001. Her research interests include examining the practices and products of literary culture to reconstruct the history of religions in South Asia. Her book *Imagining a Place for Buddhism: Literary Culture and Religious Community in Tamil-Speaking South India* (2001) examines the two extant Buddhist texts composed in Tamil. Her current research project considers the role of aesthetics and moral vision in the articulation of a distinctly Hindu religious identity in twelfth-century South India. Both point to a larger focus on the ways in which aesthetics and ethics define religious identity and community in South Asia, as well as to the creative and productive encounters among competing sectarian religious communities. Future research projects will explore the relationship of Hindu devotional and philosophical literature in Tamil to its Sanskritic forebears, as well as consider the transmission of South India strands of Buddhism and Hinduism to Southeast Asia.

CHRISTIAN LEE NOVETZKE currently teaches courses in South Asian history, religion, and public culture at the University of Pennsylvania, Philadelphia, PA. His research work is focused mainly on the time period spanning the fourteenth century to the present, and in Marāṭhī and Hindi texts. His other studies include historiography within religious traditions, the history of Orientalism in American academics, and the poetic-social cultures of "early-modern" Marāṭhī-speaking areas.

TRACY PINTCHMAN is Associate Professor and Director of the Asian Studies Program at Loyola University of Chicago, where she teaches courses on the Hindu tradition. Her publications include *The Rise of the Goddess in the Hindu Tradition* (1994) and *Seeking Mahādevī: Constructing the Identities of the Hindu Great Goddess* (2001). Her latest book is on Kārtik puja traditions, entitled *Guests at God's Wedding: Celebrating Kartik Among the Women of Benares* (forthcoming).

VALERIE RITTER is Assistant Professor in the Department of South Asian Languages and Civilizations at the University of Chicago, where she teaches Hindi and South Asian literature. Her publications on language, poetics, and gender in the early period of modern Hindi literature include "The Language of Hariaudh's Priyapravās: Notes toward an Archaeology of Modern Standard Hindi," *Journal of the American Oriental Society* (forthcoming) and a book project entitled *Modern Hindi Poetry and Poetics: Nature, Love and Instruction 1885–1935* (forthcoming). She holds a Ph.D. in Asian Languages and Literatures from the University of Washington (2001), and an M.A. in Asian Studies from the University of Texas (1995).

A. WHITNEY SANFORD is Associate Professor in the Department of Philosophy and Religious Studies at Iowa State University, Ames, IA, where she teaches courses in Religions of India and Religion and Ecology. Her recently published articles include, "Painting Words through Sound: Visions of Krishna in Paramānand's Sixteenth-Century Devotional

Poetry," *Journal of the American Academy of Religion* (2002), and "Srinathji, Dauji and Jakhaiya: Narrative as Arbiter of Contested Sites in Braj." *International Journal of Hindu Studies* (2002). She is currently working on a book entitled *Krishna and Balarama in an Idealized Braj*.

Index